Tutor Ted.

SAT®

Solutions Manual
2012-2013 Edition

By   Ted Dorsey
Ryan Harrison
Martha Marion
John Mayer
Dylan Ris
John Tchernev

For more information, visit our website: www.tutorted.com.

Cover Design: Andrew Featherston
Book Design: Andrew Featherston
Math Diagrams: Ted Dorsey
                     John Tchernev
Special Thanks to: Matt Casper
                     Anne Dorsey
                     Monica Miklas

ISBN: 1-450-51650-5
EAN-13: 978-1-450-51650-1

Table of Contents

Introduction

4   Who is Tutor Ted?
5   How to use our book
6   Self Study Guide

Solutions

9   Test 1
20 Test 2
34 Test 3
47 Test 4
58 Test 5
70 Test 6
81 Test 7
92 Test 8
104 Test 9
117 Test 10

Appendices

131 The Essay: Tutorial and Sample Essays
137 Vocabulary: Glossary by Section

Who is Tutor Ted?

In the beginning, a student (who **scored a 2210** and **got into Brown**...but I digress) stored the phone number of his SAT tutor Ted Dorsey **in his cell phone** under the name **"Tutor Ted."**

A **mini-empire was born**.

One of the most **successful** and **highly regarded** tutoring companies in Los Angeles, Tutor Ted represents a group of some of the smartest, funniest, most knowledgeable people you could hope to meet. Graduates of the top universities in the country, the members of the Tutor Ted team have **decades of experience** preparing students for the SAT.

The "real" Tutor Ted is Ted Dorsey. Ted's got a knack for acing these standardized test thingies: he achieved **perfect scores** on his **SAT** and **PSAT while in high school** and later **scored 2400 on the new SAT**. Ted graduated from **Princeton University**. He has helped prepare **hundreds of students for the SAT and SAT Subject Tests**. He is also the coauthor of the **Emotes!** series of books for young readers.

Tutor Ted (the company) offers both group and individual test prep classes in the Los Angeles area. **Tutor Ted students have achieved results that consistently and significantly exceed the improvements reported by the big, national test prep firms**.

Check out Tutor Ted's other great SAT resources, including **"Tutor Ted's Guide to the SAT"**, the crown jewel of the Tutor Ted SAT curriculum. Once available only to students in the Tutor Ted program, it is now available to everyone at Amazon.com.

For more information, visit **www.tutorted.com**.

And hey, you can always drop us a line at **solutions@tutorted.com**.

Hello!

Here's how you use our book.

The idea behind the Tutor Ted project is to give you **smart tools** for prepping for the SAT **that will improve your score and won't put you to sleep**. Here's what you need to know to get started:

This is a companion volume to the "Official SAT® Study Guide" published by the College Board®. If you don't have it, go buy it now—**it's the best book you can use to get ready for the SAT**. Plus, this book is **pretty much useless** without it.

The "Official SAT Study Guide®" (we'll call it the **Big Blue Book** from now on) has almost 2,000 realistic questions inside. The problem is that it doesn't tell you **how to solve those problems**. That's where this book comes in.

Once you complete a section or a practice test from the Big Blue Book, look that section up in this book. Check your answers, and read the explanations for any problems you don't understand.

We have included a self-study guide with schedules for completing your SAT prep. The more of the Big Blue Book that you can complete, the better, but even if you only do one practice test, you will probably improve your score. Do not try to complete all 10 practice tests in one weekend—**you may explode**.

We also included **a glossary in the back of this book** with every vocabulary word from the sentence completion problems. Use this resource as a study guide for frequently used SAT vocab words. Highlight the words you learn and review them before the test.

The essay doesn't have one correct answer, but it **does have some really useful strategies**. To find out how to improve your essay score, check out the chapter on the essay on page 131. It includes a **tutorial** as well as **sample essays** for the essay from Test 1 of the Big Blue Book.

So that's it. Go kick the SAT's a##!

Cheers,
The Tutor Ted Team

Ted Dorsey
Ryan Harrison
Martha Marion
John Mayer
Dylan Ris
John Tchernev

Self Study Guide
The best test prep for the least $$$$

The **Way-Ahead-of-the-Game** Approach   *For those with more than 6 months until their first SAT/PSAT*

Take a test. Start by taking a full, timed practice test in the Big Blue Book. Check your answers. Score it to find out your starting point. Review all the problems you didn't understand by checking Tutor Ted's SAT Solutions Manual.

Review the concepts. After finding out what you know and (more importantly) what you don't know, use the web as a resource. Research all of the concepts that you don't feel 100% comfortable with right now. If you don't know what a misplaced modifying clause is, look it up! Not sure how to calculate the slope of a line? That's on the web too.

Study vocabulary. Visit the <links> page at **tutorted.com** for a list. Study a **set number** of words each week. Make flashcards with **little notes/drawings** to help distinguish the words. Get your parents to help you by quizzing you...and find out how many words *they* really know.

Do one section every day from the Big Blue Book. Hey, I didn't say this was the *fun* approach. It's crazy productive, though. Complete a section, check your answers, look at the solutions in this book, repeat. If you're worried about running out of tests before you get to the real SAT, don't sweat it: you can start from the beginning of the book and do it all again. I had one student who worked through *four* copies of the Big Blue Book. No joke! He got a 2340, just so you know.

The **Sensible** Approach   *For those with 3 months until their first SAT/PSAT*

Take a test every week. Surrender to the Big Blue Book. Repeat to yourself, "this book is my friend, this book is my friend." Pick a time (Saturday mornings, Tuesdays at 3:37am) and take one test per week. You can break up a test and take a couple of sections each day if you want. Just make sure to take one complete, uninterrupted test at least once a month.

Review your test. Once you've finished the test, take a break! Just walk away. Come back after a day or two, check your answers, and review what you did right and wrong.

Study vocabulary. Learn the words from each practice test that you did not know. Highlight them in the glossary at the back of this book. You might think that the College Board won't reuse the same words from their own book. You are wrong, my friend! The CB reuses words like they are going out of style.

The **Just-In-Time** Approach | *For those with about a month until their first SAT/PSAT*

Take 1-2 tests every week. Do at LEAST one full, timed practice test each week. One is great and two is better. If you have to break it up a bit and complete a few sections one day, a few the next, that's OK. Just make sure you sit down for a fully timed test at least once before the real thing. And don't just work on sections that you like—you've got to practice all of it to get better. Just work through the book in order.

Review your test. Use this book to review the tests/sections that you complete. If there are any concepts that you're missing regularly, be sure to ask one of your teachers for help on that topic. You can also go to the internet, where there are plentiful, free resources to teach you math and grammatical topics.

Study vocabulary. Learn all the words that you come across in the practice tests. Highlight them in the glossary in the back of this book. If making flashcards is how you memorize best, then make flashcards.

The **"Oh s#*$!"** Approach | *For those with a week or less until their first SAT/PSAT*

Don't panic. Just remember: you can take the SAT more than once. The College Board gives seven SATs a year, and for regular admission, you can take the test as late as January of your senior year! So there is almost certainly time to take it again. Prepare as well as you can, then think of this first test as a chance to get to know the SAT and to shake off any first test jitters.

Take a practice test. Just because you started test prep late doesn't mean that you should be COMPLETELY unprepared. Set aside 3 1/2 hours. Sit at a table where you won't be disturbed or distracted. Go to the library if you have to. Turn off your cellie and laptop. Find out what it's like to sit for the full test. I'll give you a hint: it's not fun. Better to discover that in practice than on the real test, yo.

Review your test. Use this book. Figure out what you know and what you don't know. Pick a couple of major concepts to review. Adding a couple of new elements to your game WILL improve your score.

Study vocabulary. Learn these 5 words:

Pragmatic (adj) practical
Equivocal (adj) intentionally misleading or vague
Censure (v) criticize
Qualify (v) to limit the meaning of; moderate
Temperate (adj) mild

Test 1
Section 2: Critical Reading

Question 1: (A)
Clue words "accurately predicted" point to (A) "foresight."

Question 2: (B)
Clue words "simple and direct" point to (A) "candid."

Question 3: (A)
Clue words are clear: "impulsive nature and sudden whims," but the vocab is hard.
Capricious means "impulsive"
Bombastic means "pompous"
Loquacious means "talkative"

Question 4: (D)
This one is more about understanding the situation than anything else. She chose her career based on "gut-instinct" (that's what "visceral" means). In the first half, visceral is contrasted with "deliberate." and in the second half rational is contrasted with "instinctive."

Question 5: (C)
College Board bringing out the heavy guns here. "Bureaucratization" may be the longest word ever to be a correct answer on the SAT. "Ossified" means "hardened or became inflexible," which works perfectly with "adaptability destroyed" and "rigid policies." You may want to skip a question with words this tough.

Question 6: (D)
The horses don't notice the beauty of the night sky on a clear night, so it's good to be human because we get to enjoy those things. I don't usually think of stars and the night sky as "nature's beauty," but it's definitely the best option here.

Question 7: (B)
"Appeal to emotion" is very tempting here, but even though there is some feeling here, the passage is not primarily trying to tug at your heartstrings. Stuff like "feathery fishing lure" and "stars winked" points to metaphorical language.

Question 8: (C)
On a short passage, main idea should be easy: go back and look at each sentence to see what the author is getting at. Here, it's the fact that Ada King is super-famous. Also pay attention to key words that make answer choices wrong. It's not all about her interest in "computer science" (A) and it's not a character analysis (B).

Question 9: (A)
This is a tricky one because it relies on just one detail from the story. In lines 7-8 we find out that people are interested in her partly because of her famous father. Thus, the author would disagree with (A). The process of elimination will help you get rid of some of the others and eventually point you in this direction.

Passage: Africa and America
Main idea: Black Americans are drawn to Africa because people instinctively seek out their own histories.

Question 10: (D)
This answer has one of my favorite College Board tricks: using vague, generic language to disguise the correct answer. What is the "ongoing relationship"? Oh, the relationship between Black Americans and Black Africans.

Question 11: (B)
Notice the colon after the sentence with "message" in it. Your answer is going to be there. Strong language like "cannot flourish" points to cautionary advice. Also note why the other answers are wrong: it's advice, not a proposition, recollection or prediction.

Question 12: (C)
The answer choice is sitting right there for you in the sentence that follows the proverb, proving once again that reading the line reference in context is the key to getting to the right answer. Check it out: "this is a maxim that conveys the seemingly instinctive pull of one's heritage." That's (C). Funny proverb, though, isn't it? Advice on how to steal a baby? Strange.

Question 13: (E)
This is kind of tough because "unsubstantiated" isn't a typical definition of "shadowy." But here it makes sense, as these "imaginings" aren't real things. They have yet to be substantiated. Again, getting rid of wrong answers helps. These are certainly not "gloomy" or "sinister" imaginings, and they're not "secret" or "concealed" either.

Question 14: (E)
When the question asks about a transition, look for a transition! Here, it's from disappointing first encounters to connections that have made the world "take note." Doubt to pride.

Question 15: (B)
A LOT of students get this wrong. We're looking at technique here. How did the author write this passage? Oh, with sweeping statements like "We have sought to understand each other ever since we were separated long ago." That's pretty broad. Also pretty general.

Passage: Mona Lisa
Main idea, Passage 1: The Mona Lisa's crazy fame is due to Leonardo's innovative painting technique.
Main idea, Passage 2: A lot of people have theories as to why the Mona Lisa is famous.

Question 16: (C)
See the first paragraph of P1 and the first line of P2. Voila! Everyone loves the Mona Lisa. It's even in a Bob Dylan song. "Visions of Johanna." Great song with the line: "But Mona Lisa must have had the highway blues, you can tell by the way she smiles."

Question 17: (A)
One of P2's ideas is that the Mona Lisa may be famous because it is famous. All the hype just increases its renown. And line 66 clearly points to (A): "I start with the assumption that the renown of a masterpiece rests on a sequence of events and history agencies." There it is!

Question 18: (E)
What's the contrast? That the subject was "nobody special" but that her portrait "set the standard for High Renaissance paintings." Boom. Again, look for clue words that are clearly wrong. There's nothing about her "untimely demise" (C) or "lack of charisma" (D) or the painting's "monetary value."

Question 19: (B)
This is just a description of the effect that Leonardo was able to achieve. Line 23 "this technique" and his comment "in the manner of smoke" point to (B).

Question 20: (A)
"And then there's that famous smile..." You had to know that line would come into play somehow, right?

Question 21: (D)
Replace "position" with "view" and it makes perfect sense. Treat these type of Critical Reading questions as Sentence Completions. "Policy" is headed in the right direction, but far too strong. The only one that works is (D).

Question 22: (E)
TOUGH one. Very specific. See "three-dimensional features" in lines 21-22 and "sense of texture and depth" in 56. Wow, that's hard. Getting rid of clearly wrong answers will really help you here, but it's still very difficult.

Question 23: (E)
On the SAT, quotation marks almost ALWAYS "imply skepticism." The author put the word in quotes to say "I don't agree with the standard usage of this word."

Question 24: (C)
Use process of elimination here. Treat it like a two-word sentence completion question. If one part of the answer doesn't work, it's out. That'll get you right to (C). There's something wrong with at least one part of each of the others.

Section 3: Math

Question 1: (A)
Plug 4 in for x to find the biggest one. That's (A), which is 5 X 6 = 30.

Question 2: (E)
Just keep careful track of which train is faster than which. If B is 7mph, then A is 21mph and C is 42mph.

Question 3: (B)
As on almost all average problems, set up the average formula. In this case $(x+5x+6x)/3=8$. Then use algebra to solve for x.

Question 4: (D)
For those of you who remember the definition of a function, that's what we're playing with here. (D) is right because at any one x-value there is only one y-value on that graph.

Question 5: (C)
The 9 in the butterfly circle represents those who ONLY study butterflies. Put that over 30 (the total number of kids), multiply by 100, and you're done!

Question 6: (C)
First find the length of CD. It stretches from -4 to 6, so it's 10 units long. AB stretches 3 units in the positive direction so it must stretch 7 in the negative.

Question 7: (D)
The easiest thing to do here is to find the value of x^2 (it's 4) and y (it's 3), then multiply them. 12.

Question 8: (D)
You need to be pretty careful on this problem. The radius of the largest circle is equal to the diameter of B (8) plus the radius of A (2). It's easy to get confused between diameter and radius, so make sure you're managing the information in the problem carefully.

Question 9: (D)
To get from 2 to 42, we had to make 5 "jumps" down the number line. We can figure out the value of the length of one of those jumps like so: $2+5n=42$. Solve that for n, and we learn that each jump is 8 units. X is 2

jumps bigger than 2, so it's 2+2(8)=18.

Question 10: (C)
You can ignore the 70 degree angle and solve for x by subtracting 110, 30 and 90 from 360.

Question 11: (B)
The most reliable way to solve a remainder problem is to find a number that fits the definition. One easy way to do that is to take the divisor (7) and add the remainder on. 13 is a number that fits the bill, because when you divide it by 7, 7 goes in 1 time with 6 left over. Add 2 to 13 to get 15, and divide that by 7. It goes in 2 times with 1 left over.

Question 12: (D)
The numbers in the chart are ugly. Thankfully we don't need to compute with them; we just need to look at the relationship. At depth = 0, pressure = 14.7. That means we have a positive y-intercept. As depth goes up so does pressure. Those two facts make (D) the only choice.

Question 13: (E)
Draw out the terms carefully. 1, -2, 4, -8, 16, -32.

Question 14: (E)
There is an easy way to do this and a tedious way. Let's do the easy way. When we multiply these two factors together, we get $4x^2-25=5$. Add the 25 over and we're done.

Question 15: (B)
Label the point on the graph. Slope of the line will be (r−0)/(p−0) because the line passes through the origin. If r/p is the slope, the line goes up and to the left (negative slope), and the absolute value of p is greater than that of r, it has to be (B).

Question 16: (A)
Subtract b from both sides of the original equation. Now we have 3a+3b=0. 6a+6b is simply twice that value. What's two times zero? Still zero.

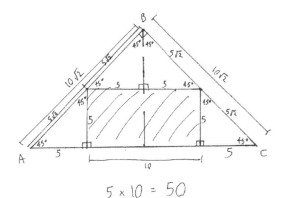

$$5 \times 10 = 50$$

Question 17: (C)
See diagram. 45-45-90 triangles abound here, and the √2 should tip you off. Since F is the midpoint of BC, then it splits that segment into two, each with length 5√2. If the hypotenuse of that little triangle on the right is 5√2 then its legs are 5. Same is true for top two triangles. The height of the rectangle is one leg long (5) and the width is two legs long, so the area is 5x10=50.

Question 18: (D)
Work with the easy values from the table and plug them into your equation. When x=0, then k*a^0=1/2. Anything to the zero power is 1, so a^0=1 and k must equal 1/2. Now plug in that k=1/2 for the next ordered pair in the table. You'll get 2=(1/2)*a^1. Solve for a and you get a=4.

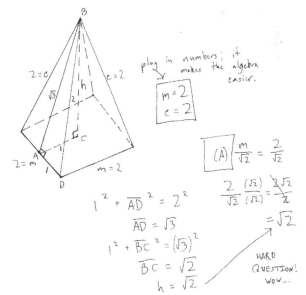

Question 19: (A)
See diagram. This one is the hardest question on the section. You're going to have to visualize right triangles within this 3D solid to get it. First, make life easy on yourself and pick a number for m that we can use to get a value for h; otherwise, the algebra will give you

a headache. I picked m=2. We need to find the slant height, which is the length of the line segment from the peak of the pyramid to the midpoint of the side labeled with m. If e=m, then e=2 as well. We've got a little right triangle there on the side, and the slant height is $\sqrt{3}$. Now use that length as the hypotenuse of another right triangle. Use Pythagorean to find that h=$\sqrt{2}$. Now use your value of m=2 and the answer choices to find which yields the same h value. That's (A).

Question 20: (A)
Plug in a value. Set k=10. The salesperson should make 10 percent of 28,000, which is equal to 28,000*0.10=2800. Go to the answer choices and plug in your value. (A) is the only one that gives the same result. This is pretty easy for #20, but where students get tripped up is the use of k as a percentage. We say that k=10, and even though we convert it to 0.10 in order to compute with it, the k value is still 10.

Section 5: Critical Reading

Question 1: (C)
Straightforward. What kind person "eagerly welcomes" people to her house? One who is known for her hospitality.

Question 2: (B)
If the people who wanted to preserve the forest were disappointed, what must have happened to the plan to save it? It got derailed. The other answer choices are positive or neutral; this is the only negative.

Question 3: (C)
Clue words "increases brain activity" point directly to "stimulus".

Question 4: (A)
Getting tougher now. We're looking for words that mean similar things but that vary by degree. Concessions is more extreme version of negotiating, so it's our winner. Also remember that if one of the words in an answer choice doesn't work, the whole answer is wrong. Process of elimination!

Question 5: (D)
The two blanks must match the two clues ("taken from another artist" and "poorly executed") IN ORDER. "Derivative" is the only one that works for the first word, and "inept" fits too.

Question 6: (B)
The most tempting wrong answer here is (A), because "affordable" is perfect and "cheapened" SEEMS like it works. But "cheapen" really means "to lower the quality of," so it's not what we're looking for. "Transformed/viable" works because it's the only pair with two positive words.

Question 7: (D)
One of my favorite vocab words, "supercilious" has the best derivation ever. "Super," meaning above, and "cilia," referring to little hairs, in this case the eyebrows. Someone who is supercilious raises their eyebrows. Try it -- it makes you look like the key word "haughty" (which means "behaving in a superior, condescending or arrogant way").

Question 8: (C)
The sentence is easy; we just need a word that means disloyalty. "Perfidy" breaks down as follows: "Per" means "damage to" and "fid" means "faithfulness." So perfidy means damaging to faithfulness. That's disloyalty.

Question 9: (A)
The fundamental disagreement between the authors of the two passages is whether or not Thoreau was saying that nature is threatened by industrialization. P1 says yes, P2 says no.

Question 10: (B)
From P1's perspective, the machine represented a destructive force against nature's "pastoral harmony."

Question 11: (E)
How would P1 respond to the direct quote from Thoreau saying that he actually kind of LIKED the railroad? By saying that he didn't feel that way most of the time. In other words, that one quote is atypical of his attitude toward mechanization.

Question 12: (C)
This is the toughest one in a set of tough questions. P1 says, "Generations of teachers have assigned Walden… as an illustration of the intensity with which…America protested the intrusion of…industrialization." It's a long sentence, but the cause-and-effect is that teachers assign it as a text of protest against industrialization. Thus, the interpretation in P2 is not representative of the way most teachers teach the book.

Passage: Cities
Main idea: The author disagrees with the widespread notion that human cities are unnatural.

Question 13: (D)
"Vision" in this case means "idea." Best choice is "conception."

Question 14: (D)

Many of the questions on this passage ask you to keep the author's perspective separate from the one that he is arguing against. OTHERS say that cities represent something non-natural. Our author disagrees. Thus, this "happier state" is a fictional state, or false supposition.

Question 15: (E)
Now we're looking for the author's perspective on how the other side thinks. He says that the Industrial Revolution "represents a wrong turning" to those folks who don't think cities are natural. Points directly at (E).

Question 16: (E)
Our author thinks that those "environmental thinkers" are flat out wrong. That's "erroneous." If you aren't sure about the definition of "erroneous," getting rid of clearly wrong answers should get you there anyway.

Question 17: (B)
There is a positive comparison made in this sentence between cities and the other two phenomena. We are all part of the same "web of life." The key to this answer is in the sentence following the referenced lines 33-36. This is common. Always read in context when choosing your answer. Including the sentence before and the sentence after is a great idea.

Question 18: (E)
The author really likes cities, right? He talks about all of the natural elements of a city, like sunlight and food-stuffs. It's hard to see that he's actually appreciating the trash of an urban center, but that's at least the only answer that gets back to the main idea, that the author loves cities.

Question 19: (A)
The three levels explore, in increasing depth, ways that the author can claim that cities are natural phenomena. He convinced me, at least. Yes, the answer choice is vague and might not jump out at you, particularly the "in support of a fundamental claim" part. But if you get rid of the clearly wrong choices, you'll get to the right one.

Question 20: (D)
What word would you substitute for "peculiar"? I'd pick "unique." Since it's not there, "distinctive" is the closest synonym. Always treat questions like these as sentence completion questions and put your own word in the blank.

Question 21: (A)
How would the author feel about a field of science dedicated to studying the ecology of cities? He'd LOVE it, of course!

Question 22: (C)
The way this paragraph is written, a comparison is clearly being drawn. "Both systems grow and evolve… Both require energy…"

Question 23: (E)
The discussion of the fact that bonds between atoms dictate both the maximum heights of trees and of skyscrapers points to our answer. (E) is written in such a stiff, formal tone…very typical of College Board to disguise a correct answer that way.

Question 24: (E)
The author warns us: "So let me state this explicitly…" Then he repeats his main claim. The function of this paragraph is restatement, or emphasis.

Section 6: Writing

Question 1: (C)
The phrase "by falling" creates cause and effect, and keeps the sentence short and clean.

Question 2: (C)
Note the College Board's hatred of the word "being." "Because" creates a cleaner, stronger link.

Question 3: (B)
The fires occurred "last summer." This is past tense verb in the plural. Some tempting choices here – look for the simplest.

Question 4: (C)
"When she showed" is the key to the sentence. Always read through the WHOLE sentence once first. Verb tense.

Question 5: (E)
First off, is this fact true or a product of the College Board's imagination? It sounds like a stretch to me. Anyway, there is a lot of information here. Semi-colon is a good way to link the two parts of the sentence. And remember that "however" frequently comes after a semi-colon.

Question 6: (A)
Parallel construction. "Begin" and "culminate." Simple, short and clean. The other answer choices make incomplete sentences or no sense in context.

Question 7: (D)
Misplaced modifier in the original. "Dressed in a crisp, clean uniform" would HAVE to be followed by "the tour guide." In the end, the uniform ends up being the subject of the sentence.

Question 8: (A)
Lots of commas, but still, the shortest one works. You can pull those appositive clauses out to see if the sentence works, like this: "A cure for some kinds of cancer may be found within the next decade." Boo-ya!

Question 9: (E)
Parallel construction. "Confusing because of its unusual structure" matches "elegant because of its…" perfectly.

Question 10: (C)
Pretty tough because of the length. The SUBJECT of the sentence ends up being the act of "Building new windmill farms." Tricky. If you're lost on one of these questions, use the process of elimination to get rid of clearly incorrect choices and you'll get there eventually.

Question 11: (E)
Memorize this one; the College Board loves this sentence construction. Take out the appositive "as many people assume" and it sounds terrrrrrrific. Notice how helpful this trick of taking out the appositive is. It's very helpful.

Question 12: (C)
Larissa and Tariq can't become just one entomologist. They do not have magical transforming qualities. Or maybe they do, but it won't fly on the SAT. Should read that they plan to become "entomologists."

Question 13: (E)
No problems here. Remember, something must be clearly incorrect. A lot of the no error choices might sound weird, but there's nothing grammatically incorrect.

Question 14: (A)
Things smell bad, they don't smell badly. Some students are fooled into choosing "had put" (C). But by the time the science teacher comes over, they HAD ALREADY PUT something smelly in the casserole. Get it? Great!

Question 15: (C)
Verb tense. See that Jerome "referred." That's past tense. He "sought out" their work. Notice how often they test tense like this. Always be on the look out for answer choices like this.

Question 16: (D)
"Thought it wise TO SUPRESS." That's an idiom. Also, "suppressing" does not work grammatically in context. You'd need a comma if you wanted to use it here, though it would still be incorrect.

Question 17: (C)

Here we want the adverb. How has it risen? Noticeably. LY. There will most likely be at least one adverb question per test. Learn to spot them automaticalLY.

Question 18: (A)
Neither / nor is correct. Also, either / or (though not in this case). Be on the lookout for these, they love to test 'em.

Question 19: (C)
Passengers are plural, therefore "their" is correct. This is another thing they love to do. Always pay attention to pronouns and make sure they are used correctly.

Question 20: (E)
No error. You might be tempted to pick (B), thinking it should be "65 and older." You COULD say it that way, but it's not wrong to say it this way.

Question 21: (B)
This is a classic faulty comparison. You can't compare Rockwell's PAINTINGS to Rauschenberg THE MAN. The College Board LOVES this type of question. They will ask it over and over again.

Question 22: (E)
This "No error" is meant to throw you by including a lot of awkward phrases. Don't be fooled; only pick something if you KNOW that it's wrong.

Question 23: (C)
Subject-Verb agreement. Spears ARE released. As the questions get trickier at the end of the section, they'll separate the subject from the verb to trick you. Take out the additional information separated by commas ("each trailed by a poison thread") and it's obvious.

Question 24: (E)
Another wacky "No error." When the questions get harder, count on seeing at least one really funky sentence that doesn't have an error.

Question 25: (C)
Idiom: capable OF distinguishING. Definitely a tricky one since there's nothing wrong with "to distinguish" other than the fact that we just don't say it that way. It does sound kind of weird if you read it aloud.

Question 26: (D)
Tricky! Hershey is the only subject in this sentence. The pronoun has to refer to it, so it should be singular. "One of ITS most famous residents," not "their."

Question 27: (E)
Another good one to memorize. Check out page 777, #29 in the Big Blue Book. They just love this sentence!

"Long since" is weird but not wrong.

Question 28: (D)
Subject-Verb agreement. "Low grades REQUIRE," not "requires." See? Notice the patterns in this section. Lots of subject-verb agreement questions.

Question 29: (D)
Tougher faulty comparison. No story is more dramatic than "THAN THE STORY OF...Hank Aaron." You need to add some words so you're not comparing stories to a person.

Passage Revision: Castles

Question 30: (C)
Palaces are mentioned a couple of times and we're told that they're different, but we're not told HOW they're different. It would be nice to learn a little more about palaces.

Question 31: (C)
We need to link these two sentences. It's all about how difficult it is to storm a castle. Adding "those who defied such obstacles did so at their own peril" is a nice connector.

Question 32: (E)
Definitely a very hard question. This requires you to do a LOT of reading. Eliminate answers based on grammatical problems. In (A), "could be found there" sucks. (B) is short, but that opening clause is very awkward. (C) is really tempting. The second part of the sentence is not parallel to the first when it says "were to be found." (D) gets palaces and castles confused. (E) is right by not being wrong.

Question 33: (C)
Yeah, it's ironic—castles were meant to keep people out but now they attract people instead. If that's hard to see, notice how the other four answers do not fit or make sense. Employ the process of elimination, dogg.

Question 34: (D)
We need a transition between the two sentences since 11 is a well-maintained tourist attraction and 12 is a decaying relic. (D) gets us there nicely.

Question 35: (B)
And we need a capper to finish off this FASCINATING essay on castles and palaces. I don't know about you, but I loved it. Again, the right answer gets in the late idea that some castles are not preserved but instead have become part of the modern landscape.

Section 7: Math

Question 1: (E)
Count up the little houses for the time periods 1961-1970, 1971-1980 and 1981-1990. There are 14. Multiply by 2000.

Question 2: (B)
Use vertical angles to find two other interior angles of the triangle with w in it. Subtract (35 + 45) from 180 to get 100.

Question 3: (E)
Working backwards from the answers is probably the easiest way to get this one. Start in the middle with (C) 6 tables with 5 people. See if it works. You only can seat 82 with that arrangement, so increase the number of tables until you find your answer. Alternately, you can write a system of equations. $x + y = 19$ and $4x + 5y = 84$, where y is the number of 5-person tables.

Question 4: (D)
Substitute $a = 4$, then factor it out of the trinomial to get (D)

Question 5: (A)
The side of the square is equal to the diameter of the circle, so the radius of the circle is 1. Find the area of the circle, using $A = \pi \times$ radius squared. The area is π. Then we take one-fourth of that amount, which is the fraction of the circle that's shaded. It's $\pi/4$.

Question 6: (C)
The diagram is not that useful here. Use your algebraic knowledge of slope instead. Rearrange the initial equation so that you have $y = -x/3 + 4$. The slope of that line is $-1/3$. The slope of a perpendicular line must be 3, so (C) is our answer.

Question 7: (E)
The sum of any two sides of a triangle must be greater than the third side. Because 5 plus 5 is not greater than 10, you can't make a triangle out of those sides.

Question 8: (C)
The easiest way to do this one is to split the vote total in half. The two candidates got around 1,400,000 votes each. To make the margin of victory 28,000, add 14,000 to 1,400,000 for the winner and subtract 14,000 from 1,400,000 for the loser. That'll create a difference of 28,000 between winner and loser. Now put the winner's tally over the total. Boom. Over.

Question 9: 9
Square both sides to clear up the radical. $2p = 18$ and $p = 9$.

Question 10: .2 or 1/5
1.783 rounded to the nearest integer is 2 and to the nearest tenth is 1.8. 2 − 1.8 = 0.2

Question 11: 15
That 2/5 probability means that of every 5 towels, 2 are brown. Set up a proportion: 2/5 = 6/x, where x represents the total number of towels. Cross-multiply and x=15.

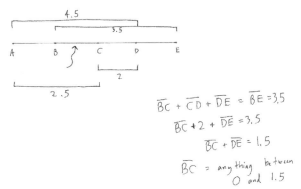

Question 12: 0<x<1.5 or 0<x<3/2
See diagram. This is a strange little number line. In the end, you don't need to know the length of AD. BE is 3.5 and CD is part of BE and is 2. That means that BC and DE must make up the other 1.5. BC could be anywhere from nearly zero to nearly 1.5.

Question 13: 6
With a ratio, add up the parts of the ratio to start. Now you can make a fraction. 3/5 days were rainy. Set up a proportion. 3/5 = x/30. Cross-multiply and x = 18. That means there were 12 sunny days, and a difference of 6.

Question 14: 117
To jump three terms from 3rd to 6th, we had to add 60 total. That means we added 20 each time. To get to the 8th term add 20 twice more. 77 + 2(20) = 117.

Question 15: 2.5 or 5/2
Chances are that on a medium or difficult math question that employs absolute value you're going to have to find the negative value. Do both, but in this case, the least value is the one where you solve x − 3 = −1/2.

Question 16: 5940
Tricky one, for sure. Logic is your friend here, not algebra. Which is the easiest number to guess at, for starters? I'd say Z, because it's the smallest (it's 5 less than W). Start with a small digit. If you pick Z=1, then W=6, Y=5, and X=12, which is not a digit. Too big. Try it with Z=0. Bingo.

Question 17: 90

All of the triangles here are equilateral, even the one created by the dotted lines (because it's angles are 60 degrees because they belong to the larger equilateral triangles). That means that the little guy has sides of 10, which means that the notch in the flag has sides of 10. Add it up: 30 on the right side, 20 each on top and bottom and 20 in the notch.

Question 18: 4.2 or 21/5
The zeros of the graph that you can see are at 3 and −3. If g(a−1.2)=0, then a−1.2 must give you one of those zeros. a−1.2=3 gives you the positive value for a, 4.2.

Section 8: Math

Question 1: (D)
Count all of the grey-shaded columns and add up the results. You should get 4+2+5+1+1=13

Question 2: (E)
Fairly tricky for #2. The two diameters create congruent triangles ABC and ADE. Thus the bases, CB and ED, must have equal length. You could also solve this one visually. If the problem doesn't say "Figure not drawn to scale" then the figure IS drawn to scale.

Question 3: (A)
There are a lot of ugly problems early in this section. Don't let them get you down! Here, this symbol looks pretty horrible. It's not so bad, though. See how 5 is in the box where a used to be? OK, plug 5 in for a. Likewise with 2 for b and 6 for c. You should then have the statement 5^2−5*6+6. That equals 1.

Question 4: (C)
Draw this out. The other two vertices will be at (-2, 2) and (2, -2). The side length of the square is 4, so its area is 16.

Question 5: (B)
Here you have to be a detective. Steph is the youngest. That's good news. Owen has both an older brother and an older sister, so he must be the second youngest. Chadd is not the oldest, so he must be the second-oldest. That makes Daria the oldest.

Question 6: (E)
In a parallelogram (which is what we have here), opposite angles are equal. Thus 2(x+y) is actually the sum of all four angles, which in any quadrilateral is 360 degrees.

Question 7: (A)
Like every other time we see average on the SAT, you

should write out the problem using the average formula. It should be (x+y+z)/3=12. Multiply the three over and you'll have x+y+z=36. This will eliminate (C) and (D). The second equation in (A) then represents the sum of the two smallest numbers (x and y) minus the greatest one (z) which equals 4.

Question 8: (B)
On an exponent problem, always try to write each element using the same base. For example, 81 is the same as 3^4. Substitute that in as a great first step. Then use your properties of exponents: 3^2x * 3^2y = 3^(2x+2y). Now that we have the same base equal to two different exponents, we can set the exponents equal to each other. 2x+2y=4. Divide both sides by 2 and x+y=2.

Question 9: (B)
F values are y-values. Where does this graph have it's maximum y-value? On that bump to the right of the y-axis. Count the hash marks: that's where x=4.

Question 10: (B)
Just a little careful algebra here. Multiply the three over. Now you have 3k=x. To find out what 3x is, multiply both sides by 3 again. Now you have 9k=3x.

Question 11: (A)
Cubes have 6 sides, so there must be 4 white sides. Divide that total area of 64 square inches to find out that each face has an area of 16 square inches. Because each face of a cube is a square, the side lengths must be the same, and must be 4 inches. Now we can find the volume. V=l*w*h, or 4*4*4, which is 64.

Question 12: (B)
This is just tedious. The best/only way to get this is to take the values of the letters off of the number line (v= -0.75, w= -0.5, x=0.25 and y=0.75) and calculate all of the values of the answer choices.

Question 13: (D)
When you add another term to this set, you'll have 7 terms. Whenever a set has an odd number of terms, one of the terms in the set IS the median. If we make n a small integer, like 2, then 6 will be the median. If n = 15, then 7 is the median. Our new number has to be an integer, so it can't be 6.5. I and III only.

Question 14: (B)
5 choices for color 1, then 4 choices (because we have to use different colors) for color 2. 5*4=20

Question 15: (E)
Pick a rectangle with easy dimensions to play with. I chose a 10x10, because the values are easy to work with and its area is 100. 10 increased by 30 percent is

13 and 10 decreased by 30 percent is 7. A 13x7 rectangle has an area of 91. That's a 9% decrease from an area of 100.

Question 16: (B)
The hardest one in the section. When you plug 10 into the equation as the input (t) value, you'll get –150+k. The easiest way to finish is to plug the answer choices in to see which will give you the same result. Alternately, you could solve the equation for the other input, like this: (t^2)/2–20t+k=–150+k. That'll turn into a quadratic. Either way, 30 yields the same result. This is definitely a problem you'll need 2-3 minutes to solve. If you didn't get this one, don't beat yourself up.

Section 9: Critical Reading

Question 1: (B)
"Free of tricks" means direct and not misleading. That's "straightforward."

Question 2: (C)
We've got a "resurgence of popularity" for the team. The crowds must be large and the cheers must be loud. That's (C).

Question 3: (B)
You really need to use the answer choices here, as the sentence doesn't quite have enough specific clues to know the words. Trying all of the combinations, the only one that remotely makes sense with this situation is "altered/revolution," though "revolution" does seem like too strong a word choice in this sentence.

Question 4: (E)
This is tough, because most students will avoid "currency," thinking that it only refers to cash money. But the other first words that work—credence, acceptance and momentum—are paired with other words that really don't work at all. "Currency" in this case means "general acceptance." Paired with "inconclusive," it's perfect.

Question 5: (B)
Here it's a straight-up vocab challenge. Which word means "virtually transparent?" Only diaphanous. Here are some of the other definitions:
Palpable: obvious, easily observed
Variegated: marked by patches of different colors
Anomalous: deviating from the norm

Question 6: (D)
Look up "iconoclast" and you'll realize that these sentences are practically ripped from the dictionary.
Dilettante: someone who's good at a lot of stuff but

not great at anything
Egalitarian: someone who believes in equality
Dowager: an older, respectable woman
Purveyor: someone who sells stuff

Passage: Shirley and Mr. Sympson
Main idea: Shirley, a young romantic, and her uncle Mr. Sympson, an old, mean fart, can't agree about who she should marry.

Question 7: (C)
This passage, in general, is long and tough to get into, but the questions aren't actually that bad. Here, this is a basic main idea question. (C): they don't get along and don't agree at all.

Question 8: (C)
To match the word 'romantic,' (C) is really the only possibility, especially given what else we learn about her personality.

Question 9: (E)
He "anxiously desired" to get her married; that means he just wants to get it over with! "Impatience" words perfectly.

Question 10: (E)
Marrying Sam Wynne would yield a sweet estate and "good connections." Those are social and financial advantages!

Question 11: (A)
Toughest one on the passage, because it asks you to understand this phrase: "despicable, commonplace profligacy." I don't know about you, but I don't throw the word "profligacy" around in conversation very much. It means "lewd, or wildly extravagant." Apparently Mr. Wynne is not very well behaved. In other words, he acts in an undignified manner.

Question 12: (B)
He asks her a question. She says, "I don't have to answer that." You got served, Mr. Sympson! And is that really how you spell your name? Not Simpson? Really? Hm.

Question 13: (D)
Note that this question starts with "The passage as a whole suggests…" That's because we have to remember that good ol' uncle was only her guardian up until adulthood, and now she's free of his authority (see the italics).

Question 14: (A)
This is a hard question. He tells her to "take care," and she turns it around and says, "Scrupulous care I will

take… Before I marry I am resolved to esteem – to admire – to LOVE." She twists his words to suit her meaning. This works for the correct answer, (A), but may not be immediately obvious. The other choices, however, all contain an incorrect word. She's not "turning the BLAME back on him" (B), she's not "childishly mocking the TONE" (C), she's not "lamenting his failure to SYMPATHIZE" (D), and she's not "JUSTIFYING" anything (E).

Question 15: (D)
She is speaking in an "unknown tongue" because she doesn't expect that Mr. Wynne could possibly understand her talk about love. Tongue, used in this old-school context, means "language."

Question 16: (B)
"To what will she come?" is an expression of frustration, not a real question. He thinks she's making a huge mistake…

Question 17: (C)
…and she pretends like he is asking a real question, and answers it as such. I'm definitely not marrying that guy, she says.

Question 18: (B)
See lines 80-82. "Before I marry, I am resolved…to love."

Question 19: (E)
He doesn't want her to marry a poor man and she doesn't want to marry an undignified man. So they can agree on one thing: her husband should not be both poor AND undignified.

Section 10: Writing

Question 1: (D)
"Challenges" is the subject of the sentence, and the word is plural, so "There are many challenges" is what we need to start. Then, "associated" is cleaner, shorter, and more idiomatically correct than "which associate."

Question 2: (C)
The right answer in this case does two good things. The first part of the choice clarifies which watercolors (the ones "on display at the museum"), then gets straight to a strong main verb: "represent." Together, they make a strong, tight sentence.

Question 3: (B)
"Origins" is the subject, so we need a plural verb. And all of those guys can't have just one presidency—they have to have the plural "presidencies."

Question 4: (E)
You can't start this part of the sentence with "she" because it'll be ambiguous—are you talking about Sheila or Lucy? The other choice you have to make is about verb tense. This sentence is written in the simple past tense, so we want (E).

Question 5: (C)
We lead off with a modifying clause here. WHAT was carried by the strong winds? It has to be the dust. That leaves us with (C) and (D). The extra word "that" in (D) makes it an incomplete sentence, so it must be (C).

Question 6: (E)
How do we link these two clauses? The regulations have SO complicated the process THAT no one wants to undertake the task. Those words work together; the others don't.

Question 7: (D)
Even the right answer here kind of stinks, but it's better than the others. "Is because" does not work in this sentence. (D) is right because the two reasons given in the second part of the sentence are parallel. Adults are 1) getting fewer cavities and 2) becoming more vain. Isn't that a little judgmental, College Board? Don't be hatin' just because y'all have nasty teeth!

Question 8: (E)
We've got another modifying clause here. I love those things! They make picking an answer so easy. "If asked to name a musical group..." must be followed by WHO is being asked to name the group. It's "most people"! If you recognize that simple thing, you'll go straight to the right answer.

Question 9: (E)
We need a strong subject and a main verb in the missing portion of the sentence. That's the US and Canada, and the verb is "set."

Question 10: (A)
The clause after Ruben Blades's name is an appositive to sneak in one more fact about him before we get to the meat of the sentence. Also, remember how much the College Board hates the word "being."

Question 11: (D)
We're looking for parallelism, but more than anything else we're just trying to get through a whole heap of text here. Get picky on each of the answer choices. "Being" is horrible in (A), so that's out. "It reconciling" sucks in (B). The semicolon and "as such" don't make sense in (C). The part that comes after the semicolon in (E) is not a complete sentence, so that's not it. (D) is long, but it's parallel and complete.

Question 12: (D)
Parallelism again here. Note that on some of these questions, in order to be parallel you actually have to be fairly wordy. "Adults are overharvested, their eggs are disturbed, and their nesting habitats are destroyed" is long, but it's parallel.

Question 13: (C)
Ah, a short one. Yay. Tricky subject here: it's "improper diet and lack of exercise." That's two things, so "contribute" is correct.

Question 14: (E)
Yet another parallelism question, and another good one to memorize. Check out page 775, #11. Same question. They even have the same answer! Not very creative, College Board. Alexei's acquaintances have two things to say about him, first, that he is "annoying because of his unpredictability." The other comment has to match that one's structure exactly. That's "delightful because of his imagination." That's a word for word parallel. For the record, I know Alexei, and I don't think he's annoying.

Test 2
Section 2: Math

Question 1: (D)
The missing term is twice the previous term plus 2. So, we multiply (10)(2) = 20 and add 2 to get 22.

Question 2: (A)
Let's convert one hour to 60 minutes. Now we can set up a proportion:
24 cartons / 60 minutes = x cartons / 5 minutes.
We cross multiply to get 120 = 60x. x = 2.

Question 3: (A)
In May, Cathy sold 48 cars. In January and February combined, she sold 20 plus 18 cars, for a total of 38. So, compared to the number 38, the answer is that in May, Cathy sold 10 MORE cars.

Question 4: (C)
This one involves some effort! A circle graph (a.k.a. "pie chart") has slices based on proportions of the total. So, first we need to know the total cars sold in 6 months. 20 + 18 + 22 + 30 + 48 + 42 = 180 total cars. If we use the number of cars sold in April (30 cars) out of the total (180), we can now make that a proportion to the sector we want of the circle (out of 360 degrees). Huh? Did that make sense? It's easier to explain in math terms:
30 cars / 180 total cars = x degrees / 360 total degrees
We can cross multiply and solve for x, which is 60 degrees.

Question 5: (D)
Here's a cool idea: rotate your book 90 degrees and look at it! Yes, you're allowed to do that! Now rotate it back real quick and see which answer it looks like before you forget. (Note: papers may go flying in every direction).
A more systematic thing to do is to look at a specific part of the original figure. I like the two little squares sticking out in the top right corner. When the figure is rotated, they should be in the top left corner, and should be pointing upwards. Only answers (C) and (D) fit that description. The difference between (C) and (D) is the indent on the bottom of the figures. Back in the original figure, that indent is on the left hand side, and it is in a position that is equivalent to (D).

Question 6: (D)
Let's math-ify the sentence:
3 + 2x = 10. So we solve for x. 2x = 7. x = 7/2.
BUT they want four times that number. So 4x = 4(7/2) = 28/2 = 14.

Question 7: (A)
Since a < 0, a must be a negative number. The bigger the number we multiply times a, the more negative it gets. So 8a is much MORE negative. Don't believe me? Pick any negative number for a (it can be an integer or a fraction). For example, if a = -5, then 2a = -10, 4a = -20, and 8a = -40. The GREATEST of those options is the original number, a itself, because the rest are MORE negative. Sneaky!

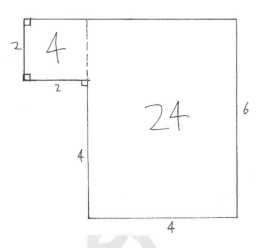

Question 8: (B)
See diagram. Draw a line straight up, chopping off the little square. We now have a big rectangle and a little square. The area of the rectangle is (6)(4) = 24. The bottom of the little square is labeled 2. Do we know it's a square for sure? Yes, because the height of the whole figure on the right hand side is 6, so the height of the figure on the left hand side (the part marked "4" plus the height of the square) must also equal 6. So the little square has a base of 2 and height of 2. Its area is 4. The area of the rectangle plus little square is 24 + 4 = 28.

Question 9: (D)
We can square root both sides, but we have to remember to add a plus and minus sign on the right hand side. So we have two options: x − 2 = +5 or x − 2 = -5. They tell us that x is less than zero, so that helps. Let's focus on x − 2 = -5. If we solve for x by adding 2 to both sides, we get x = -3. Sweet! (We can double-check by plugging it back into the original equation).

Question 10: (E)
The two triangles must be similar because they have two congruent angles (they share angle P, and they both contain an angle that is x degrees). The cool thing is that it doesn't matter what x is.
For similar triangles, we can use proportions. The question is asking for PT/PS, which is the ratio of a side of the smaller triangle to the corresponding side of the

larger triangle. We can set that equal to the ratio of a different side of the small triangle (the side that is 8 units) to the corresponding side of the bigger triangle (the side that's 10 units). So:
PT/PS = 8/10 = 4/5.
For some reason, this math section has a LOT of proportion questions in it!

Question 11: (D)
The quick way to do this is to pick a point on the graph and use its coordinates. For example, at week 7, the length is 70 mm. Then we can just plug those numbers into the answers and see which one works. Answer (D) pretty clearly works: L = 10W, which means 70 = 10(7). If we want to be extra sure, we can plug in the coordinates of any other point into answer (D), and that equation still works.

Question 12: (A)
It's much easier to see what's going on if we arrange this list of numbers in order. I'll leave out the missing number, n, for now:
5, 5, 5, 5, 6, 6, 6, 7
Since mode is the most frequent number, and we're told that it is 5, that means the missing number can't be a 6. If n were 6, then 6 would be as frequent as 5, and that would mess up everything, and the world would stop making sense and people would run through the streets screaming and tearing out their hair. So the answer is that n can't equal 6.
If n is any number bigger than 6, it will be added to the right hand side of the list in the appropriate order, and the median will be 6, like it's supposed to be. So (A) gives us the only value of n that won't work.

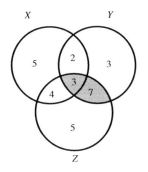

Question 13: (C)
See diagram. We need to look at the areas where circles Y and Z overlap. The number 7 is in the area where they overlap, so that counts, but we also have to count the number 3 in the middle of the whole figure (it's where X, Y and Z overlap, which is technically inside Y and inside Z). So there are 7 + 3 = 10 total elements in the intersection of Y and Z.

Question 14: (E)

Since m = t^3, we need to take the equation w = m^2 + m and plug in t^3 anytime we see "m." So we get w = (t^3)^2 + (t^3). We can multiply the exponents in the first chunk and get w = t^6 + t^3.

Question 15: (B)
This one involves doing several painstaking steps of calculations carefully, and then thoroughly checking the answers. Yay. The triangle symbol just means that we take whatever number is next to it and plug it into (x − 1)(x + 1). So, first let's evaluate 6 in that way. (6 − 1)(6 + 1) = (5)(7) = 35. Now let's plug 5 into the same formula. (5 − 1)(5 + 1) = (4)(6) = 24. So, 6(triangle) minus 5(triangle) is really just asking for 35 − 24. Our answer is 11.
BUT, we have to see which answer choice equals 11. Now we just have to use trial and error. Since our earlier answers for 6 and 5 were so large, I'd start by trying smaller numbers. It turns out that answer (B) works. (3 − 1)(3 + 1) = (2)(4) = 8, and (2 − 1)(2 + 1) = (1)(3) = 3. And 8 + 3 gives us the 11 we were looking for. Like I said earlier, "yay."

Question 16: (D)
We need to use trial and error on the answers. The easiest way to start is to use the fact that we're told x/y is not an integer. (Of course, we all remember that the word "integer" means a whole number with no decimals or fractions, right? Awesome. I'm glad we all remember that from, like, third grade).
So we can go through the answers and eliminate any answers where x/y IS an integer. That means that (A) can't work. Neither can (C) or (E). We're left with (B) and (D). Now we can check those by squaring x and dividing it by y. Now we WANT to get an integer! (D) works because 6 squared is 36, and 36/4 = 9, which is a whole number.

Question 17: (B)
The absolute value of any graph takes the parts of the graph that were negative (y-values less than zero) and reflects them around the x-axis. In other words, the positive parts of the graph stay where they are, and when the graph touches zero, it "bounces" back up into positive territory instead of going into negative territory. Answer (B) has a picture that represents this idea. Another way to solve this one is to plug numbers into the equation given (the one with the absolute value) and use the resulting coordinates to plot the graph on your own. Or just graph it in a graphing calculator.

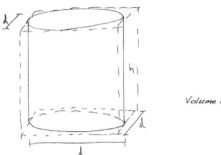

Volume of Box = *lwh*
= *d* x *d* x *h*
= *d²h*

Question 18: (B)

See diagram. Envision a cake inside of a rectangular box. The box will have the same height as the cake. Now we need to figure out the size of the base of the box. The base of the cylinder is a circle. The base of the box will be a square with the circle inscribed inside of it (it's a square because circles are symmetrical). The circle touches each of the four sides of the square, meaning that each side of the square is the same length as the diameter of the circle. And finally… (drum roll please)… the area of our rectangular box is the area of the square base times the height, which equals $(d^2)(h)$.

Question 19: (E)

This one's kinda nasty! First, let's turn the sentences they gave us into math equations. We have two equations:
$x^2 = 4(y^2)$
$x = 2y + 1$
We can solve these using the substitution method. Let's plug the right hand side of the second equation in for x in the first equation:
$(2y + 1)^2 = 4(y^2)$. Now we can FOIL the left hand side.
$4(y^2) + 4y + 1 = 4(y^2)$. We can subtract 4 y-squared from both sides.
$4y + 1 = 0$. Now solve for y.
$y = -1/4$.
We need the value of x, so we can plug this value into the second equation we had when we started (I would avoid the first equation because it involves messy squaring).
$x = 2(-1/4) + 1$. So, $x = -1/2 + 1$. Finally, $x = 1/2$.

Question 20: (E)

The trick here is that perpendicular lines have slopes that are negative reciprocals! So, we can find the slope of line L and use that to find the slope of line Q. The slope of line L is rise/run = (change in y)/(change in x) = $(1 - 0) / (2 - 0) = 1/2$. That means the slope of line Q is -2/1. Now we plug in the points that are on line Q into the slope formula:
$-2/1 = (t - 1)/(0 - 2)$. Then we simplify to get:

$-2 = (t - 1)/(-2)$. Now we can multiply both sides by -2. $4 = (t - 1)$. We add one to both sides to discover that t = 5. Hooray!

Section 4: Critical Reading

Question 1: (C)

Here's a sentence where we might not be 100% sure what the story is after the first read-through. The best clue is the phrase, "once you knew…" When you knew what happened to the hero, you could "foresee" what happened to the villain. Thus, the movie is "predictable."

Question 2: (B)

See the keyword "actually" there? It indicates that the first word is the opposite of what came before it. The opposite effect of reducing pollution has to be either (B) "contaminating" or (E) "polluting." In the second half of the sentence we get the phrase, "even the most well-intentioned…" That word "even" suggests another contrast. Thus, it's "backfire," which is the opposite effect that a well-intentioned plan should have.

Question 3: (A)

The last phrase is the definition of the missing word. "Dispassionate" means exactly that. Even if you didn't know that word, you might be able to break it into parts and figure it out. "Passionate" means "with a lot of emotion," and as a prefix, Dis– means "not." So, "Not with a lot of emotion."

Question 4: (B)

You definitely need to take your time to understand the story behind this sentence. So there's a belief that the Taino people all perished (died). But modern Taino descendants have come forward. Ah. That belief then appears to be untrue. Looking at the second words, only "misconception" and "delusion" are possibilities. Now, that belief is no longer considered TRUE. "Erroneous" means false (think "in error" when you see "erroneous"), so that can't be it. By elimination, it's (B).

Question 5: (E)

Not too complicated. The "although" is a clue that we need a word that's the opposite of "angered," and in this case that's "mollified," which means "soothed."

Question 6: (A)

Here's another one where it's obvious what you're looking for but the choices are fairly obscure. If you don't know right away which answer means "the crap floating in space," do your best to eliminate words that DON'T mean that. You can probably get it down to "flotsam" (discarded objects and debris) and "raiment" (clothing). Obviously, it's flotsam.

Question 7: (A)
Keys here: first, finding a contrast to "physiology" (related to the body). Second, figuring out what "irascible" means. The first word should be something that means personality. Now, notice that "personality" is there as an answer choice. "Disposition" could work too. "Irascible" is related to "ire" which is anger. That matches "cantankerous" (easily irritated) better than "laconic" (using few words).

Question 8: (A)
Easy clue words ("unpredictable"), tough vocab words. Think of the element mercury when you see "mercurial". Mercury is a metal that's a liquid at room temperature. As far as metals go, that stuff is unpredictable!

Question 9: (D)
P2 directly challenges P1 for assuming that "empty" land does not already have a use and could be utilized to house more people. Just because land appears to be unoccupied doesn't mean people could live there. So P1 is focusing on the wrong factor in assessing overcrowding.

Question 10: (C)
"...is as widespread as it is WRONG." That's a pretty strong choice at the end, isn't it? Although "dismayed" is tempting, that word means "discouraged." The tone of that sentence is more forceful. "Emphatic" means "with emphasis," so that's the right answer.

Question 11: (C)
One of the SAT's favorite questions involves the use of quotation marks to indicate that the author doesn't agree with the common use of a term. It's like using airquotes to indicate sarcasm. When P2 puts quotes around "empty," it's indicating disagreement with P1's use of that word.

Question 12: (A)
What can these two guys agree about? That there is plenty of land on earth where people don't live.

Passage: Canoe Trip
Main idea: Three characters discuss the contrast between wilderness and civilization as they plan a canoe trip.

Question 13: (B)
The map seems to have a will of it's own, as if it's choosing to unroll and show it's colors. "Animate" means alive, so that's perfect here.

Question 14: (C)
This question just asks what the function of these 6 lines is. The narrator is really just making an observation here about his friend Lewis's manner of speaking. That's "note an impression."

Question 15: (D)
Notice how the hand "seemed to have power over the terrain" and that "all streams everywhere quit running"? That's a powerful hand! "Omnipotent" means all-powerful. So there's your winner.

Question 16: (E)
Figure out which word works best in the sentence. Although "flowing" might be tempting because it's related to rivers, what's really happening here is that the river is NOT flowing (because of the power of Lewis's hand...see the previous question). "Suspended" is best in the sentence, meaning "stopped in mid-motion."

Question 17: (E)
Alaska is "wild," which to Lewis means untouched by man, or "undeveloped."

Question 18: (A)
So Lewis is a guy who likes stuff to remain wild, right? He wants to get up to this wild area BEFORE the real estate people get hold of it, as if to say that they will spoil it. He is contemptuous of those people.

Question 19: (E)
Does Lewis REALLY think it'll be like heaven? Quite the opposite, actually. He's being ironic.

Question 20: (B)
This one takes a bit of work and perhaps looking at the answer choices to imagine which one might work. When you look at (B), notice how the author really does imagine two different states: man-made and wild. Of course, this answer probably won't jump out at you, but getting rid of all those wrong answers that don't fit at all will get you there.

Question 21: (A)
This sentence in the passage is all about the narrator's physical awareness and eagerness ("felt ready"). Thus, "physical anticipation."

Question 22: (A)
Again, you've got to figure out which one works best in the original sentence. On the map, the narrator is finding ("locating") a spot on the map.

Question 23: (D)
This is a vocabulary question that sneaked onto the reading passage. Lewis is about to make a big, edu-

cational point for his friends, right? "Didactic" means "fond of instructing others." Boy, is that perfect. If you don't know that word, you've just got to eliminate bad choices and take a guess.

Question 24: (C)
Try to find clues in this section, like "strictly his own" and "evolve a personal approach." That should lead you to (C).

Question 25: (C)
Beware the SAT's sense of humor: it isn't very humorous. Bobby Trippe is no Zack Galifianakis here (he's not even Dane Cook), but he is trying to be funny. The previous paragraph lets us know that he's about to say something to deflate Lewis's self-important speech. He does so using a bit of sarcasm that the SAT considers humorous.

Section 5: Math

Question 1: (B)
If $3x = 0$, then divide by 3 to get $x = 0$. Plug that into the second expression and get $1 + 0 + 0^2$, which is still just equal to 1.

Question 2: (E)
The diameter of circle A is 3 times the diameter of circle B. Let's plug in numbers and say that the diameter of circle A is 24, in which case the diameter of circle B is 8. Since the radius is always half the diameter, the radius of circle A is 12, and the radius of circle B is 4. The ratio of those is 12 : 4, which can be reduced to 3 : 1.

Question 3: (D)
If every number in a set is doubled, then their average will also be doubled.
Don't believe me? Fine. For a simple example, let's say that set N is just the numbers 2 and 4. Their average is 3. Set M is double those numbers, so it contains the numbers 4 and 8. If we average them, $(4 + 8)/2 = 12/2 = 6$.

Question 4: (C)
When we multiply by 10^{-2}, that means we move the decimal two spots to the left (it's the same as dividing by 100). So, if our original number was 654, for example, then the new number would be 6.54.

Question 5: (E)
This is a little crazy looking at first! $k + n < k$. It's easier to see what's going on if you put in a number for k. For example: $5 + n < 5$. So basically, we are adding n to a number, and the result is less than the number we started with! That means that n must be negative. It's

reducing the value of the left hand side of the expression. So the correct answer is the one that shows that n is a negative number, which is: $n < 0$.

Question 6: (A)
Wow, the SAT writers really put a lot of time into that very detailed drawing of a truck, didn't they? A boxy shape with one wheel. Those are some very impressive drawing skills, SAT writers! Don't quit your day jobs. Since slope is rise/run, that means we can set up a proportion where $7/16 = y/x$. We're told that $y = 3.5$, so we put that into the proportion. $7/16 = 3.5/x$. Now we cross multiply and solve for x. $7x = 56$. $x = 8$.

Question 7: (B)
By the rules of parabolas, in the equation $y = ax^2 + 2$, the "+2" part is the height of where the parabola crosses the y-axis, and the value of a determines the shape of the parabola (skinny or wide). Larger values of a make the parabola skinnier, and smaller values of a make the parabola wider. So in the second equation we're given, $y = (a/3)(x^2) + 2$, the parabola will cross the axis at the same height, but the a-value is smaller, so the shape will be wider!

Question 8: (B)
Meredith is clearly desperate for attention.
The best way to do this is to systematically make a list of the possibilities. Let's say she wears a red hat. Then she needs something white and something blue. She can wear either a white sweater, and blue jeans, or she could wear the blue sweater and white jeans. We could write those options down as:
RED hat, WHITE sweater, BLUE jeans
RED hat, BLUE sweater, WHITE jeans
If Meredith starts with a blue hat, she also has two options:
BLUE hat, RED sweater, WHITE jeans
BLUE hat, WHITE sweater, RED jeans
And finally, (starting to see a pattern) if she starts with a white hat, she again has two options:
WHITE hat, RED sweater, BLUE jeans
WHITE hat, BLUE sweater, RED jeans
Those are all the possibilities. She has a total of six options!

Question 9: 4.5 or 9/2
Let's turn the sentence into a math equation! $2x + 5 = 14$. Subtract 5 from both sides. $2x = 9$. Divide by 2 to get $x = 9/2$.

Question 10: 135
Ah, parallel lines, how you love to show up on the SAT. Between parallel lines, there's a theorem that says that angles on the same side add up to 180 degrees. So x +

y = 180. Since y = 3x, we can rewrite the first equation as x + 3x = 180. Therefore, 4x = 180, and x = 45. We plug that into y = 3x to solve for y. So y = 3(45) = 135.

Question 11: 32
If we stand the CD cases up flat on their edges and put them into the box that way, the dimensions will line up perfectly. The box has a width of 4 inches and a height of 4 inches, which matches the CD cases' width and height of 4 inches. Now, we just have to look at how deep the box is. It's 8 inches deep, and each CD case is 1/4 inch thick. So the questions is really just asking how many 1/4 inch thick CD cases will fit in an 8 inch deep box. 4 CD cases would be a total of one inch thick, and there are 8 inches, so we multiply (4)(8) to get 32.

Question 12: 1/15, or .066, or .067
There are a couple of ways to do this one. Probably the fastest way is to cross-multiply the two fractions:
(3x + y) / y = 6/5
5(3x + y) = 6y
15x + 5y = 6y
15x = 1y. Now we want to solve for x/y, so we divide both sides by y.
15x/y = 1. And to get x/y by itself, we divide both sides by 15.
x/y = 1/15. Tada!

Question 13: 1750
To find the average increase, the trick is that we first need to find the average profit for the stores for each year. They were nice enough to already give us the to-tals. You can IGNORE all of the individual profits in the table! Awesome! For Year 1, the three stores earned a total of $21,000. So the average profit that year for the three stores was 21,000/3 = 7,000 per store. For Year 2, the average profit was the Year 2 total divided by 3, which is 26,250/3 = 8,750. Then the last step to find the INCREASE is just to subtract those two average profits. 8,750 – 7,000 = 1750.

Question 14: 4.25<x<8.5 or 17/4<x<17/2
This one is a little bit nasty. When they ask for a value of a where f(a) < a, that means that they really want you to find a set of coordinates where the y-value, which is the same concept as f(a), is less than the x-value, which is the same as a. Since the original equation is an absolute value function, if you have a graphing calculator, it's worthwhile to graph the function and take a look at what's going on. Now if you also graph the line y = x, then the correct answers are the range of values where the absolute value function dips BELOW the line y = x.
If you look at the graph, the function touches the x-axis (has a height of zero) at an x-value between 5 and 6. (Specifically, it touches at 17/3, which is 5.667). Any

x-value around that area will work. For example, if you say that a = 5, and plug it into your function, you can calculate that f(a) = the absolute value of (3)(5) – 17 = 15 – 17 = -2. The absolute value of that is 2. f(a) = 2, and 2 < 5. So a = 5 is a correct answer! It also works if a = 6. It turns out that any value of a that is between 4.25 and 8.5 will work.
The way to solve this more "officially" is to mathemati-cally state that we want the absolute value of 3a – 17 to be less than a. To solve absolute value inequali-ties, we have to get rid of the absolute value sign and rewrite them as two inequalities, one with a negative value out front:
3a – 17 < a AND -(3a – 17) < a. Then we simplify both.
2a < 17 AND -3a + 17 < a.
a < 17/2 AND 17 < 4a
a < 17/2 AND 17/4 < a.
That means that the correct value for "a" is any value that is bigger than 17/4 (a.k.a. 4.25) and smaller than 17/2 (a.k.a. 8.5).
The fastest way to solve this problem? Guess and check.

Question 15: 8
This problem gives us more info than we need. We can ignore how much candy is left in the jar! Just think about the candy that Ari has. Mmm… He has 3 red pieces and 4 green pieces. He takes 13 more pieces of candy, and we want him to have a total of more reds than greens. Well, the 13 pieces of candy can be split up into various amounts of red and green. Let's say that out of the 13 pieces, 7 are red and 6 are green. Then Ari's total of red candy is the original 3 plus 7 more = 10. His total of green is 4 + 6, which also equals 10. For him to have MORE red candy than green, he needs to take any number of red candies more than 7. If he takes 8 red candies and 5 green, that works. So 8 is the right answer.

Question 16: 9
A little bit tricky! The best way to do this is to just focus on the fact that we need three consecutive integers. For example, 1 x 2 x 3 = 6. That would work. The problem doesn't say that the consecutive integers have to be POSTIIVE, so we have to think about whether we need to include negative integers or zero. For example, how about -1 x -2 x -3? But that doesn't work, because that equals -6. The product of any three negative numbers will be negative, and the problem says we want posi-tive products, so we can ignore negatives. Likewise, if zero is one of the consecutive integers, like 0 x 1 x 2, those are consecutive, but the product is zero, so it isn't positive. So, we can safely start with the smallest posi-tive integers, and then if we carefully make a list, we'll find that we get all the products less than 1000 pretty quickly:

1 x 2 x 3 = 6
2 x 3 x 4 = 24
3 x 4 x 5 = 60
4 x 5 x 6 = 120
5 x 6 x 7 = 210
6 x 7 x 8 = 336
7 x 8 x 9 = 504
8 x 9 x 10 = 720
9 x 10 x 11 = 990
That's it! The total is that there are NINE integers that are tri-factorable.

Question 17: 40
We need to write two equations, one for the cost of using each long distance carrier. It's easier to start with carrier B, and it's simpler to do everything in terms of cents instead of dollars. Carrier B costs 6 cents for every minute. So the cost = 6t.

For carrier A, the cost is the flat rate of a dollar (that's 100 cents) plus 7 cents for every minute ABOVE 20 minutes. For example, if t is 35 minutes, we subtract 20 to find that t was 15 minutes over the first 20. As an equation, that can be written as the cost = 100 + 7(t – 20).

We are looking for the time where the costs of using the two carriers are equal, so we can set the two equations equal to each other and solve for t.

$6t = 100 + 7(t – 20)$
$6t = 100 + 7t – 140$
$6t = 7t – 40$
$-1t = -40$
$t = 40$ minutes!

Question 18: 8/5 or 1.6
We need to find the area in terms of k and the perimeter in terms of k. Let's do area first. Each little square has sides of length k, so the area of each little square is k^2. There are 10 little boxes, so the area of the total figure is $10k^2$.

To find the perimeter, we just need to CAREFULLY count up how many little line segments are included in the perimeter. The base of the figure is four units across. The right hand side is 4 units tall. And the messier "steps" part of the figure is made up of 8 little line segments. That all adds up to a perimeter of 16k. Now we set the area and perimeter equal to each other. $10k^2 = 16k$. We can divide both sides by k, to get $10k = 16$. Now we divide by 10 and find that k = 16/10, which reduces to 8/5.

Section 6: Writing

Question 1: (D)
Ellen wants to read and relax RATHER than practice. Pretty lazy, but grammatically correct.

Question 2: (E)
Take out "winner of the 1902 Nobel Prize for Physiology or Medicine" and it's obvious: "Sir Donald Ross… identified the mosquito…"

Question 3: (C)
Who was "traveling through Yosemite"? "We" were, so "we" must follow the comma. "Being" is bad so (D) is out.

Question 4: (C)
Keep these sentences simple, like a news article. The poet composed it "to recount" the history is keeping it simple.

Question 5: (B)
"Has enriched" is the proper verb form since she has already done it. The answer choice that uses this verb correctly and is the most direct is (B).

Question 6: (C)
The sentence starts with: "Leslie Marmon Silko has said that…" Then comes the underlined portion, followed by a "but." So you're only looking for what she has said, stated clearly. (C) is the only option if you look at the choices in this context.

Question 7: (C)
Really? The Baltimore waterfront is fascinating? We'll take your word for it, Antonio. That opening adjective clause, "Finding the Baltimore waterfront fascinating" has to be immediately followed by Antonio because he's the one who has this strange fascination.

Question 8: (A)
This one is about verb tense. The "with" takes us into the present tense – this just happened, "with each of the members SHAVING several seconds."

Question 9: (D)
All of the answers but (D) incorrectly use "they" or "their." We can't tell if the plural pronoun is referring to people or bats or bat houses or backyards. It is kind of funny to read them as written, though. (A) seems to imply, for example, that certain people are building bat houses in their backyards because these people can eat large numbers of insects. So why don't they build insect houses in their backyards? Discuss.

Question 10: (A)
Chances are you might have been scared to pick (A) because "for all their talk" sounds a little odd. Maybe you don't love it, but the other four are incorrect so it has to be (A). Get rid of what's wrong to get to what's right.

Question 11: (A)
Some very tempting answer choices here, but only one uses parallel construction. Always be on the lookout for this. "The enforcement of waste-disposal regulations" = "the education of the public." End of discussion.

Question 12: (B)
"Cindy, Leroy, and I." Do this trick = "I was so startled" or "Me was so startled." Which sounds better? Go with that one.

Question 13: (D)
The key here is "early in her career." Oh, so she wrote these awhile ago? Oh, so it must be "the lurid thrillers she wrote early in her career."

Question 14: (C)
Follow the clues! If the character "SAW himself," then he "BELIEVED" that he could do no wrong. Verb tense.

Question 15: (B)
Neither/nor. 'Nuff said.

Question 16: (C)
Verb tense = "40 years after it WAS written."

Question 17: (D)
We are talking about the many workers here. They weren't collectively one slave laborer, they were essentially "slave laborers."

Question 18: (C)
Who is "they?" We don't know. It's a mystery.

Question 19: (E)
This is okay. Also true, apparently. Is there such a thing as too much garlic? Plan and write an essay on this topic using examples taken from literature, history and your own experience.

Question 20: (B)
Subject/verb agreement. "The managers always HOLD us responsible."

Question 21: (C)
Big warning bells should go off every time you see "being." Parallel construction = "strength and AGILITY."

Question 22: (D)
"Obsession" is only one thing and this particular obsession with saving time and money "IS" absurd.

Question 23: (A)
"Arrived to" is incorrect. No one arrives TO a place. One might arrive IN a place, though.

Question 24: (E)
This is okay as written. Also disappointing for the publicity subcommittee. Maybe they should have printed more flyers?

Question 25: (C)
Subject/verb agreement that is kind of hidden by the aside about sophisticated technical equipment. Take that phrase out and you have: "Peter Pan's seemingly effortless flights…CONTINUE to delight." Very nice.

Question 26: (D)
We don't say that sides had refused offers FOR assistance. Rather, we say they had refused offered OF assistance. Annoying, yes, but also true. This is an example of a difficult question.

Question 27: (E)
This one is okay, but purposely wordy and difficult to get through. Don't be tempted to choose "with even" even though it looks weird. It's not wrong so there is no error.

Question 28: (C)
This one can be hard to see and is another example of a question with the highest difficulty ranking (meaning, very few students got it right on the actual test). So don't feel bad if you missed it. Don't get mad, get even. The thing here is, we don't know if "her" (C) is referring to Ms. Perez or Ms. Tanaka. Only one of them can have Sam as her son. Get it? Mmmmmm.

Question 29: (E)
Great example of how "no error" sentences can be purposely convoluted and confusing at the end of the section as the problems get harder. This one might simply sound wrong, but it's not. There are no errors. If you got this one wrong, look at what you chose and ask yourself what is grammatically incorrect about your choice. You'll see it's actually okay. If you're getting a lot of these wrong one way or the other, try circling your "no error" answers and checking them again at the end of the section. Go through each answer choice and ask yourself: what COULD be wrong with this underlined thing. Now is anything actually WRONG here?

Passage Revision: Film Remakes of Classical Works

Question 30: (E)
All we're doing here is clarifying what "purists" are. No need to get too wordy with it – a simple comma followed by the explanation is fine.

Question 31: (C)
This is definitely an "in context" question. Look at sentence 2 and you'll see it's talking about reviews. "Ones"

in sentence 3 is referring to these reviews.

Question 32: (C)
Again, if it says "in context," read it in context. The sentences before this one are talking about ROMEO AND JULIET, so sentence 5 is providing another example with CLUELESS. "Another supposed outrage" is the best way to make this clear.

Question 33: (A)
This one might be hard to see if you didn't quickly read the whole passage first. The second paragraph is the crux of the passage's argument: that updating and modernizing classic works is cool. The first paragraph's topic sentence, however, is about how modern critics think these remakes are disrespectful and a waste of time. The rest of the first paragraph applies this point of view to a couple examples, before refuting it in the second paragraph. So (A) is right. HOWEVER, even if you didn't see all that, you should be able to eliminate the other four answer choices and get to (A) anyway. There is something wrong with all of them. Incorrect key words = (B) "personal experience," (C) "objective analysis," (D) "writing fiction," (E) "reveal playfulness." Point is: getting rid of clearly wrong answers is the key to finding the right one.

Question 34: (E)
This one is simply about grammar. He would recognize the swaggering teenagers AS distant relatives.

Question 35: (B)
"In context" again. This sentence shifts the discussion to Austen from Shakespeare so a transition is necessary. The only good one is (B).

Section 7: Critical Reading

Question 1: (D)
Geoffrey was SUCH a disgrace that any chance of him being elected was "eliminated." Sorry, Geoff.

Question 2: (C)
This is definitely a tricky one for question #2. Your best clue is the word "Although," which tells us that there is going to be an opposite setup here. We can eliminate answers that aren't opposites of each other. That leaves us with (A), (B) and (C). Now, what does the "uneven quality of the material" suggest? In this case, that they didn't do a good enough job of editing down the material. In other words, the editors were too "inclusive." They should have cut some more material.

Question 3: (D)
First word means brief and the second means instruc-

tive. Only (B) and (D) work for the first word. For the second, "enlightening" (informative; instructive) is way better than "elaborate" (complex).

Question 4: (E)
The key here is that the magazine has a large circulation. It's very successful. That suggests "preeminence," which means supremacy or distinction.

Question 5: (A)
Easy clues, tough vocab. We need a word that means "left no doubt." That's exactly what "unequivocal" means. Learn that word! It's a very high frequency SAT vocab word.

Question 6: (D)
Notice that the sentence is constructed like a definition would be: "a movement is…" It's just a clarification of a term before the author starts his/her argument.

Question 7: (B)
Look for where Black writers and artists are mentioned in the passage—it's in the last sentence. That should point you squarely to (B).

Question 8: (C)
Note your topic sentence here. It tells you exactly what's going on in this passage. We're talking about "cool" and how "cool" has been around for much longer than most slang words.

Question 9: (B)
Fashion designs here are used as an example of something WITHOUT staying power (as opposed to the word "cool"). Now we need a word for something that means "temporary" or "fleeting." That's "ephemeral"—another good vocab word to store away.

Passage: Venus
Main idea: A discussion of several theories about why Venus is so different from Earth.

Question 10: (E)
Here's a restatement of the main idea from above. The trickiest thing about this one is the "astronomical enigma" part. What is that referring to? Oh, it's Venus. Very tricky, College Board!

Question 11: (A)
The sentence is set up so that you might logically make a comparison to Earth but then at the end it says "—but this is emphatically not so." This sentence raises a plausible idea and denies it, all in one.

Question 12: (E)
Check out the topic sentence: "Yet opinions differed."

The author then presents some opinions. How many? Two. Hence, (E).

Question 13: (B)
Tough one! The answer comes AFTER lines 28-30. Look at 34-38. There's a statement that directly links an atmosphere of pure carbon dioxide to the impossibility of a lush, green world. If you don't see the answer in the immediate spot that the question references, make sure to look above and below until you find it.

Question 14: (B)
This is even harder than the last one: Mariner 2 gave us our "first reliable information." What does that IMPLY? That the information that came before must NOT have been reliable. That's (B).

Question 15: (D)
Tone is all about identifying key choices that the author made. Here, it's the use of "can only lie in its…" The author clearly believes only one conclusion can be made, and that's a decisive tone.

Passage: New in New York
Main idea: A young girl moves to New York from Puerto Rico and has to adjust her identity in addition to adjusting to a new environment.

Question 16: (C)
We need a word here that means "regular" but also captures the sense of the city that the narrator is trying to relate—that the city is flat, imposing, and goes on forever. "Unvarying" is the best choice.

Question 17: (B)
There are several "vivid" images here: "dim silver glow", "glistening sparks" and "ephemeral jewels."

Question 18: (E)
Mami and Tata tease about the streets not being paved with gold. They don't think the narrator literally expected golden streets. It's a metaphor for expectations that could never be realized.

Question 19: (B)
This plays out like a tone question, though the question doesn't tell you that it will. Look for clues: "hard to tell," "vertical maze," "sharp corners and deep shadows." I'm not crazy about (B), but it's the best match to those clues.

Question 20: (E)
I think this one boils down to either choice (D) or (E). Are they suspicious of each other or not? "She appraised me shyly; I pretended to ignore her." They're a little bit hesitant but not explicitly suspicious; that's why

it's (E).

Question 21: (D)
The conversation between the girls is about what it means to be "Hispanic" in New York. That's definitely (D).

Question 22: (B)
The author is thinking that this new word "Hispanic" might apply to her too now. She is concerned that she is becoming "someone else." Thus, being Hispanic will mean the loss of her previous identity.

Question 23: (E)
"This isn't Puerto Rico," says Mami, as if to say "you can't live life in New York the way you did in Puerto Rico." Another way of saying the same thing is (E), that different rules now apply.

Question 24: (D)
Check out the key tone/mood words at the very end of the passage, especially "greater dangers lie ahead." Clearly the narrator is feeling scared and thrown into doubt. That's (D), right?

Section 8: Math

Question 1: (B)
The phrase "what fraction of the film" tells us that we need the total length of the film to be on the bottom of the fraction, and we put the 15 minutes elapsed on top. So we get 15/90, which reduces to 1/6.

Question 2: (D)
Length JK has to be the longest because it's the hypotenuse of a right triangle, and there's a theorem that says a hypotenuse is always longer than the legs of a right triangle. HL is only part of one leg, and JL is the hypotenuse of a smaller right triangle (it has one leg the same as the big triangle and one leg shorter than the big triangle), so none of the other options can be longer than JK.

Question 3: (C)
Because this is a linear function, that means that the difference between terms is constant. If we look at the values of f(n): 7, 13, 19, we can see that we are adding 6 between each term. So term p will be what we get when we add 6 to 19, giving us an answer of 25.

Question 4: (C)
Maly's time building houses is represented as n. Charlie has built houses for 5 years less than twice n. Algebraically, that's 2n − 5.

Question 5: (B)
Since AD is a straight line, that means it is a total of 180 degrees. Thank goodness for straight lines! We know that the first angle is 80, which means that we have 100 degrees left over for angle BPD. Since BPD is bisected, we chop 100 in half and get 50 for angle CPD.

Question 6: (C)
Every OTHER integer is odd, which means that there is a distance of 2 between odd integers. (For example, from 5 to 7). So, if x equals 5, for instance, than the next odd number, 7, should be written algebraically as x + 2.

Question 7: (A)
Watch out! This question has one sneaky trick. For those who remember what Quadrants are, point P is in Quadrant IV, meaning that the x-values are positive but the y-values are negative. For those who don't remember what Quadrants are, um… they tell us that P's x-values are positive, but the y-values are negative. So in the coordinates of P(a, b), the letter b ALREADY represents a negative number (and "a" represents a positive number)! Point T is in Quadrant III, which means that both terms should be negative. Since b is already negative, the correct answer is (-a, b).

Question 8: (A)
Let's start at the end of the problem and go backwards. We need to find out how many beads of each type are in the box. We are told there are 12 red glass beads. Since the probability of a red glass bead being chosen is three times the probability of a blue glass bead being chosen, that just means there must be three times more red beads than blue beads. So the blue glass beads are 12/3 = 4. Now, we're also told there are 4 times as many glass beads as wood beads. Notice that now we are talking about glass beads in general, meaning all of them. So we add up 12 red glass beads plus 4 blue glass beads to get 16 total glass beads. That is 4 times the number of wood beads, so there are 16/4 = 4 wood beads. The GRAND TOTAL is the total number of glass beads (16) plus the number of wood beads (4), which equals 20.

Question 9: (A)
When it's reflected about the x-axis, that means that a graph is flipped upside down! The graph isn't shifted left or right, just flipped in place, so the answer that matches it is answer (A).

Question 10: (C)
With an algebraic question like this, it is sometimes hard to know for sure what the right approach is. One clue is to use what the question is asking for. They want to know xy, so we need to find out a way to get

an xy term.
In this case, it turns out that the best thing to do is FOIL (expand) each binomial. $(x + y)^2 = 100$ can be expanded into $x^2 + 2xy + y^2 = 100$.
Likewise, $(x - y)^2 = 16$ can be expanded into $x^2 - 2xy + y^2 = 16$.
We've got some xy terms, which are what we want. Now, if we line up the two equations and subtract the second equation from the first one, we can get rid of the other junk.
$(x^2 + 2xy + y^2 = 100)$
$- (x^2 - 2xy + y^2 = 16)$
This gives us $4xy = 84$. Now to get xy by itself, we just divide both sides by 4. $xy = 21$.

Question 11: (A)
We need to solve the inequality for x. First we add 5 to both sides to find that 4 is less than or equal to 4x. Then we divide both sides by 4 to get that 1 is less than or equal to x. That's the same thing as saying that x is greater than or equal to 1. Answer (A) shows the correct graph of that.

Question 12: (E)
Trick question! Circles are perfectly symmetrical, so that means that if a rectangle fits inside it, you can rotate the amount you want and it will still fit. In other words, we could inscribe another triangle the exact same shape as PQRS, just rotated 10 degrees clockwise. Or 18 degrees clockwise. Or 7.8 degrees counter-clockwise. There are infinite rectangles of the same shape that can be inscribed in this circle! That's what "more than four" means here: infinity.

Question 13: (B)
The quick and easy way to do this one is to plug in a number for n. Let's say that n = 3. Then $2^n = 8$. And $2^{(n+1)} = 2^4 = 16$. So $2^n + 2^{(n+1)} = 8 + 16 = 24$. Our value of k is 24. Now, let's calculate what they are asking for: $2^{(n+2)}$. If n is still 3, then that gives us $2^5 = 32$. Cool. The last step is to look at the answers. Since our value of k is 24, we need to plug 24 into the answers and see which one gives us the value of 32 that we're looking for. The correct answer is (B).

Question 14: (E)
We know that side AB is NOT the same length as side AC, but we don't know which one of them is the same length as side BC. In fact, we don't really know enough to pick any answer about side BC. But, before we give up all hope and cry ourselves to sleep, we can look at the angles. The rule is that larger angles are opposite larger sides. The angle opposite of side AB is angle z. The angle opposite side AC is angle y. Since side AB is longer, that means angle z must be bigger than angle y. Answer (E) is the answer we're looking for: y can't

equal z.

Question 15: (D)
Tom's total expenses were $240. Since his hotel room was 20 percent of his expenses, we can calculate (.20)(240) = 48. Tom paid $48 for his share of the hotel room. But he shared the cost of the room with three OTHER people! That means that FOUR people, including Tom, stayed in the room. The total cost of the room, therefore, is 4 times what Tom paid. (4)(48) = 192.

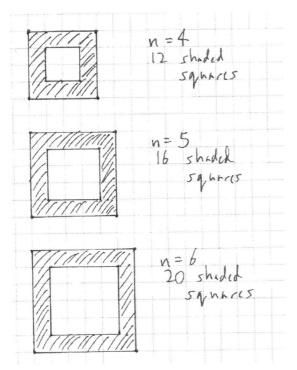

Question 16: (E)
See diagram. It's a good idea to draw a picture here and see what happens. Let's say that we have a square gameboard that is 5 rows of 5 squares each. In other words, n = 5. Then, if we count all of the squares along the boundary (the edges) we end up with 16. We can't just add up the length of each of the 4 sides (5 each) because we would be counting each corner twice. If we had a gameboard that was 6 by 6 instead, the total squares along the edges would be 20. If we keep doing this, we'll see the pattern that the number of squares along the edges keeps on increasing by 4. k increases by 4, and it's also a multiple of 4. Some possible values for k would be 12, 16, 20, 24, 28...The only answer that is a multiple of 4 is 52. It's mean that they made the biggest answer choice be the right one. But 52 definitely works – it's the number of squares along the edges if the gameboard is 14 rows of 14 squares each.

Section 9: Critical Reading

Question 1: (C)
"Desolate" means bleak and empty. It's easy to feel isolated and lonely in that kind of setting.

Question 2: (B)
"Hybrid" is a mix of two different things. For instance, those "hybrid" cars everyone is driving combine a gasoline engine with an electric battery.

Question 3: (A)
The key word is "rigorous"; you are basically looking for its synonym and "stringent" is the only choice that comes close.

Question 4: (D)
The key here is where the author writes that freedom of expression causes folks to feel "LESS threatened." So that first blank has to more or less be a word that would cause a threat. "Divisive" and "militant" would both work. Then you move on to the second blank. Now we need an opposite for "encourage." "Restricted" is the word you're looking for.

Question 5: (A)
No logic here, just straight up vocab. If you know the word "bucolic," you know that it specifically relates to rural settings.

Question 6: (E)
That first blank has to be a synonym for "foolish," right? So that eliminates C and D. All the others could work. Now the second blank has to be related to "skewed data." Out of your remaining answer choices (A, B and E), only E fits the bill with "chicanery." Definition: The use of trickery to achieve a purpose.

Passage: Comic Books: Pro and Con
Main idea, Passage 1: The author says that comics serve no useful purpose and are anti-educational. Main idea, Passage 2: The author says that comics are junk but give kids a useful psychological relief.

Question 7: (C)
The first author downright hates them and the second author likes them—but not for any sort of educational value. After all, he calls them "junk."

Question 8: (A)
You have to go back to line 4 to get some context for this word. Sometimes these types of questions are just straight up vocabulary questions in disguise. Not here.

They want you to note how this word, with multiple definitions, fits into a particular sentence.

Question 9: (C)
Choice (C) basically paraphrases what the author says in the very next sentence. All the other choices diverge off onto tangents.

Question 10: (D)
Remember, the guy isn't blaming the children. He's blaming the comic books themselves. Answer choice (C) doesn't blame the children either, but it goes way too far by indicting the entire education system.

Question 11: (E)
P2 author refutes this claim in his very first sentence. Choice (E) paraphrases that sentence. Simple as that.

Question 12: (C)
This information mostly comes from the second-to-last paragraph. Also note how easy it is to eliminate answers (A), (D) and (E) because, whether or not they're true, they're never addressed in the essay. Remember, you're never asked to bring in outside knowledge of a subject for reading comprehension.

Question 13: (B)
"Fanzines" isn't a known term to most readers. All these quotes do is identify it as a term. The other answer choices are reading way too much into those quotes.

Question 14: (D)
He's saying that people have tried to produce "educational junk." With that in mind, you can eliminate (B) and (E). But he thinks this junk is just plain stupid, so only (D) will work. The word choices in (A) "unpolished" and (C) "misunderstood" don't accurately reflect the author's disdain for educational junk.

Question 15: (E)
Once you check the cited line, you'll see we're basically looking for a synonym for "basest," which means really low and vulgar. "Degraded" is really the only choice under that criterion.

Question 16: (D)
This is pretty darn similar to question 12, but no matter. The author is clearly discussing the positive aspects of comic books, so we can eliminate (A) and (B). He's talking about their effect on children, so we eliminate (C). And he establishes early on that he does not view comic books as educational tools, so there goes (E). The answer is clearly (D); comic books are a therapeutic diversion.

Question 17: (E)
Remember, Passage 1 guy is all about ripping into comic books, not students or society at large. So (A), (B) and (C) are out the window. Between the remaining choices, (E) is far better because Passage 1 deals with comic books' contribution to inadequate intellectual growth among children.

Question 18: (C)
Half analysis question, half vocab question. If you know the meanings of "conversational," "sarcastic," and "analytical," you know those words don't work. Perhaps you considered "facetious," but that word means being inappropriately humorous and flippant when facing a serious issue. Well there's nothing humorous about Passage 1. The answer is clearly "severe."

Section 10: Writing

Question 1: (B)
Remember that shorter is better and we're trying to avoid those "-ing" words when possible. This answer accomplishes both.

Question 2: (C)
This answer puts all the information in order. We start with where Isabel was born and raised and end with where she now resides. Between those two statements, we identify Isabel as author of "The House of Spirits" via a dependent clause. And most importantly, we only have one true verb in the sentence: "resides."

Question 3: (C)
We substitute that unfortunate word "being" for a neat, succinct verb: "was." The sentence is otherwise unchanged.

Question 4: (B)
Why try to squeeze two sentences into one? Using a prepositional phrase like "at the risk of being eaten" keeps the sentence simple and focused.

Question 5: (E)
This sentence describes cause and effect. Choice (E) best explains how the museum's "creative and persistent effort" led to the Picasso acquisition. Plus why use the pronoun "it" (like they do in the original sentence) when we're obviously still talking about the museum?

Question 6: (E)
Remember that an introductory clause has to match up properly with the thing it's describing. The original sentence doesn't do that. Answer choice (E) gets rid of the introductory clause altogether and makes the sentence

as simple as possible. Simple = good!

Question 7: (A)
This one was right the way it was written. "Should" and "would" are both the same tense (and that would of course be "future-perfect-in-past-tense"...DUH!) But beyond that, it just sounds right, and sometimes that's a valid reason as well.

Question 8: (D)
Consistency, folks. Ability in math and in foreign languages. "Math" and "foreign languages" are both the same kind of thing (school subjects) so why not introduce them with the same preposition?

Question 9: (A)
The tip-off should be that all the so-called "improvements" they offer state the same exact information but with extra verbs, prepositions, clauses and other extraneous nonsense. Why not say it in fewer words?

Question 10: (B)
You've gotta appreciate the irony that this sentence describing Szechuaun cooking reads like a poor translation from the original Chinese dialect. Choice (B) says everything the original does, but it does so without any "-ing" verbs or instances of "to be."

Question 11: (D)
We're talking about Gershwin's music, not Gershwin himself. Therefore, his music has to be compared to other music, not other composers.

Question 12: (E)
Remember that if you see the word "being" in the grammar section, it's probably wrong. So get rid of it and simplify the sentence. But simpler doesn't always mean shorter. Note that answer choice (B) is even shorter than (E) is, but it actually creates a run-on sentence!

Question 13: (A)
Yet another agreement question. The introductory clause talks about "their desire to extend free enterprise." Whose desire to extend free enterprise? Well it must be some group of people. Only answer choice (A) has a group of people as its subject (Canadians).

Question 14: (C)
Let's keep our subject consistent here. If "researchers" are the subject of the sentence's first half, they should probably be the subject of it's second half if possible. But we can't have a run-on sentence, like we would if we picked (D). So choose (C), which not only keeps a single subject but also separates two independent clauses with a comma and a conjunction.

Test 3
Section 2: Math

Question 1: (A)
Start by solving the second equation for y. $20y - 5y =$ 15. $15y = 15$. $y = 1$. Now plug that into the first equation: $1 = x - 5$. Add 5 to both sides to find that $6 = x$.

Question 2: (C)
4 blue buttons plus 3 red buttons equals 7. Out of the nine buttons in the bag, that leaves 2 buttons that are yellow. The probability of picking a yellow button is 2/9.

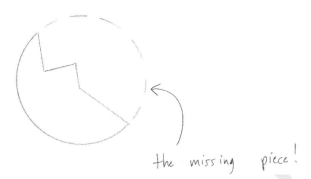

the missing piece!

Question 3: (B)
See diagram. A cool trick is to trace along the circular arc in the original figure, and then continue to sketch along the same arcing path until you've completed the full circle. Try to be careful, but it doesn't have to perfect. The SAT doesn't give you extra points for having art skills, even if you're the next Picasso. Now you should be able to see pretty clearly the shape of the piece that you need to complete the circle. It matches answer (B).

Question 4: (D)
25 percent of the circle means imagine dividing it into four quarters (each with a right angle at the center). Now, if we look at the wedges that are in the drawing: Chocolate is definitely bigger than a quarter of the circle. Vanilla is also slightly bigger than a quarter. The other four flavors are all less than 25 percent each: Strawberry, Mint, Peach, and Pecan.

Question 5: (E)
Two angles in the triangle are 37 and 58 degrees. The three angles inside the triangle must add up to 180, so we add up those two ($37 + 58 = 95$) and subtract 95 from 180 to find that the missing angle in the triangle is 85. Now, we use all the straight lines! Angle x forms a straight line with the 85 degree angle, so they must add up to 180 together. $x + 85 = 180$. That means x $= 95$. Angle y forms a straight line with the 37 degree

angle. $y + 37 = 180$. $y = 143$. Angle z forms a straight line with the 58 degree angle. $z + 58 = 180$. Angle z $= 122$. Finally we can add up $x + y + z$. $95 + 143 + 122 = 360$.
The super-fast way to do this is to realize that the three angles we are looking for are all parts of straight lines. The total degrees for all three straight lines is $3(180) =$ 540. Out of those 540 degrees, the three angles we DON'T want are all inside the triangle. The 3 angles in any triangle add up to 180. So we subtract those 180 degrees from 540, and we are left over with the sum of the angles we're looking for: 360.

Question 6: (B)
$6x + 4 = 7$. Subtract 4 from both sides to find that $6x = 3$. But they are asking for $6x - 4$. So we subtract 4 from both sides again. $6x - 4 = -1$.

Question 7: (B)
There's an easy way and a hard way to do this one. The hard way is to calculate all the arc lengths by dividing the circle into five equal sectors. The easy way is to realize that arc ABC includes exactly two sides of the pentagon. Arc AEC includes exactly three sides of the pentagon. All the sides are the same length. So the ratio of ABC to AEC is 2 sides to 3 sides, or "2 to 3".

Question 8: (D)
There are four tick marks from zero to 1, so that means each tick mark signifies a distance of 1/4. If we square the fraction (-1/2), we get positive 1/4. Which is the same as the first tick mark to the right of zero, at point D.

Question 9: (C)
The phrase "how much greater than" means that we subtract. So the problem is telling us to start with (s + t) and subtract (s + w).
$(s + t) - (s + w)$ can be simplified by distributing the negative sign:
$s + t - s - w$, and that simplifies to just $t - w$. There's our answer!

Question 10: (D)
The term "organisms" is very vague. Let's assume the biologist is a mad scientist creating an army of evil clones. What we need to do is plug in the numbers they give us for t. First, let's plug in $t = 4$. The population of evil clones at that point is $(3000)(2)^{(4/4)} = (3000)(2) = 6000$ evil clones. Now, we plug in time t $= 16$ and see what value we get. $(3000)(2)^{(16/4)} = (3000)(2)^{(4)} = (3000)(16) = 48000$ evil clones. Wow, that's a pretty substantial army of evil clones! To find out how much the population increased, we subtract $48,000 - 6,000$ to get 42,000.

Question 11: (E)
We can write an equation for the average that we are given: $(3 + s + t) / 3 = 5$. Now we can solve that equation for $s + t$. First we multiply both sides by 3: $3 + s + t = 15$. Now we subtract 3 from both sides. $s + t = 12$.

Question 12: (D)
We're looking for the areas where A and B overlap. The number 5 is inside both circles A and B. The number 2 is also inside both A and B (it's OK that it's also inside circle C). So the total overlap is $5 + 2 = 7$.

Question 13: (D)
800 students have been accepted so far, and 40 percent are male. How many actual people is that? $(.40)(800) = 320$ dudes. If the school eventually wants to have 1000 kids, and have half of them be dudes, that means they want to accept 500 dudes total. If they have 320 dudes so far, they need 180 more dudes to get to their target of 500.

Question 14: (C)
The quick and good way to solve this one is to realize that the first inequality is talking about subtracting two perfect squares. If we list the first few perfect squares, we get: 1, 4, 9, 16, and 25. As the numbers get bigger, the difference between perfect squares increases. We are told the difference between them is less than 6. There are only two possibilities that work: $4 - 1 = 3$. 3 is a difference less than 6. And $9 - 4 = 5$, which is also a difference less than 6. Out of those options, we want $t + k$ to add up to more than 4, so let's go with the bigger numbers. To get the numbers 9 and 4, our values of t and k would be 3 and 2. And $3 + 2 > 4$. It works! Bwa ha ha! So the value of t is 3.

Question 15: (A)
Answer (A) is correct. We can multiply 618 by 1/2 first to get 309, and then take 23 percent of it. In answers (B) and (D) they are wrongly multiplying by a half TWICE. In answer (C) I don't know what's going on. (I guess they SUBTRACTED one half?? Of a percent?!) That's just very wrong. And in answer (E), they forgot the percent sign, which is a no-no.

Question 16: (A)
This looks much more painful than it really is. They tell us $g(x) = f(3x + 1)$. We want to find $g(2)$, which isn't so bad, because $g(2) = f(3(2) + 1)$. The right hand side simplifies to $f(7)$. Now we go to our chart and look for what the value of $f(x)$ is when x is 7. In the next to last row, the value of x is 7, and the corresponding value of $f(x)$ is -5. That means our answer is -5. Awesome!

Question 17: (C)
Okay, this requires a few steps. First, notice that arc AB and arc CD (the shaded one below the line) if they were slid together would form a full, shaded circle with radius of 1. The area of that would be πr^2, which is just π in this case.

Arcs AC and BD form the top and bottom halves of another circle. This one has a radius of 2. The area of this circle is $\pi(2)^2$, which is 4π. This circle includes all of the white area AND the smaller shaded circle we calculated before. So the area of just the WHITE regions is $4\pi - \pi = 3\pi$. Finally, we need the area of the whole big circle, which has a radius of 3. That area is 9π. We found that all of the white regions add up to 3π, so we subtract that from the total of 9π, leaving us with a total shaded area of 6π. Whew! That one will make you go cross-eyed if you stare at it too long!

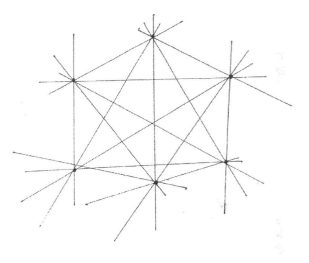

Question 18: (A)
See diagram. Let's draw 6 points in space, without any three of them being on the same line. One easy way to do this is to arrange them like the six vertexes of a hexagon. If we start at one point and draw a line from it to each of the other five points, one at a time, we will have drawn 5 lines. If we then move on to the second point, there is already a line between it and the first point. But from that second point, we can draw lines to the other 4 points. From the next point, we can draw 3 new lines. From the next one, 2 new lines, and 1 from the last point. The total number of lines is $5 + 4 + 3 + 2 + 1 = 15$.

Question 19: (C)
Since $b = a$, that means $f(b) = f(a)$. Now we can examine each statement:
Statement I is true. $f(a + b)$ is equivalent to $f(a) + f(b)$. and since $f(b) = f(a)$ from above, we can replace $f(b)$ with $f(a)$ to get $f(a) + f(a)$, which is the same as 2 times $f(a)$.

Statement II is false. Squaring f(a) is a whole different thing. We only have enough information to make conclusions about adding functions or multiplying them by two. We don't know anything about what they will equal when they are squared.

Statement III is true. f(b) + f(b) can be rewritten as f(b + b), which is the same as f(2b). Since b = a, that also equals f(2a).

Question 20: (B)

The area of the rectangular area is 4000, the length is x and the width is y. So we can write xy = 4000. In terms of x and y, we can also write an expression for the total lengths of rope needed. There is one rope of length y in the drawing and four ropes of length x (the two sides of the rectangle, plus the two partitions dividing it into sections). So the total length of rope needed is y + 4x. We can take the earlier equation, xy = 4000, and solve it for x by dividing both sides by y. So, x = 4000/y. Now we plug that in for x in our expression for the total length of rope. y + 4x turns into y + 4(4000/y). That can be simplified to y + 16,000/y.

Section 4: Critical Reading

Question 1: (B)

You've got two clues and two missing words: perfect! The first word goes with "extensive travel" and the second completes the phrase "creative ------- for his writing." "Worldly" and "inspiration" work just swell for those two spots.

Question 2: (E)

We need a word that works well with "deepen." Another word that suggests that our awareness grows through art is "extend."

Question 3: (D)

This is a long-winded way of saying that the chief executive got fired. A fancy word for that is "ousted."

Question 4: (C)

Again, two clues and two blanks. The first one should mean "surprising" and the second "undermining accepted theories." By elimination we should definitely arrive at (C).

Question 5: (C)

Which of these words would help to explain the rapid growth of the Asian American community? Only "expansion."

Question 6: (D)

What's the deal with bears? They're surprisingly -------, but we should still exercise caution. I'd start with that

second blank. Once you find a good word there, look for an answer choice that has a word that's the opposite for that first clause. "Far from being aggressive, bears are surprising placid." I don't know about you, but this sentence doesn't make me any more likely to go and pet a bear.

Question 7: (D)

Your definition is given in the second part of that sentence; to get this one right, you just have to study your vocab! It's "clairvoyant," which unsurprisingly means "a person with insights beyond normal human perception."

Question 8: (C)

The definition is within the sentence, something like "capable of noting subtle differences." What makes this one really hard is that we all have a strong association with the word "discriminating," and it's not a positive one. In the dictionary, though, discriminating just means "recognizing differences; discerning." That devious College Board!

Question 9: (A)

P1 tells us that "a reform movement...is afoot," whereas P2 suggests that journalism is doing well and that its critics are misrepresenting the truth. The best answer choice for that is (A).

Question 10: (E)

This one is tough because it is based on one little tiny eensy-weensy detail: the mention of "robust media profits" in line 15. P1 doesn't talk about money, so there's your answer. Man, that's picky.

Question 11: (D)

As we discussed on question 9, P2's perspective is that journalism is actually in great shape and doesn't need these reform efforts. That's why the initiatives are "unwarranted" (unnecessary).

Question 12: (E)

I'm going to go ahead and say this one is tricky. The "irony" that's being highlighted is that the heads of the reform movement want to fix journalism but in doing so they are not being very good journalists, because from P2's perspective, they are not citing the facts in making sweeping and untrue judgments about the state of journalism. The people who want to fix journalism are violating the first rule of journalism. Oh, the irony.

Passage: Yawning (or "Who the *$!@ has the nerve to put a passage about yawning on the SAT?")

Main idea: Yawning is not a very good way to

track sleepiness.

Question 13: (C)
The unstated assumption of those two lines is that there is a relationship between yawning and sleepiness. You know it, I know it, but it wasn't stated in those two lines, so it's an assumption.

Question 14: (B)
Whoever thought you'd have to take the time to define what a yawn is? But here we are, and we're doing it: a yawn is "that slow, exaggerated mouth opening…" Man, I'm yawning just thinking about it!

Question 15: (E)
Anecdote is a word you definitely want to learn if you don't know it already. An anecdote is a story, usually a brief one. When the author describes the personal experience of watching skydivers yawn, he or she is telling a story, which means he or she is using anecdote.

Question 16: (E)
The mention of the coffee break indicates that these divers had just gotten caffeine, so they should not have been tired. It points to the mystery: why were they yawning when they could not possibly be tired? Thus, the coffee shows that the yawning was unexpected

Question 17: (A)
This is tough because you might not know what "the power of suggestion" means. It's the way we influence each other. When one person yawns, like I'm doing right now, it causes someone else to yawn (did you yawn?). That's the power of suggestion.

Question 18: (D)
Definitely the trickiest question on this passage. If you got it, congrats; if not, don't sweat it. We're looking for evidence that would undermine (detract from) the idea that people yawn to increase their oxygen intake when carbon dioxide levels are high. The one that would reject that idea is (D), because it would show that people in oxygen-deprived areas, who you would expect to yawn MORE, actually yawn LESS.

Question 19: (E)
With all of this talk about yawning, you might have forgotten that the reason brought up yawning at all was in the context of sleep research. In 55-57 we return the discussion to the topic raised in the first paragraph.

Question 20: (D)
As always, look to replace the word in the sentence with its closest match. We're talking about people's "ambition and drive." The nearest match is vitality, which means liveliness or energy.

Question 21: (B)
This is another challenging one. The other instances are when people admit that they drink a lot of coffee but don't realize that they drink the coffee in order to prevent sleepiness. In other words, people might not even be aware that they are sleepy.

Question 22: (B)
The "simple definition" states that you fall asleep faster when you're more tired. (B) directly undermines that by saying, no, if you're extremely sleepy you may actually have difficulty falling asleep.

Question 23: (C)
All of the EXCEPT questions are a pain. You just have to go through and try to match each answer to something you read about. It'll be quickest to do it from memory but you may also have to look back. Here, it's (C): yawning as a means of clearing your ears is not mentioned, so that's your winner.

Question 24: (A)
Here's a tone question. Overall, there isn't a lot of emotion or controversy here. Just a lot of yawning. And a lot of information. (A).

Section 5: Math

Question 1: (A)
Dave owns 44 comic books, which means that the other two guys own a total of 128 − 44 = 84. The average for the two of them is 84/2 = 42.

Question 2: (B)
Because circles are symmetrical, point P is the same distance from the origin as the point we're given, (6, 0). But now the distance is 6 units along the y-axis instead of the x-axis, so the coordinates of P are (0, 6).

Question 3: (D)
We have to pay a flat rate of one dollar plus ten cents for each copy. That would be written mathematically as 1.00 + 0.10n.

Question 4: (B)
This is a weird one! One way to think about it is that each "a" in a term is worth one point. If the term has two "a"s, it's worth two points, if it has one "a", it's worth one point, and if it has no "a"s, it's worth zero points. We can now label each term with its points.
aa = 2 bc = 0
ab = 1 aa = 2
ac = 1 ba = 1
If we add up all the points, we get a total of 7.

Question 5: (A)

The diagonal divides the square into two 45-45-90 right triangles. The ratio between the hypotenuse and the legs of a 45-45-90 right triangle is $\sqrt{2}$ to 1. Since the hypotenuse is longer, we DIVIDE our hypotenuse of 4 by $\sqrt{2}$ to get the length of each leg. Each leg has a length of $4/\sqrt{2}$. The area of the square is that leg squared, which is $(4/\sqrt{2})^2$. That simplifies into $16/2 = 8$.

Question 6: (E)

If x is inversely proportional to y, that means y is directly proportional to $1/x$. If we square one term, we have to square the other. That means $1/(x^2)$ is proportional to y^2.

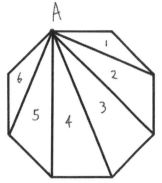

Question 7: (C)

See diagram. The polygon has 8 vertices (8 corners). It's an octagon! From point A, it is possible to draw a maximum of 5 diagonals. That's because two vertices are next to A (one on each side, along the edges). You can't draw a diagonal to those points (a diagonal has to go through the inside of the figure). So out of 8 vertices, two are along the edges, and one of them is point A itself. That leaves 5 other vertices that point A can be connected to by diagonals. If you draw all 5 diagonals, the region inside the octagon will be divided into SIX triangles.

Question 8: (B)

FOIL (distribute) the left hand side of the equation. $x^2 - 8x - kx + 8k = x^2 - 5kx + m$. We can subtract x^2 from both sides, canceling that out. Now we have: $-8x - kx + 8k = -5kx + m$. Basically, the terms that have an x in them on the left hand side must equal the term with an x in it on the right hand side. And the constant terms (those without variables) on the left and right hand sides must be equal. So, we can split it up into two separate equations: $-8x - kx = -5kx$, and also $8k = m$. Let's focus on the first equation, solving it for k. First, we add kx to both sides. $-8x = -4kx$. Now we can divide both sides by x. $-8 = -4k$. And now we divide both sides by -4, to get $2 = k$. Finally, we plug

2 in for k in our other equation, the one where the 8k term equals m. $8(2) = m$. $m = 16$.

Question 9: 93/2 or 46.5

Divide the total distance of 62 by 4 to find the distance the bird flew in one hour, then multiply that by 3 to find out how far it flew in 3 hours. That equals 186/4, which reduces to 93/2.

Question 10: 4

The four points all lie on the circle, and the distance from the center of the circle to any point on the edge is the length of the radius. So the distance from P to each of the other 4 points is 1. The total of the four distances is 4.

Question 11: 1, 2, or 4

10,000 can be rewritten as 10^4 power. So $10^{ab} = 10^4$. The terms a and b are two positive integers that multiply together to equal 4. That means term a is any positive factor of 4: it could be 1, 2, or 4. You get to choose whichever one you want to grid in! No really, go wild with it!

Question 12: 13

Since the line $2x - 3y = c$ passes through the point (5, -1), we can plug those coordinates in for x and y and solve for c. $2(5) - 3(-1) = c$. $10 + 3 = c$. $13 = c$.

Question 13: 1992

One thing that helps for doing this problem quickly is to draw in the line $y = x$. This is a diagonal line with a slope of 1 going up to the right through the middle of the data. It should go through the point (600, 600), the point (700, 700), and so on. Any points on that line – like the point labeled 1999 – are where the male and female students were perfectly balanced. The further a point is away from that line, the greater the difference between male and female students. The point labeled 1992 is the furthest from that line. In that year, there were 800 female students and only 650 males, with a difference of 150. So 1992 is our answer.

Question 14: 5/4 or 1.25

Five times a number is the same as the number added to five. We really should turn this into math. It can be written as $5x = 5 + x$. To solve, we can subtract x from both sides. $4x = 5$. Now we divide both sides by 4, to get $x = 5/4$.

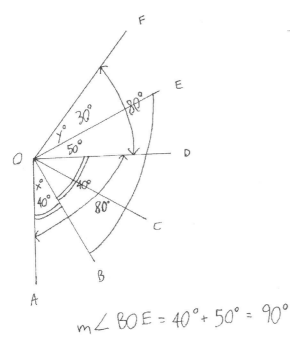

$$m \angle BOE = 40° + 50° = 90°$$

notch). So within one piece of the pattern, the bold line goes straight along 3 inches, then 2 inches around a notch, for a total of 5 inches. Then it repeats. Since the pattern happens 20 times, the total length of the bold notched edge is 5(20) = 100.

Question 18: 1/2 or .5
The area of the square is 64, meaning that each side has a length of 8. We can now find the coordinates of point R. R is 8 units above the origin, and 4 units to the right of the origin (because half the square is to the right of the origin). That makes the coordinates of point R (4, 8). We can plug those in for x and y in the parabola's equation y = ax^2. 8 = a(4)^2. 8 = a(16). 1/2 = a.
Note: We know that exactly half of the square is to the right of the origin because the square touches the parabola on both sides, and parabolas are always symmetrical.

Question 15: 90
See diagram. This would have been a lot easier if they had drawn it to scale! It's best to work backwards from the end of the problem. OB bisects angle AOD. We know one of the halves of angle AOD is angle AOB, which is labeled x... it's 40 degrees! So angle BOD is the other half... it's also 40 degrees. Angle AOD is in total 80 degrees. The beginning of the problem told us that OD bisects angle AOF. Which means that the WHOLE diagram (same as angle AOF) is twice as big as AOD, so the total is 160. The other half of AOF is angle DOF, which also must be 80. We know that y is 30. The rest of DOF is angle DOE. Out of 80 degrees, if y is 30 degrees, angle DOE must be the remaining 50 degrees. Now we finally know everything we need to. The measure of angle BOE is angle BOD (40 degrees) plus angle DOE (50 degrees) for a total of 90 degrees.

Question 16: 67
Before the integer 12 appears in this sequence, the number 1 appears once, the number 2 appears twice, and so on. We have to count how many terms appear before 12. The answer is 1 + 2 + 3 + 4 + 5 + 6 + 7 + 8 + 9 + 10 + 11, which adds up to 66. Then the number 12 will appear after that as the NEXT term, term number 67.

Question 17: 100
Clearly there is a pattern going on here. Every four inches, the pattern repeats. The strip is 80 inches long, so that means the pattern repeats exactly 20 times. Each piece of the pattern has three straight inches, and then a triangle. Each triangle is equilateral with a base of 1, which means each side of it is 1. The bold line goes along two sides of the triangle (the sides of the

Section 6: Writing

Question 1: (B)
This sentence is all about Norman Rockwell so start with him. Only (A) and (B) do this. (A) incorrectly uses "that" instead of "who" (Norman Rockwell is a person, not a thing).

Question 2: (B)
The second half of this sentence happened as a result of the first half. "After" is the best way to get this point across. "Because of" (A) is grammatically incorrect.

Question 3: (A)
A lot going on here – great time to bring in the semicolon. (B) is not a complete sentence, (C) incorrectly uses "fighting" instead of "fought," (D) is a run-on without the semicolon and also weird, and (E) incorrectly uses "in fact" – we know it's a fact, it's telling us what happened next. (A) is best: "fought" is correct, "however" turns the sentence around and keeps the content clear and both sides of the semicolon are complete.

Question 4: (B)
Nursing and physical therapy are two things – they "are EXAMPLES." "Where" is not correct in (C), the only other answer choice that correctly uses "are examples."

Question 5: (D)
There are definitely two distinct parts to this complex sentence. We need the semicolon in the right answer. The other four are run-ons.

Question 6: (C)
Parallel construction = the company "maintains" and

"manages."

Question 7: (E)
Parallel construction again. "Studying dance" = "practicing difficult steps" = "PERFORMING FREQUENTLY."

Question 8: (D)
Misplaced modifier in (A) and (B) – Jackson Pollock needs to follow the comma. "Having once been" is bad in (E) and (C) is not a complete sentence. Also, (D) is so nice and pretty!

Question 9: (D)
Take out the whole middle clause and it's very simple: "Legendary nineteenth-century endurance rider Frank T. Hopkins…IS the hero…"

Question 10: (A)
Only (A) uses the right pronoun ("its") and the right verb (the past tense "sold," which matches with the fact that the fans "shared" the music).

Question 11: (B)
Parallel construction: "inhabit Ecuador" as "inhabit North America."

Question 12: (D)
"They are hard" does not complete the list correctly with parallel structure. Whatever goes there should be a simple adjective like "beauty" and "luster."

Question 13: (D)
Faulty comparison – this sentence compares Mary's science project to Jim, not Jim's science project.

Question 14: (A)
"Being" is bad. "Was unfounded" would work well.

Question 15: (A)
Subject/verb agreement. "Waterways…POSE challenges…"

Question 16: (D)
The sentence as is implies that the antique store itself was wandering in the city. "While wandering" fixes this.

Question 17: (C)
Either/or. "And" is wrong.

Question 18: (E)
This one is fine. Isn't it nice?

Question 19: (B)
Subject/verb agreement. Horse psychology is one thing, so it HELPS trainers.

Question 20: (C)
Parallel construction is missing. Other types of deserts "can be sown" and "can be watered."

Question 21: (D)
Amazing! As written, the sentence says that the vacuum cleaner presses its own button to empty its own dust bag. While this would be really cool, it's probably not true. It should read "when a button is pressed."

Question 22: (A)
"The gecko" is one thing, "famous for ITS sticky feet."

Question 23: (B)
We've got a subject-verb agreement issue here. "Both her work AND her dedication HAVE gained…"

Question 24: (A)
Verb tense. This uprising happened in 1911! Take out "has," so it "LED to the establishment of a Chinese republic."

Question 25: (D)
Faulty comparison. The sentence as is compares Mark's paintings to the other artists, not their paintings.

Question 26: (B)
Verb tense. This one is kind of hard to figure out at first. Written correctly, the sentence would read: "by the time Brianne finally arrived at the theater, we HAD waited for her for an hour."

Question 27: (C)
The university is one thing. "Their" should be "its."

Question 28: (E)
This one is okay.

Question 29: (D)
This is a mean one and a lot of people got it wrong on the actual test so don't feel bad about it. "Each year" is unnecessary because it's redundant with "annually." Yeah, it's tough.

Passage Revision: Seeds of Peace Camp

Question 30: (E)
This one is just about getting the order of the words right. Syntax, baby, SYNTAX. (E) is the best answer – direct and clear. There's a lot of the passive voice floating around the other answers, by the way. Gross.

Question 31: (B)
Just get rid of the answer choices that don't have anything to do with the first paragraph. That pretty much

gets you down to (B). Getting specific about which countries and presumed "enemies" we are talking about here would help.

Question 32: (D)
Well, it feels out of place where it is now – kind of tacked on and strange. But it does fit best in the second paragraph, which gets specific about what daily life is like for the campers. Only (D) keeps it in the second paragraph and moves it from its current weird position.

Question 33: (A)
This one says "in context," but you can really treat it like an improving sentences question (the first part of the writing section). (C), (D) and (E) are run-on sentences and far too wordy and confusing to be correct. (B) has a misplaced modifier: it says that the COUNTRIES are unaffiliated instead of the CAMP ITSELF. (A) is the best one anyway.

Question 34: (C)
"Being that" is always gross. Change it!

Question 35: (E)
This paragraph is all about Wallach and his philosophy, right? So keep it in the family: (E) talks about his convictions and his resulting success. Does this camp sound like a great idea? You know, most of these passages can be pretty awful, but this one is okay.

Section 7: Critical Reading

Question 1: (E)
From "too faint," it's pretty clear that the second word should mean something like "read" or "understand." Only (C) and (E) work for that, and only (E) works for the first blank.

Question 2: (D)
Here we're missing two words that are positively related to each other, but we might not know exactly what they are from the sentence. "Wider interest" is a nice clue, suggesting that Jean Ritchie might have made Kentucky music more popular, and indeed that is the case. "Catalyst… stirred" is the right way to complete this mini-story.

Question 3: (E)
From the setup, it's fairly clear we're looking for words that means "lacking any." Now it's just a matter of eliminating. You'll probably get to "bereft of" best by elimination.

Question 4: (C)
Simple setup here: we're just looking for a word that

means something that is statistically very small. That word is "anomaly," or in plural, "anomalies."

Question 5: (A)
Hmm…is there a word that means "neither written nor spoken"? Why yes, there is! It's "tacit." Not too difficult for #5.

Question 6: (B)
In the previous sentence, the author discusses "self-expression" as a motivation behind drawing. In 6-8, drawing and poetry are linked. So both of those activities serve that purpose of self-expression.

Question 7: (C)
This is a little tricky. Notice that parenthetical comment "(too seriously!)" which is a bit self-critical and explains the "naïve" part of the correct answer. Now it's up to us to interpret the list of goals at the end as a grandiose ambition. To do all those things would be ambitious.

Question 8: (D)
What are the important elements of this passage? First, the impact of World War II on people's lives. Second, how Chinese American women responded in particular. That definitely points us towards (D), which gets both of those elements in there.

Question 9: (B)
The second paragraph presents specific details that justify the claims made in the first paragraph.

Passage: The Shopkeepers of Greek Street
Main idea: The lifestyle of a shopkeeper is one indication of how the world has changed in the machine age.

Question 10: (B)
Look for key phrases. Here, they're "might as well have happened in another country in another age." That's definitely dismissive.

Question 11: (B)
The order is put in, and days later goods arrive. (B) is the definition of that kind of order.

Question 12: (C)
Here, the phrase benign monster represents the world of manufacturing, which most people do not see. It's benign ("kind") because it gives us goods like soap, and a monster because its factories belch smoke.

Question 13: (E)
The word compensation means "pay." This takes a bit of a leap in logic, but why do the shopkeepers do what they do, anyway? For charity? Probably for profit, right?

Compensation refers to how much money they take home.

Question 14: (C)
The shopkeepers are in a hurry "in case someone with money should come along." You never know who might walk by and want to buy something.

Passage: Clovis and the first Americans
Main idea, Passage 1: The Clovis people were thought to be the first settlers of the Americas until some recent discoveries.
Main idea, Passage 2: Most people think that any travel to the New World must have been before or after the ice age, but it's possible that settlers traveled there by boat.

Question 15: (C)
This is a tough one because this fact is not explicitly stated in P1. It's implied by lines 26-30, but not stated overtly. It is stated in P2, in 38-41. (D) may be tempting, because these authors do not draw definitive conclusions as to when America was settled, but neither author states that "we may never know."

Question 16: (C)
Pick the choice that completes that sentence best. The groove, or flute, is the last thing that is done to finish—or complete—the arrowhead.

Question 17: (E)
This quote summarizes what has been previously stated just in time for the next line to suggest that reality may be different than what people had thought was true.

Question 18: (D)
Plug in your answer choices to find which fits the context best. "Indication" is definitely the champ when you do so.

Question 19: (B)
The evidence in 25-36 suggests that somebody was living in the Americas earlier than the Clovis. P2 would view this as evidence that yeah, somebody came by boat DURING the ice age.

Question 20: (D)
We're looking for something to suggest that people traveled by sea during the ice age. Boat anchors, dude. Boat anchors that are more than 13,500 years old.

Question 21: (E)
These geologic studies suggest that there may have been places to "hang out" and "chill" for sea-going adventurers looking to start a new people in the Americas. These findings go to support the claim that people

could have come by sea.

Question 22: (C)
You've got to take a look at each of these numbered statements and assess it. I is definitely in both, II is definitely not. III is the hard one. P1 mentions mammoths in line 18 and P2 talks about salmon in line 53. So I and III, (C).

Question 23: (B)
Just a picky little question. Each passage quotes a dude with an opinion. Once you find those quotes, you know you got this one right.

Question 24: (D)
The right answer is a nice summation of this passage. P1 first states the old idea that Clovis was the first settlement, then mentions this new study that threatens to blow that idea up. P2 then gives one theory of how people would have traveled to the New World pre-Clovis.

Section 8: Math

Question 1: (C)
This can be math-ified into the following equation: $(3/4)x = 18$. We are looking for $(1/4)x$, which is the same as dividing both sides by 3. $(1/4)x = 6$.

Question 2: (B)
We plug in 5 for k in the expression $k(k-1)$. $5(5-1) = 5(4) = 20$.

Question 3: (D)
The question is just really asking where the dotted line on the graph crosses the solid line on the graph. The answer is at 45.

Question 4: (A)
In five days, the total number of hours is 24 hours per day times 5, which is 120 hours. Toni spent 2 hours per day commuting, so in 5 days, she spent 10 total hours commuting. I'm sure Toni would be sad to realize she spends so many hours commuting each week. Out of the total hours in her day, Toni spent 10/120 hours commuting, which can be simplified to 1/12.

Question 5: (C)
We can just square both sides of the equation. On the left hand side, the square root sign will cancel out, and we will be left with the number 3, which is equal to $(x + 1)$ squared.

Question 6: (A)
There's a rule in Geometry that the longest side of a

triangle is always opposite the biggest angle, and the smallest side of a triangle is opposite the smallest angle. You might be wondering why you're expected to memorize that rule, because it seems like something you'll never need again in your life. Well, you'd be surprised. Whatever job you want to have when you grow up, you'll definitely need to know that rule about triangles. You'll use it every day. Okay, that's a lie. You'll never need it. But you need it now, so let's focus:
The longest side is 10, which means the biggest angle is the one opposite it, angle x. Angle t is opposite the shortest side, so angle t is the smallest angle. In order, the angles can be written: t < r < x.

Question 7: (A)
The fastest way to do this one is to plug in the answers and see what works. If we plug in -3 for y, we get the absolute value of 6 – 5(-3) > 20. This simplifies to 6 + 15 > 20, and so 21 > 20. Answer (A) is the one that works! Cool.

Question 8: (D)
A right triangle with sides that are twice as big as those in triangle ABC would have sides of length 6, 8, and x. We can use the Pythagorean Theorem to find x. 6^2 + 8^2 = x^2. 36 + 64 = x^2. 100 = x^2. x = 10. The perimeter, therefore, is 6 + 8 + 10, which equals 24. It's a good idea to memorize that 6-8-10 triangle, by the way—the College Board loves it.

Question 9: (C)
For each row of the table, we can find the ratio by dividing the number of Foreign Locations by the number of United States locations. For company A, 4000/1400 = 2.857. For company B, the ratio is 2.538. For company C, it's 3.575. For company D, it's 1.826. And for company E, it's 2.756. Company C has the highest ratio.

Question 10: (E)
The markings in the figure can help us find the slope of line L. From the y-axis, it goes down one unit and over three to cross the x-axis. That makes the slope of line L -1/3. Perpendicular lines have slopes that are negative reciprocals, so the slope of line N is 3/1.

Question 11: (E)
We can subtract 5 from both sides of the equation to get 2x = 3kx. Now we solve for k by dividing both sides by 3x. The x's cancel out, and we are left with 2/3 = k.

Question 12: (B)
We only need to have one positive number as the bare minimum to make all the numbers add up to zero. For example, out of the 11 integers, ten of the numbers

could be -1, -2, -3, …, -9, -10. (The negative numbers from 1 to 10). These would add up to a total of -55. We can have our 11th integer be positive 55, which will cancel out all of the rest of them and make the total be zero.

Question 13: (E)
It's best to try to make a systematic list of ways to get tokens to add up to 17. Starting with using the fewest number of tokens:
You could have one 10-point token, one 5-point token, and two 1-point tokens.
You could have three 5-point tokens and two 1-point tokens.
Or one worth 10 points and seven worth 1 point.
Or two worth 5 points and seven worth 1 point.
Or one worth 5 points and twelve worth 1 point.
Or seventeen tokens, all worth 1 point.
The total is six possible combinations!

Question 14: (D)
Multiplying the entire function by 2 will STRETCH it vertically, but it won't move the graph left or right or shift it up or down. Answer (D) shows the graph being stretched vertically.

Question 15: (C)
This one is sneaky! It's helpful to keep writing out terms a little further than the SAT does (it's almost as if they're not trying to be helpful):
2, -4, 8, -16, 32, -64, 128, -256, 512…
The first six terms are all less than 100. After that, the positive terms are greater than 100, but keep in mind that the negative terms are not! Out of 50 terms total, the first six are less than 100, leaving 44 terms. Half of those are positive and half are negative, meaning 22 negative terms. Counting those and the first 6, we get a total of 28 terms less than 100.

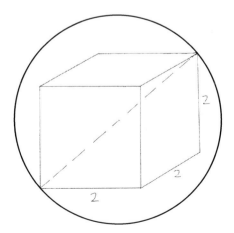

Question 16: (D)

See diagram. The volume of a cube is equal to the side length cubed. So if the volume is 8, each side has length two. There is a three-dimensional distance formula, which is kind of similar to the Pythagorean theorem, which says that the distance between two points in three dimensions is $d = \sqrt{(x^2) + (y^2) + (z^2)}$, where x, y, and z are the distances between the points in each of the dimensions.

In our case, because of the symmetry of a cube and a sphere, opposite corners of the cube will touch the sphere on exactly opposite sides of the sphere. That means that the straight distance between two opposite corners of the cube (along an internal diagonal) is equal to the sphere's diameter. So, for example, that would be the distance from the top-right-front corner of the cube to the bottom-left-rear corner. The good news (yes, there's good news) is that each edge of the cube is just 2, and so the change in each dimension from one corner to the opposite corner is just 2. From the top-right-front corner, we go across 2 units of height, 2 units of width, and 2 units of depth to get to the bottom-left-rear corner. In our distance formula, we plug in 2 for each variable. $d = \sqrt{(2^2) + (2^2) + (2^2)}$. This simplifies to $d = \sqrt{4 + 4 + 4} = \sqrt{12} = 2\sqrt{3}$. And that is the diameter of our sphere! Now, let's go take a nap.

Section 9: Critical Reading

Question 1: (C)

From the first word, "paradoxically," we know we're looking for opposites. The only pair of words that are opposites of each other are "liberating" and "repressive."

Question 2: (D)

He's plagued by doubt; that means he has feelings of inadequacy. Look for that second word first. It could be (A), (C) or (D). Then go to the first word. He could not get rid of these feelings. That's "dispel."

Question 3: (A)

First word: blatantly proud, second word: offensively bold. Once you know that, it's just a vocabulary bee (do they have those? Like a spelling bee, but with vocab words? They should). Cross off one word at a time that doesn't work, leaving words you don't know. Then take a guess. The words are hard but match those clues perfectly: "haughty... impudent."

Question 4: (B)

Wow, is this one specific. I'll be honest: I didn't know this vocab word until I saw this question. Eliminate words based on what you know does not mean "two points that are exactly opposite each other on a globe" and take your best guess. Antipodes. Now try to use it in conversation.

Question 5: (A)

Ken cares for his mother; thus, he takes his family responsibilities seriously. An adjective describing "family" is "filial." Tough.

Question 6: (A)

You have to know that abashed means embarrassed, for starters. Then you know for sure that the orchestra sounded terrible. What's an adjective for terrible sounding? Cacophonous: sounds like crap.

Passage: A Trip to the Library
Main idea: A young reader who loves taking trips to the library discovers a favorite book.

Question 7: (E)

In the line that is referenced, the excursions are regarded as a "piece of perfection." She really really really likes them. Therefore, "delight."

Question 8: (C)

Look back at those lines and hunt for the distinction. You "could miss it" from the outside, but once you were inside, "you could never mistake it for anything else." The contrast is between the exterior and interior of the library.

Question 9: (C)

Words like "you could never mistake it" convey a strong sense of reality, or conviction.

Question 10: (D)

She sure loves the library! The ceiling is described as "great." The angels carry books and "other instruments of learning." What does that express about the author? Definitely (D).

Question 11: (A)

Read through the whole sentence that mentions Africa. The author used it as a way to remind herself of political struggles there that paralleled the civil rights movement in America.

Question 12: (C)

Why is Daddy arguing with the television? Because he has some strong feelings about the matter that they are discussing: civil rights.

Question 13: (D)

The author admits that her only real knowledge of Africa comes from Tarzan movies. The question she poses in the parentheses emphasize the fact that she didn't get a lot of useful information from those movies.

Question 14: (C)
The fourth paragraph basically lists types of books that she read and intellectual discoveries that they led to. She doesn't "provide several examples" of science experiments, just one, so (E) is wrong.

Question 15: (D)
Part of the discussion in the highlighted section talks about how boring titles can disguise great books, and vice versa. Hence, book titles can be misleading.

Question 16: (A)
Here the author includes a long quote from "Little Women." It's almost as though we are sitting in the library, engrossed like she was in the book. It helps to convey the excitement and significance of sitting down with this one particular book.

Question 17: (C)
The choice here that fits the context of the sentence is definitely "equitable."

Question 18: (E)
Have you ever sat down and just read a book without any interruptions? It usually happens when you absolutely fall in love with a book, when it "captivates" you. Or when the book report is due the next day and you haven't started.

Question 19: (D)
The list of Jo's characteristics helps the author to justify the idea that they are "kindred spirits," or two very similar people.

Section 10: Writing

Question 1: (A)
First off, get the verb right: "assured" (this happened in the past). (B) has "them" and we don't know who "them" is and (C) gets the syntax wrong.

Question 2: (B)
This one is just about getting the middle clause set apart correctly as an aside. Getting rid of clearly wrong and wordy choices should get you to (B).

Question 3: (C)
Sometimes, the right answer is right and the wrong answers are wrong and there's not much to say. You need "although" because it's important to point out that she finished the painted despite feeling tired. The wrong

answer choices have wrong verbs, wrong tenses, wrong words, wrong commas and wrong content.

Question 4: (D)
First off, keep the verbs parallel: the men and women "hike" and "return." Secondly, keep your answers clean and simple like a news article.

Question 5: (C)
Lots of words here, lots of stuff going on. Every answer choice but (C) has incorrect parallel construction and verb usage. Get rid of the wrong ones one at a time and leave answers that are okay or on the fence. That'll get you to the right answer on this question in no time.

Question 6: (D)
There are two separate pieces to this sentence so a semicolon is needed. (D) is clearly better than (E) – it's simpler and contains one less "so."

Question 7: (B)
Students are often scared to start a sentence with "because," but it's okay a lot of the time. Really. It's simple: Because of this…this! (A) is passive and backwards. (B) gets it right.

Question 8: (C)
This sentence can be confusing to pick apart. The point is that the buffalo herds trampled vegetation and this was GOOD because it HELPED. "Thereby aiding," though a little clunky, is the best way to make this clear. Not only this, but the other answer choices have parallel construction issues and incorrect verb form usage.

Question 9: (E)
Either/or and parallel construction. "To renovate" = "to replace."

Question 10: (B)
The College Board LOVES starting sentences with "because." See question 7 if you don't believe me. "Because" is the clearest and best to start this sentence. "Is the reason why" is redundant and too wordy in answer choice (A) so it's (B).

Question 11: (A)
Put Theodore Roosevelt up front because he is the subject of this sentence. (A) does this correctly, uses the semicolon correctly and maintains the whole point of the sentence: that in addition to being a great reformer, Teddy was also a great president. He was responsible for the national park system. Well played.

Question 12: (E)
This one is hard to see. The trick is paying attention to the second part of the sentence that is NOT underlined:

"politically active, was created in 1996…" The comma, followed by "was," tells us that the whole middle section needs to be an appositive clause. What was created in 1996? Jesse Jackson's Rainbow PUSH Coalition. (C), (D) & (E) all correctly put a comma after "Coalition," but only (E) correctly completes the middle part of the sentence.

Question 13: (E)
"Including forcing" is best because it gives an example of the many difficult choices Jane Eyre must make.

Question 14: (A)
This is a hard one and a lot of students got it wrong when it was on the actual test. Let's use the good 'ol workhorse: THE PROCESS OF ELIMINATION. (B) is wrong because it's a run-on sentence! (C) is wrong because "in addition to being" is bad! (D) is wrong because "that contained" is past tense and we're in the present, yo! (E) is wrong because "and being also" is gross! So it has to be (A). Even if you don't like (A), it's the best choice. So it's (A). Now, the BEST way to write this is: "Nicknamed the supergrain of the future, quinoa is a complete protein that contains all the necessary amino acids and is high in fiber." But that's not an answer choice, is it? So go with (A), which is less good and more confusing (thank you, College Board).

Test 4
Section 2: Critical Reading

Question 1: (D)
Clue word is "surprise." He wants to be surprising, so he wants to "avoid" being predictable, which is the opposite of being surprising.

Question 2: (C)
Since the pandas are already weak, you should infer that a harsh winter would be extremely bad for them. Catastrophic.

Question 3: (A)
Tricky sentence. In this village, marriage was mostly about economics. That's not to say that married couples didn't love each other—it's just that love was a secondary consideration. This points to the fact that it was not necessarily "devoid" (lacking) of love, but that it was mostly a practical "arrangement."

Question 4: (B)
A "procrastinator" is a person who delays. Since Maggie is a procrastinator, she would be naturally inclined to "temporize," which means to draw things out and "prolong" which means the same thing. The other answers make her a different kind of person.

Question 5: (C)
Windows are described as doing two things: letting in light and keeping in the heat (insulation). Since some gases are like windows they do those two things too: Admit light and contain heat.

Question 6: (C)
The speaker is described as being stylish but vacuous (which means lacking real substance). Rhetoric is the art of speaking. She moved listeners because she was good at speaking, but the listeners were too naïve to see that her speeches lacked substance.

Question 7: (D)
These vocab words are hard.
"Fastidious" mean "fussy or particular"
"Sedulous" means "sincerely or diligently"
"Vindictive" means "vicious or spiteful"
"Mercenary" means "in it for the money"
"Petulant" is like a baby throwing a temper tantrum. This actor gets irritated when anything doesn't go his way -- like a baby.

Question 8: (A)
Again, these are hard words but an easy question. People say the films are overly-sentimental. "Treacly" means "overly sweet."

You can get rid of "cursory" (brief or curt), "prosaic" (boring, pedantic), "meticulous" (detail oriented), or "consecrated" (sacred).

Question 9: (C)
Though Balzac showed a "penetrating intuition" -- an insightfulness -- in his work, he did not act like this in his personal life. (E) is tempting but it's wrong because people's expectations were reasonable, since they came from Balzac's work.

Question 10: (B)
In the prior sentence, the author has made a distinction between Balzac's "sensitivity" (or lack thereof) and his "imagination." This last sentence is used to drive that point home. The other answers are off-topic.

Question 11: (E)
She says herself "his being so good really makes it very difficult." His being good makes it difficult only because of being compared to him.

Question 12: (C)
The paragraph is not exclusively about (A) the medical profession or (B) her childhood. It's also not about (D) her father as a potential collaborator. And her attitude is not one of "gratitude." It's about how she compares to her father as a doctor. He is her model for this role.

Passage: Middle Class women in the 19th century
Main idea, Passage 1: Women were regarded differently in the workplace than men in the 19th century, and as the century came to a close, the role of women had become even more restricted. Main idea, Passage 2: The opportunity for unaccompanied travel outside of England for increasing numbers of woman in the 19th century was a way for woman to transcend the narrow confines of their traditional roles.

Question 13: (A)
This sentence asserts that men and women were different because a man's self-worth ROSE with economic exertions. For woman, it was the opposite.

Question 14: (C)
In this context, "occupation" is referring to a person's livelihood and profession. This is "vocation."

Question 15: (E)
This problem is confusing because of all of the dates. The passage is making a distinction between the seventeenth century, where men and women were portrayed as equals in business (with both names on the coins) to the late eighteenth century, where women had largely withdrawn from business life.

Question 16: (D)
Go looking for them. They are all there. Now don't get confused just because the queen is MENTIONED in the passage, because she is not mentioned as evidence of women's diminished social status. In fact, she is an exception.

Question 17: (D)
Answers (B) and (C) do not support the argument -- they weaken it. Answer (E) gives you information about the seventeenth century but we have nothing to compare it to. Answer (D) is specifically about a CHANGE WHICH IS TAKING PLACE wherein a women's role in business is being diminished.

Question 18: (D)
Plug the choices in. They "welcome" the opportunity. None of the other choices make much sense.

Question 19: (E)
This one is tricky. Answers (A) and (D) can be ruled out. The words "Striking inconsistency" makes answer (C) tempting, but her British citizenship is really not relevant. And though Mary Kingsley may have been "opposed to" these campaigns for women's rights, the paragraph says nothing about her being "antagonistic." It's (E) -- her motives are misinterpreted.

Question 20: (C)
"Scientific research" is an educational pursuit and "missionary" work is a humanitarian concern. "Entrepreneurial interests" refers to business, which, according to the passage, was not a part of women's agendas.

Question 21: (A)
Answer (A) involves a middle-class woman traveling alone. None of the other options offer such a scenario and so don't exemplify the argument in the passage.

Question 22: (B)
The "fifth class" is a class of women confined largely to the house. The "caged birds" are confined to the parlor.

Question 23: (B)
These questions are tricky. Neither of these passages feel emotional. Not "nostalgic" or "personal" or "indignant" or "hostile." They feel like a cool presentation of the facts.

Question 24: (A)
What assumption is being made in P2? That England was constrictive for women. Since they were pursuing their vocations abroad, we assume that they were discouraged from doing so back home, which is the subject of P1.

Section 3: Math

Question 1: (E)
Treat an inequality like an equation and solve by subtracting 1 from both sides and then dividing by 3. The value of b must be less than 3. So that means it's NOT 3.

Question 2: (A)
Rewrite 16 as a power of 2. It's 2 to the 4th power. So then x has to just be one.

Question 3: (E)
Plug in any number for r and try it out. If r = 10, then r + 5 = 15, and r – 2 = 8. And 15 is 7 greater than 8.

Question 4: (E)
This is all about visualization. When the vertical edges that are 2 units long are cut and flattened, they will not be touching. If it's hard to visualize, you could also add up the surface area of the sides and bottom of the original box, and then add up the areas of the rectangles in each answer.

Question 5: (B)
This is a logic question – start counting the pathways and make sure to be thorough. If you go up from A, you have to go straight up for the length of two boxes. Then you have the choice of either going up for one more box or turning right and then going up. Then you have no more choices until you get to D. If you go RIGHT from A, you'll reach a similar point where you have two options. So the total different paths are 4.

Question 6: (A)
They want to trick you into multiplying 42 by 3/7. Don't do it! "3/7 of n" means that 3/7 is being multiplied by n. So to solve for n, you have to multiply both sides by the fraction upside down (the "reciprocal" if you want to be fancy). So n = 98. Then 5/7 of n (now we can just multiply) is 70.

Question 7: (E)
A probability question involving geometry shapes can be solved with the area of the part you want divided by the area of the whole figure. Since they don't tell you any side lengths or areas, you can just make up a number. If we say that A has an area of 1, the B and C are also 1, and D, E, and F are each 2. The total area of the six boxes adds up to 9, so the area of F divided by that is 2/9.

Question 8: (E)

Plug in odd numbers for a and b and CAREFULLY test each option. Being careful is generally a good rule of thumb on the SAT math. (a + 1) turns out to always be an even number. In option I, an even times an odd gives you an even answer. But an even plus an odd number or an even minus an odd number both give you odd numbers, so II and III must be correct.

Question 9: (D)
They're trying to scare you when they ask for long numbers involving hundreds of zeroes. But just follow the pattern the problem sets up. After the 98th 1, there must be 98 zeroes. Then there's a 1 and 99 zeroes. Then there's a 1 and 100 zeroes. Then you have arrived at the 101st 1, so stop. Add up all the zeroes: 98 + 99 + 100 = 297.

Question 10: (D)
When it asks for f(2), it means that you need to plug in 2 for x. Then simplify the fraction to get -5/2.

Question 11: (A)
The diagram here is the opposite of helpful. We don't know the exact measures of angles x and y, but we know that they're NOT right angles, even though they sure look like it. We're told that x > 90. And what we DO know is that x and y combine to form a straight line, so they must add up to 180. So maybe x is 100. Then y would be 80. Or x is 91, in which case y is 89. No matter what, y must be less than 90.

Question 12: (D)
The easy way to do this one is to realize that if the point (a,b) is on the x-axis, then the height is zero. So b is zero. We substitute zero for y in the equation of the line and solve for x (which is equivalent to a, which turns out to be 2).

Question 13: (E)
When a median is involved, it's helpful to put the numbers in order from smallest to biggest, if they're not already. If we do that, leaving out t for now, we get 27, 33, 40, 44, 50, 68. The median is the middle number. So 40 is supposed to be in the middle of those numbers, but right now there are two numbers to the left of 40 and three to the right. So t must be inserted into the list to the left of 40 to balance out the list. So t must be less than or equal to 40.

Question 14: (D)
This question becomes a LOT easier if you draw a line from left to right connecting the bottom two points of the diagram. Now we have a square with sides of length 6. The bottom corners of the square must each be 90 degrees, so we can find the base angles of the triangle by subtracting the 30 degree angle from 90

degrees on each side. Then the triangle has two base angles of 60 degrees, which means it must be equilateral. Since the bottom of the triangle is 6, each side is 6. The original figure has five sides, all of which are length 6, for a perimeter of 30.

Question 15: (C)
Using a factor tree is the best way to find prime factors. The greatest prime factor of 38 is 19. And the greatest prime factor of 100 is 5. So m + n equals 24. Sweet!

Question 16: (C)
The one sneaky thing here is that they don't say WHERE line K intersects line L. We don't know if line K goes through the origin. All we know is that any perpendicular lines have negative reciprocal slopes, so if L has a positive slope, K's slope must be negative.

Question 17: (A)
What's with the arrows?! They're just a made-up function. Just ignore them and substitute 1 and 2 for a and b in the fraction (a + b)/(a − b). That turns into 3/(-1). Now substitute 2 and x into the original fraction for a and b. So now the equation is 3/(-1) = (2 + x)/(2 − x). Cross multiply and solve for x.

Question 18: (A)
This is an awesome problem for plugging in numbers! Lets say x is 20 dollars, and z is 5 dollars. Then the first shirt costs $20, the second shirt costs $15, and the third shirt… also costs $15. (Not $10! We're only subtracting $5 from the original price!). Now let's say n = 4. The customer's total cost is 20 + 15 + 15 + 15 = 65. Check each answer by plugging in our values for x, z, and n. Answer A will give you $65. Aha!

Question 19: (A)
The area of this sector (pie slice) of the circle has to be found using a proportion for the circle's total area. But we're not told the circle's area or the circle's radius. All we know is a stupid arc length. So we have to first use a proportion where we set 30/360 equal to 6π/C (where C is the circumference of the circle). C = 72π. Now we can find the radius, since C = 2πr. The radius is 36. And now the area is π time r squared, which is 1296π. Finally, we can do the proportion we wanted to do at the beginning. 30/360 = x/1296π. Solve for x, and the sector's area is 108π.

Question 20: (E)
This looks really simple, but since it's the last problem, it's gonna have at least one sneaky trick. Avoid that by plugging in a number for n. Let's say n = 125 men. Then the number if women is 200. So the total enrolled is 325. The percent of those enrolled who are men is 125/325, but we need to multiply that answer by 100

to convert it to a percent. Approximately 38.5%. Now we plug 125 in for n in each of the answers and E gives us 38.5.

Section 5: Critical Reading

Question 1: (B)
If you're detail-oriented, you're going to be "adept at" (good at) keeping track of particulars.

Question 2: (E)
It's always good with these to put in words of your own. "Rebellion," "conflagration," or "uprising," would all work for the first part. For the second part, I would put in the phrase "put down." This is the same thing as "quelled."

Question 3: (E)
The vocab here is tricky. You know that the word in the blank has to be bad because inbreeding causes genetic problems.
"ineffable" means: incapable of being expressed in words
"articulated" means: made up of two or more sections connected by a joint that can pivot
"consummate" means: excellent, skillful, or accomplished
"presumptive" means: based on what is thought most likely or reasonable
"deleterious" means: with a harmful or damaging effect on somebody or something

Question 4: (A)
We don't have a lot of info here, though we know that since his colleagues are "accusing" him, he must have done something wrong. Then we have to find which two options are in the right relationship to each other. "Vacillate" is bad, and it's in the right relationship to "inconsistency."

Question 5: (E)
"Judicious" means "even-handed." This is "equitable." "Eulogy" fits as well because eulogies are meant to be kind celebrations, and this is the extreme that is opposite "indictment."

Question 6: (B)
P2 doesn't talk at all of working conditions on the farm, which is the main thrust of P1.

Question 7: (D)
Such phrases as "brutal… schedule" (P1) and "great discomfort" (P2) make farm life seem very unromantic.

Question 8: (B)

The "majority" sees farm life as "superior to any to any other kind of life in this country." But the author of P1 knows how difficult the realities of farm life are.

Question 9: (E)
No quotes in passage two. Politicians can be authorities, you know.

Passage: June's Life Importance
Main idea: A Chinese American author considers her relationship with her Mother and her culture.

Question 10: (A)
By the way people react to Waverly's statement, it's clear that he is making fun of June. So answers (C), (D), and (E) are out. And the ad isn't convoluted, so it must be answer (A).

Question 11: (A)
She was surprised about how humiliated she felt -- surprised by her own feelings.

Question 12: (D)
It's all about the word "again," yo!

Question 13: (C)
The way the passage is structured leads us to believe that June is more upset by her mother's betrayal than by anything else that had occurred.

Question 14: (B)
Elimination is probably the best here. The Passage ends with June's realization that the bartender doesn't know what the pendant means. So answer (B) is verifiable. The other answers all seem off-topic or somehow false.

Question 15: (A)
Elimination again. June sees many people wearing these jade pennants around town. This makes us feel that this is a widely observed tradition. Again, this makes answer (A) verifiable and the other answers are unverifiable.

Passage: Bats aren't bad
Main Idea: People have a longstanding fear of bats that prevents us from appreciating bats' potentially useful qualities.

Question 16: (E)
Though the first paragraph is specifically about bats, the rest of the passage is about how humans think and feel about bats.

Question 17: (D)
"Well-known" and "elegant" both fit into the sentence pretty well, but "elegant" isn't really a synonym for "classic." It's gotta be "well-known."

Question 18: (A)
Process of elimination here. The reason the author talks about the usefulness of bats here is that, usually, when we think of bats, we think of them as scary creatures. Certainly we don't think about their usefulness.

Question 19: (C)
An author uses quotes to express skepticism. He is expressing skepticism about what is normal time and what is not. Don't be drawn towards answer . He's not saying suggesting that we're "obsessed with time," but rather that we have prejudice about what time is "normal."

Question 20: (E)
Process of elimination again. The first four answers all detract from the author's assertion that humans are scared of bats because we are uncomfortable with the night.

Question 21: (A)
All these anecdotes (except the one from Bram Stoker) are drawn from different historical human cultures. That is anthropology, the study of human culture.

Question 22: (C)
The first sentence in this paragraph is a thesis: humans think bats are freaky dudes. The other sentences are examples of how different cultures have imagined their freakiness.

Question 23: (B)
Ancient Egyptians used them for medicine. And they built the pyramids!

Question 24: (B)
"If vampires were semi-human…" This kind of "what if" scenario has everything to do with human perception.

Section 6: Math

Question 1: (D)
Try plugging in each answer. Just be careful and you'll see that (3 + 12)/2 gives you the right value.

Question 2: (D)
With two parallel lines crossed by another line, the corresponding angles (the ones in the same position above and below) are equal. So angle 2 equals angle 6, and angle 4 equals angle 8.

Question 3: (A)
In this chart, you can fill in the first column because

27,000 must be added to 21,000 to total 48,000. Then if you move from left to right along the middle row, 500 must be added in the middle box to add up to 21,500. And that's the value you're looking for.

Question 4: (E)
Put 15 into the equation as the value of k, and solve for A, which then equals $30.

Question 5: (D)
The quick way to do this one is to realize that since v equals xr and v also equals kr, that means xr and kr must be equal to each other. Then divide both sides by r to see that k is equal to x.

Question 6: (B)
The secret number is 5. If there are two white eggs for every three brown eggs, then two out of every five TOTAL eggs is white. So the total number of eggs in the basket must be divisible by 5 or else you will end up with pieces of eggs and a very messy basket.

Question 7: (C)
Since the problem says that r has to be larger than t, we can try to make t smaller by factoring it. 18 factors into 9 x 2. You can pull the 9 out from under the radical sign by square rooting it. So a 3 comes out and is multiplied by the 18 out front. The 2 is still trapped underneath. That results in $54\sqrt{2}$. And r multiplied by t equals 108. Aw snap!

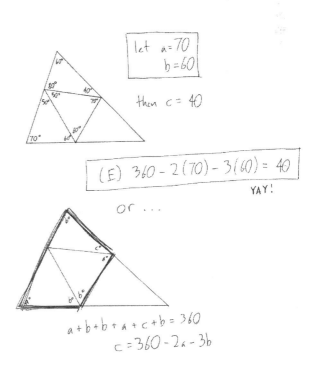

Question 8: (E)
See diagram. There are two manageable ways to solve this one. The most reliable way is to plug in values for a and b and let them determine your c value. The other way is to look at the left portion of the diagram as a quadrilateral. Now that is fancy!

Question 9: 1404
No need to solve for t using a cube root. The problem is just asking for 4 times the number that they gave you!

Question 10: 57.5
Halfway in between two numbers is the same as their average. Add up 53 and 62 and divide by 2.

Question 11: 110
If two angles of the triangle have the same measure, then two sides of a triangle must also have the same length. It's one of those – whatchamacallits – theorems. So the third side must be either 30 or 50. Since we want the least perimeter, we pick 30 instead of 50, and add up our three sides: 30 + 30 + 50.

Question 12: 9
The quick and awesome way to solve this problem is to remember the formula for the difference of two squares: $x^2 - y^2 = (x + y)(x - y)$. The left side of the equation equals 77, and 11 can be inserted into the equation to replace the whole chunk $(x + y)$. In other words, $77 = 11(x - y)$. Divide by 11. $x - y$ equals 7. Now we have two simple equations with 2 variables: $x + y = 11$, and $x - y = 7$. Solve the system of two equations using the addition/subtraction method to find that $2x = 18$, so $x = 9$.

Question 13: 13, 14, 15, 16, or 17
This isn't too bad if you just pick a number between 20 and 30. If it's a number that goes evenly into 360 degrees, you'll be much happier. Like, say, 24 degrees. If you divide the circle into wedges that are each 24 degrees, you'll have 15 pieces of pizza.

Question 14: 5
NOTE: THE BOOK IS WRONG! How embarrassing for them! At least in the initial print run, the book lists the answer as 6. But the REAL correct answer is 5, not 6. The first five terms in the sequence are $a + 3a + 9a + 27a + 81a = 605$. Simplify and solve for a.

Question 15: 1/2 or .5
If you are able to correctly label the lengths of the drawing without making a mistake, then you are a very careful person. It's so easy to screw up on this one! If the ratio of QS/QV = 1/3, then we can label QS as 1 and QV as 3. So SV = 2. Likewise, we can label PT as 3

and PR as 4. Are we allowed to just assume the numbers in the ratio are the same as the side lengths? Yes, because the final answer is converted back to a ratio. With the lengths we have labeled, the area of PST is $(1/2)(3)(2) = 3$. The area of PQR is $(1/2)(4)(3) = 6$.

Question 16: 2 or 7
You gotta know how functions work to nail this one. The stuff in parentheses gets plugged in for x. So plug (2m) into the equation for x. $14 + (2m)^2/4$ simplifies to 14 plus m^2. And that equals 9m. Subtract 9m from both sides to move everything to one side of the equation. $m^2 - 9m + 14 = 0$. Factor the quadratic to $(m - 2)(m - 7) = 0$. The solutions are 2 or 7. Either one is OK, so pick your favorite!

Question 17: 149
This question takes forever. If you're running out of time on a section, skip a long one like this. To answer it, start with Type A. There are 10 clocks, and each chimes n times on the nth hour. In the time period we're looking for, the only time the hour changes is at 8:00. Each of those 10 clocks chimes 8 times, so that's 80 chimes. Keep a running total on the page. Each of the 10 clocks in Type A also chimes once on the half hour. There are TWO half hours within our time period: 7:30 and 8:30. So 10 chimes plus 10 more chimes. Our running total is now 100. For Type B, 5 clocks chime 8 times on the hour, so that is 40 more chimes (Running total: 140). Finally, the three clocks in Type C chime ONCE on the hour (3 x 1 = 3, Running total: 143), and once on each of the TWO half hours (3 x 1 x 2 = 6). The final total is 149.

Question 18: 72
The trick to finding different arrangements is to draw a line of blanks to represent the possibilities. This problem has five cards, so we need five blanks:

_____ _____ _____ _____ _____

If all five cards were allowed to be put in any spot, we could calculate the possibilities as:

5 x 4 x 3 x 2 x 1 = 120

BUT, the gray card can't be put in the first or last blank, so we need to focus on those two blanks first. There are four options for how many cards can go in the first blank, and then, once one of those four options is assigned, there are only three options for the final blank:

4 x _____ x _____ x _____ x 3

Now there are no restrictions on the three middle spots. There are three cards left (including that pesky gray card, who can finally find a home), and three spots. We can treat these three spots as a mini-problem within the bigger one, and the calculation would be 3 x 2 x 1. So, putting it all together:

4 x 3 x 2 x 1 x 3 = 72

Section 7: Writing

Question 1: (E)
Parallel construction. We're talking about museums in Great Britain and in Canada. The current sentence compares museums in Great Britain to the entire nation of Canada.

Question 2: (B)
"Which" makes it an appositive. The subject is already known (Dispatch Education) so "it" is redundant. The others are too wordy and weird.

Question 3: (B)
A hometown cannot print world news; a hometown newspaper can.

Question 4: (E)
This one is tricky because even the correct answer sounds off with the use of "thereby." A general rule is that the simplest and shortest answer always wins. The other choices are clunky and use far too many "therefores."

Question 5: (D)
The College Board loves this type of question. Who or what "thought the problem through with some care?" Misplaced modifier in the original. The correct answer is the only one which simply states: "the chairperson."

Question 6: (C)
Two parts to this one. #1. Subject/verb agreement. Students are giving multiple reasons for failing to participate so the answer has to start with "are," not "is." #2. Parallel construction.

Question 7: (A)
No problems with the original sentence. Also note: it's the simplest and shortest answer.

Question 8: (E)
Misplaced modifier in the original – the small town did not return to Dayville after ten years. The other choices either have incorrect tense agreement or are unnecessarily verbose (wordy). Isn't it nice to know that Margo's hometown is so much livelier now? What, did they put in an Applebees?

Question 9: (E)
"Having" is a stinky way to start a sentence (so is "being," by the way). "Because" is the way to go. A fun game to play = read each answer choice like a newscaster and see which one sounds the best. It's usually the right answer. For fun, read answer choice (C) like a newscaster. That newscaster should be fired.

Question 10: (C)
Whoa! Lots of stuff here. Where is Richard moving?! All of these are long and confusing, but only the right answer employs correct parallel construction.

Question 11: (C)
This is a tricky one. First off, there needs to be parallel construction in the first part of the sentence: "on the government" and "on universities." Then it's back to the good 'ol classic MISPLACED MODIFIER! Who or what is dependent on the government and universities? The space research center. Yeah! Wouldn't it be awesome if we could take vacations to other planets?

Question 12: (C)
Verb tense. This happened in the past. The Galileo "disintegrated."

Question 13: (E)
No problems here. Note = the sentences with no error will sometimes sound clunky, but there's nothing technically wrong. Look for real, hard, concrete errors. The most tempting choice is probably (D). It works because it's parallel to "satisfy." The contract WILL do two things: one, SATISFY the demands, and two, BE ACCEPTABLE to all levels.

Question 14: (B)
Either/or.

Question 15: (D)
Subject/verb agreement. Pottery shards are plural! So THEY are virtually indestructible.

Question 16: (D)
This one is hard because "only one of a kind" is an idiom. The correct way to write this sentence is "the only one of its kind."

Question 17: (E)
Nothing wrong here. Might sound too wordy – don't fall for the trick.

Question 18: (A)
Verb tense. Shelby WAS absent when his rivals voted so he is worried about missing future meetings.

Question 19: (E)
Nothing wrong here. A lot of students are tempted to choose (B) because "in those cities in which" sounds strange, but there's nothing wrong with it.

Question 20: (D)
"OF necessity" is incorrect. "Necessary" should replace it to create a parallel to the adjective "present."

Question 21: (B)
Him, not he.

Question 22: (B)
Classic parallel construction. "It is far easier TO RIDE a bicycle than TO EXPLAIN…"

Question 23: (E)
Evil evil evil no error. Even the right answer sounds terrible. "For the most part" seems wrong. BUT: there is nothing grammatically incorrect. They are deliberately messing with your head and trying to fool you. Not very nice.

Question 24: (A)
The word "since" makes this an incomplete sentence as it is written. Read it carefully. Get rid of "since" and it's okay. Not great, but okay.

Question 25: (A)
Idiom: preoccupation WITH technique.

Question 26: (B)
Mmmmm. Carlos and me, not Carlos and I. Get rid of Carlos and it becomes clear. "The foundation awarded I a grant" does not sound good. In any case, congratulations to you and Carlos. Hopefully your network of community centers will help a lot of people.

Question 27: (B)
Subject/verb agreement…but tricky. "The proposed health clinics and the proposed center WERE also supported by the commission." When they want to be mean, the College Board puts the subject AFTER the verb. Be careful!

Question 28: (C)
Pronoun agreement. Exact same deal as the last question (#27). We're talking about the potency of the tablets so "their" is correct, not "its."

Question 29: (B)
Adverb! A seafloor cannot be "constant changing," but it can be "constantly changing."

Passage Revision: Workplace Problems

Question 30: (D)
This passage is about employee/employer communication and workplace conditions. EXCITING STUFF! Good trick here = look at the concluding paragraph (particularly the last sentence). The correct answer choice is basically the same thing with the words moved around.

Question 31: (B)
Okay, so this one is mean because the whole "but

workers, too, must…" looks like a classic wrong answer. This section is all about getting rid of what's wrong to get to what's right. Nothing's going to be stellar, but at least three of the answer choices will be bad. This is a difficult question. Most of the answer are too clunky and confusing.

Question 32: (E)
This requires going back to the passage looking at the previous sentence since the sentence in question obviously refers to it. Then it's still tricky, but "treatment" is a better word choice to refer to what's going on than "concern" or "view."

Question 33: (E)
Look for the simplest and shortest answers. The other choices are all over the place.

Question 34: (C)
We need a transition from the previous paragraph to this one. So what's this paragraph about? Complaints that employers might have with employees. This gets you down to (C) & (E). Then it's gotta be (C) because employers are complaining, not employees.

Question 35: (E)
And we need a capper to finish off this FASCINATING essay on workplace conditions and employee/employer relations! The correct answer is simple, clean and straightforward. Also bland and general enough to be perfect for the SAT!

Section 8: Critical Reading

Question 1: (D)
Counsel means "advice."

Question 2: (A)
The phrase "that excitement" describes the phrase in the first blank. Excitement is like "passion." When you put in answer (A) the sentence makes total sense.

Question 3: (E)
This is a clear positive/negative relationship. Try fitting in your own words into the blanks. My first guess is that as, say, "bad" as things seemed, there were actually some "good," things that came from it. Vice versa would work too. It's gotta be answer (E). Bad = catastrophic. Good = constructive.

Question 4: (D)
If the beauty of the mountain is usually cloaked, then the clouds must be doing the cloaking. The blank should be filled by a synonym for the word "Cloak." "Shroud" is best.

Question 5: (A)
So she released her product just as everybody wanted to buy it? How fortunate! She really seized a great opportunity.

Question 6: (D)
This one's hard. Talk it out. If a scientist went into another culture and told the people that the way they practice medicine was silly and childish, that would be very condescending. That would be smug or arrogant. So it's either answer (B) or (D). The second part of answer (B) doesn't make any sense (how would scientific qualifications pursue prejudice?). It must be (D).

Passage: Television
Main idea: The arguments for the dangers of television are categorically flawed.

Question 7: (B)
We are talking here about the "manipulation" thesis, where there are those who are manipulated and those who are doing the manipulating. The "wire-pullers" are the ones doing the manipulating.

Question 8: (B)
Use elimination if this one snags you. None of the wrong answers make sense.

Question 9: (D)
This one is tricky because there are some other close answers in there. The writer is using this anecdote to say "isn't it ridiculous that people used to think that books would rot your brain? That's the same as the people who talk about television rotting your brain now." Answers (A) and (C) are both tempting, but less exact than answer (D).

Question 10: (D)
Just like in the last question, the author is saying that resistance to television is just as ridiculous and small-minded as early resistance to books.

Question 11: (C)
This paragraph is about how people won't be able to tell the difference between reality and fiction.

Question 12: (A)
This one is tricky. I'd get rid of answers (D) and (E) to begin with. Answer (B) isn't right either (this isn't only an insignificant point, it's their entire point). It's gotta be answer (A). The proponents of this theory don't really believe that people won't be able to tell the difference between an apple on tv and an apple in their hand. The author is taking their point too literally.

Question 13: (B)
Questions of attitude have to do with the WAY the author makes his argument. The way the language sounds and feels. In this paragraph, it feels like the author thinks that critics of television are some pretty dumb people.

Question 14: (E)
This question is similar to the last question. The tricky part is that, on occasion, the author uses the tactics in answers (C) and (D). But throughout the piece the author is suggesting that these arguments are weak and that the people who make them are ridiculous.

Question 15: (B)
The piece talks very little (or not at all) of politics or comedy. The critics of television seem to think television viewers are naïve, unsuspecting victims.

Question 16: (E)
It can't be answers (A), (C), or (D), because the author isn't earnest, morose, of telling lies. Neither can it be (B) because the author is not analyzing academic documentation (where are the documents?). It answer (E). He's describing the arguments while laughing at them.

Question 17: (D)
Another hard one. Answers (B), (C), and (E) don't work. But it's tricky between answers (A) and (D). Answer (D) is more exact. It's not that these critics can determine things in an "excellent" manner, but that they can determine things without a shadow of a doubt.

Question 18: (B)
If the theories are symptoms of a universal stupefaction, then that means that the critics have become stupid from watching tv, and this is why their theories are so lame. In short, the author is being a real jerk.

Question 19: (A)
This is another question of attitude. The author isn't puzzled, embarrassed, sympathetic, or resigned. He's sickened, but still having a laugh about it.

Section 9: Math

Question 1: (C)
4 boys got off the bus, and now there are half as many boys as girls. That means that 4 is half the original number of boys (and original number of girls).

Question 2: (D)
Negative slopes go down to the right. And the line has to go through the vertical y-axis ABOVE the origin to have a positive y-intercept.

Question 3: (B)
Don't pick (C) – that's too easy! The cost per donut for a box of six means you divide the price of a box of 6 ($1.89) by 6 and get $0.315 cents.

Question 4: (B)
The donuts are cheaper when bought in bulk. (You can verify that by dividing the price of a box by the number of donuts in the box to get the cost per donut). So buy one box of 12 donuts, then one box of 6 donuts. You now have 18. You can't buy another box or you'll have too many. Now buy three individual donuts for 40 cents each ($1.20 together). So the total cost is 3.59 + 1.89 + 1.20 = 6.68.

Question 5: (C)
The number 5 is the x-value of a spot on the graph. The question is asking, what is the function's height when the x-value is 5? The height is approximately 3.

Question 6: (C)
The only actual number we know here is that all of the angles combined must add up to 360 degrees. So 2x + 3x + 4x = 360. Simplify and x = 40.

Question 7: (D)
The fastest way to find x is to raise both sides of the equation to the -2 power. The exponents on the left hand side cancel, so you just have $x \wedge 1$, and the right side turns out to be 9. We know y and z are positive integers. A little trial and error will confirm that the only integers that could equal 16 are $2 \wedge 4$, or else $4 \wedge 2$. Since z is bigger than y, z equals 4. Add x and z, which is 9 plus 4.

Question 8: (C)
The cool thing about semicircles is that they're SYM-METRICAL! It's all about starting at the top of the semicircle, where the x coordinate is 4. The problem wants you to find two spots that have equal height. If you move along the curve to the left and to the right the same distance, that would do it. Two units left gives you an x-value of 2, and two units to the right gives you an x-value of 6.

Question 9: (B)
Your life will be really, really simple on problems like this if you just plug in each answer and see if it works. Let's try answer (A), where p = 2. Then 2p + 7 equals 11. If we divide by 5, the remainder is 1. No good. But if p is 3, then 2p + 7 equals 13, and the remainder is 3 when we divide by 5.

Question 10: (B)
They really want you to be fooled into thinking the answer is 24. But if Stacy is 12th tallest, then there are 11 kids taller than her. And there are 11 kids shorter than her. Add 11 plus 11 and don't forget Stacy herself. That's 23 kids!

Question 11: (A)
The rules for graphing parabolas say that if a is negative, then the parabola opens downwards. And if c is negative, then the parabola's vertex is shifted downwards from the origin.

Question 12: (B)
It seems like there's not enough information! First, draw in segment PQ and segment QR. Since PQ is symmetrical around AB, that means that half of segment PQ is inside the rectangle and half is outside. Likewise for segment QR. So half of the total distance from P to R is inside the rectangle. The distance across the rectangle from left to right is 4, so the length of PR must be 8.

Question 13: (C)
Finally, a question where calculators help! Do percent changes one at a time. Pretend the initial price is 100. Then increasing it by 10% gives you 110. Now reduce it by 25%. Multiply .25 x 110 = 27.5, and remember you're SUBTRACTING 27.5 from the 110. Now you're at 82.5, which is the answer. (82.5 out of the original price of 100 is 82.5 percent.) Cool, dude.

Question 14: (E)
4w = 4 + w. Solve for w. It equals 4/3. But those SAT jerks aren't asking for w! They want 3w, so multiply your answer by 3.

Question 15: (C)
"Consecutive even integers" means every other number. So three consecutive even integers can be written as x, (x + 2), and (x + 4). Then plug those three values into the Pythagorean theorem: $a^2 + b^2 = c^2$, replacing a, b, and c.

Question 16: (D)
I. True. y can never equal x. Let's say x = 4. Then y = 4¼. y will always be a little bit more than x.
II. False. y can not be an integer. y will always be a mixed number made from an integer plus a fraction.
III. True. Divide both sides of the inequality by x (you're allowed to because x can't equal zero). Now it says y > x, which will always be true.

Section 10: Writing

Question 1: (B)
This is going to happen in the future, so the medical researchers "hope to explore." Cool. Also, note that the

sentence as it is written is not complete: they "hope exploring the body with miniature robots sent into the bloodstream…" – will what? You'll see this a lot.

Question 2: (B)
This question demonstrates how an appositive can make something pretty simple look confusing. Take out the whole middle of the sentence, which functions almost as a parenthetical ("one of the few Black soldiers in White regiments during the early part of the Civil War"). Once you do that, the correct answer is obvious. This trick is a good weapon to have in your SAT arsenal. Know how and when to use it!

Question 3: (A)
It's okay as is, but the use of the word "for" throws people off. Remember: look for what's clearly incorrect. The other answer choices all contain something very wrong, particularly the ambiguous use of the pronoun "it."

Question 4: (B)
Parallel construction. Journalists "should present a balanced view" and "should also stir." Note: it's also the shortest and simplest answer. The SAT is boring like that.

Question 5: (D)
This sentence needs something to connect warrior and devised, right? A comma is not enough (A), a semi-colon results in an incomplete second half of the sentence (C) and (E) is just plain too wordy with unnecessary words.

Question 6: (E)
First off, the lawyers "asserted that," so (A) and (B) are gone. And (C) and (D) are far too clunky and strange to be correct.

Question 7: (E)
Another classic parallel construction. Toni Morrison was honored not only "as a great novelist" but also "as an eloquent historian." Man, you're thinking, they ask this type of question a lot! Yes. Yes, they do.

Question 8: (A)
This one is annoying because the whole sentence is up for debate. It's also tricky because there's a lot of information that the correct answer must contain. They move everything around here to confuse you, but the original sentence is the best. If it ain't broke, don't fix it.

Question 9: (D)
(A), (B) and (E) all follow the comma with "it" or "this." The problem with that is that we have no idea what "it" or "this" is referring to. There are a lot of things in

the first part of the sentence: Uranus, kilometers, the Sun and a methane cloud. So those are no good. And the sentence starts with "because," so "is the reason" (C) is unnecessary. Whew!

Question 10: (B)
Another misplaced modifier question. Ding ding ding! Get used to these. Who or what is "lacking good instruction?" The answer is "I." So you're down to (B) and (D) and (B) is clearer. (D) sounds like this person created the graph with someone named "numerous mistakes." Maybe a superhero?

Question 11: (C)
Use elimination on this somewhat difficult question. (D) is too wordy; (B) and (E) have weird logic with the "and." The decision between (A) and (C) comes down to an idiomatic thing. We are "absorbed IN" things, not "absorbed BY" things. I suppose that water could be absorbed BY a towel, but that's a different sentence altogether, isn't it?

Question 12: (D)
Misplaced modifier here: who is "entering an Internet website"? In this case, YOU are, not your order. It can only be (D).

Question 13: (C)
Parallel construction. One day we will: 1) "establish bases on the moon" & 2) "land on Neptune." How awesome will that be?! Would you rather live on the moon or Neptune? Why? Plan and write an essay in which you develop your point of view on this issue. Support your position with reasoning and examples taken from your reading, studies, experiences, or observations.

Question 14: (D)
Great example of a seemingly complicated sentence made simple when the appositive is removed. So get rid of "although their common language is English" and you will see that "the city is populated by many people who speak languages at home…"

Test 5
Section 2: Math

Question 1: (D)
Solve for x. Subtract 3x from both sides, then subtract 1 from both sides, then divide by two.

Question 2: (B)
How many times does one term go into the next? Roughly twice. In fact, each term is always double the previous term, and then plus one. So m = 2 and p = 1.

Question 3: (B)
To find the total number of combinations, multiply the number of options for Color (3 options) by the number of options for Size (4 options).

Question 4: (D)
Try each answer. Plug -3 in for x, and then plug 3 in for x, and see if the first value is greater.

Question 5: (E)
Set up a proportion using two fractions. 15 pounds / 8 cm = x pounds / 20 cm. Cross multiply. 300 = 8x. x = 37.5.

Question 6: (E)
Do yourself a favor and draw a picture!
I. True. YZ is half the total length.
II. False. ½XZ equals XY, not 2 XY
III. True. XZ is twice the length of XY.

Question 7: (C)
5s equals 2r and 5s ALSO equals 6t. So 2r and 6t are equal to each other. Divide by two to solve for r. r = 3t.

Question 8: (A)
Say there are n = 5 buses and each bus can hold x = 10 passengers. Then the five buses together can hold 50 passengers. But one bus has 3 empty seats, so the total passengers k = 50 – 3 = 47. The formula that matches this is (A), nx – 3 = k.

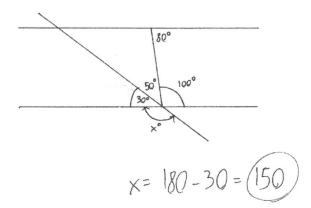

$$x = 180 - 30 = \boxed{150}$$

Question 9: (A)
See diagram. When you look at this one, doesn't it just scream out, "parallel lines cut by a transversal?" Well, it does to me. The easiest way to look at this is to check out the angle directly below the 80 degree angle. Those two angles are same-side interior angles, which have to add up to 180. Once we know that, we're almost home. If that's 100, then the little guy underneath the 50 must be 30. If that's 30, then the underside of that must be whatever's left of 180, so 150.

Question 10: (B)
Try plugging in the answers. Plug in zero on both sides and you get 0 < 0. Zero can't be less than zero! That would be crazy!

Question 11: (C)
I'll bet Senai is looking pretty stupid on her lopsided bike right about now… Anyhoo, the revolutions a wheel makes are related to its circumference. If the back wheel has a diameter of 10, its circumference is 10π. Front wheel's diameter: 5. Front wheel's circumference: 5π. A wheel of circumference 5π must make exactly two full revolutions to match one revolution of the back wheel with circumference 10π.

Question 12: (C)
If 3/5 is the probability of picking a positive number from the list, that means 3 out of every 5 numbers are positive. So let's say there are 5 numbers on the list. 3 are positive, 2 are negative. n/p = 2/3.

Question 13: (B)
This one looks gnarlier than it actually is. You've got this somewhat ugly function equation and a pair of values to plug into it. Substitute 640 for c(x) and 20 for x. Your job now is to do some careful algebra. Start by simplifying that fraction; you should get 590 for that value. Subtract 590 from the 640 and you'll find that k = 50.

Question 14: (A)
If x and y are both 1, then 2(1) + 3(1) = 5. So that could work. But if you increase the value of either x or y at all, the total will be greater than 6, so (1,1) is the only option.

Question 15: (C)
The two 60 degree angles mean triangle DEF must be equilateral. So each side is 5, and the perimeter is 15. Triangle ABC must be isosceles because it has two angles labeled x (we don't need to know the value of x!) and BC must equal AB, which equals 8. So ABC's perimeter is 8 + 8 + 5 = 21. 21 − 16 = 5.

Question 16: (E)
Plug in some consecutive odd integers. Let's say x = 3 and y = 5. Then $y^2 - x^2 = 25 - 9 = 16$. Plug in 3 for x into each of the answers and (E) gives you the correct value of 16.
OR, to be fancy and solve it algebraically, two consecutive odd integers can be written as x and x + 2. Substitute (x + 2) for y. So $y^2 - x^2$ can be rewritten as $(x + 2)^2 - x^2$. FOIL to get $x^2 + 4x + 4 - x^2$, which equals 4x + 4.

Question 17: (A)
This one is nasty! So many unknowns! The line 4x + y = k can be rewritten in slope intercept form as y = -4x + k. The slope is -4. Line L is perpendicular to it, and perpendicular lines have negative reciprocal slopes, so line L's slope is ¼. Now take a deep breath. We know line L passes through the origin, so its y-intercept is zero. Now we have an equation for L: y = (1/4)x + 0, or y = (1/4)x. Plug (t, t + 1) into that equation, replacing x and y. t + 1 = (1/4)t. Solve for t, which equals -4/3.

Question 18: (A)
The average of x, y, and z would be (x + y + z)/3. But the answers don't have x and y in them. Since the average of x and y is k, we can write (x + y)/2 = k. Multiply by two. x + y = 2k. Now in the first average, substitute 2k for x + y.

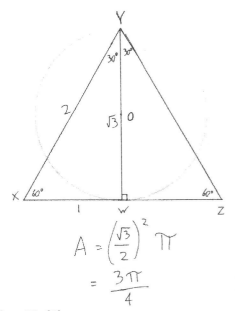

$$A = \left(\frac{\sqrt{3}}{2}\right)^2 \pi$$

$$= \frac{3\pi}{4}$$

Question 19: (C)
See diagram. Angle XYZ is cut in half by the altitude YZ, so XYW is a 30-60-90 right triangle. XW is 1 unit long, so side WY is length √3 by the immortal rules of 30-60-90 triangles. WY is also the diameter of the circle, so the circle's radius is √3/2. The area is $\pi r^2 = \pi(\sqrt{3}/2)^2 = (3/4)\pi$.

Question 20: (C)
This one requires a little thinking. If you divide 15 by some number k, and have 3 left over, then k must go evenly into 12, because 12 is 3 less than 15. what are the factors of 12? 1, 2, 3, 4, 6, and 12. BUT, to create a remainder of 3, k must itself be bigger than 3 (it's a rule), so k can only be 4, 6, or 12. Three options.

Section 3: Critical Reading

Question 1: (D)
Here we are looking for a word that is most nearly the opposite of "harmless." This is "toxic."

Question 2: (D)
"Scrutinizes" means "critically examining."

Question 3: (C)
If a country changes names, then that's a sign of political turbulence ("We will now be called the United States of King Kevin!"). The name changes "testify to" the political turbulence.

Question 4: (C)

From the first blank, we know that it has to be answer (A) or (C), because the important thing about these pods is that there are so many of them. In the second blank, we see that answer A doesn't make sense ("subtracted from fossil records?"). "Catalogued" makes sense.

Question 5: (A)
Vocab words are really hard here. If we were to fit in our own words they might be "complicated (strategies)," and "skilled (player)." "Byzantine" means "complicated." "Adroit" means "skilled."

Question 6: (B)
We are clued in to "spontaneous" by phrases like "not self-conscious," and "speaks directly."

Question 7: (E)
His letters have the same style and tone at all of these different periods in his life. Consistency.

Question 8: (C)
Wow. This question is...impossible. Definitely the hardest reading question in the book. What the passage is trying to say is that black leaders have sometimes been put on a pedestal, and that authors have been told not to explore the "humanity" (or normal human flaws) of folks like Martin Luther King Jr. That means that those folks have been portrayed as "above reproach"—too important to be criticized.

Question 9: (B)
The author uses the word "paintings," but earlier he talks about authors. Metaphorically, those "paintings" must really be books. Historical biographies, to be specific.
If these two short passages were hard for you, don't worry! They are hard for everyone. If you aced the last four questions, then congrats: you are kicking SAT butt.

Passage: Time Travel
Main Idea: Time travel is possible, though maybe not in the sci-fi movie way.

Question 10: (B)
The author is using this moment to put the idea of "two-million years" into context. He mentions Australopithecus as if to say, "yeah, dude, it was a long time ago."

Question 11: (A)
If you could do this, then that would be a kind of time travel. You could see Earth in its distant past.

Question 12: (E)
The author mentions curing a terrible disease in the

past and seeing what the future looks like. All of this would be possible with time travel. Time travel is fascinating because the possibilities are so many and so profound.

Question 13: (B)
The author wants us to know that we aren't just listening to the crazy dude on the subway platform talking about traveling in time ("I come from three hundred years in the future! Could you spare some change?").

Question 14: (C)
This one is a little tricky. Don't worry because you don't know what things like "deterministic universe" mean exactly. The point is that the author is telling us HOW time travel would be taking place, he's just talking about how much it would screw things up if it were possible.

Question 15: (B)
This one is a bit weird, too. The author is imagining that it must have been strange when clocks were invented and people realized that time was made up of perfect little intervals. So... if people ALREADY felt that that's the way time was organized, that would ruin the author's argument.

Question 16: (D)
These are examples of our own natural timepieces.

Question 17: (E)
"Ruthless" refers to time's steady progression. The process of aging is unstoppable. Answer (A) might be tempting, but it is less exact because the author is talking about TIME, not ABOUT OUR RELATIONSHIP TO TIME.

Question 18: (C)
This paragraph is about how time travel is possible... in the mind. He's trying to tell us that he time-travelled a little bit.

Passage: Middle Class women in the 19th century
Main Idea: When you remove the element of human narrative from art, most people don't know how to approach it.

Question 19: (C)
This passage tries to determine what pleasures most people about looking at art.

Question 20: (C)
"Figures," in this context, means "people" or rather, "representations of people."

Question 21: (B)

"The story of John and Susie" is meant as a stand-in for any kind of interpersonal story. The author is contrasting this with a purely aesthetic art, one that has no story.

Question 22: (D)
Most people resist modern art because there are no people in it, and no stories. They cannot connect the painting to their own lives.

Question 23: (E)
This question is really hard. Let's eliminate bad answers: "Aggressively hostile" is much too strong -- the author is speaking calmly, without too much passion. The piece does not feel "Solemn" or sad. "Puzzlement" is wrong too, because the author seems to have a very clear idea about why people feel how they do. So it's answer (B) or (E). The best place to spot the condescension is in the opening paragraph. I love this: "It is an art not for people in general but for a special class who may not be better but are evidently different." So they MAY not be better...but then again, maybe they ARE better. That's definitely condescending.

Question 24: (A)
This is paraphrasing what the author says in the final paragraph.

Section 4: Math

Question 1: (A)
Replace s + t in the second equation with 3. So (3) – 6 = -3.

Question 2: (C)
The distance from C to Q is just the length of one edge, but the distance from C to P involves going diagonally down and left through the cube. The straight edge of a cube is always shorter than the distance from one corner to an opposite corner.

Question 3: (D)
Email represents 18%, so it should be a much bigger slice of the pie than News Groups or Other. So answers (A) and (E) must be wrong. Web Sites are 78%, which should take up more than ¾ of the circle (75%), so (B) doesn't work. News Groups and Other should be equal-sized slices, so (D) is a better answer than (C).

Question 4: (D)
If the denominator is x, the numerator is x – 5. Write the equation (x – 5)/x = ¾. Cross multiply to get 4x – 20 = 3x. x = 20.

Question 5: (E)

Area of the triangle = ½ (b x h) = 18. The height of the triangle is 4. Thus ½ (b x 4) = 18. Solve for b, which turns out to equal 9. Looking at the base of the figure, the distance from left to right from 2k to 5k is 3k. The base is 3k long, and we already know the base equals 9, so k = 3. Not too shabby!

Question 6: (D)
Do exponent problems one step at a time and be extra careful. First, divide both sides of the equation by 10m. $mk^{-1} = 10$. k^{-1} can be rewritten as $1/k$. So $m/k = 10$. Solve for m, multiplying both sides by k. m = 10k. Now you can find m^{-1} by flipping both sides of the equation upside down. $m^{-1} = 1/10k$.

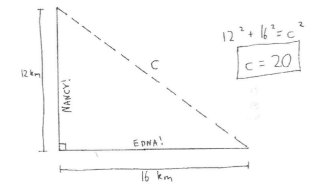

Question 7: (E)
Ah, nothing like spending 4 hours walking home from a friend's house! Edna and Nancy need to meet some people in their own neighborhood! See diagram. We need to find the distances they have traveled, so we use distance = rate x time. Edna's distance is 4 km/hr x 4 hrs = 16 km. Nancy's distance is 3 km/hr x 4 hrs = 12 km. Since one is going north and the other is going east, there is a right angle between them. Use Pythagorean theorem to find the distance from one to the other. $12^2 + 16^2 = c^2$. c = 20.

Question 8: (C)
The left and right hand sides of parabolas are symmetrical. Basically, what the question is asking is what point on the parabola is symmetrical to the point where x = 3? Since 3 is two units to the right of the vertex, go two units to the left of the vertex to find a symmetrical point. The x-coordinate there is -1.

Question 9: 7
The family needs 5 x 4 = 20 bottles of water. 20 divided by 3 is 6.6667, so we round up to 7 to make sure they buy enough water.

Question 10: 13
To get rid of the absolute value sign, split the top equation into two versions, one with a plus sign out front

and one with a minus sign. $10 - k = 3$, and $-(10 - k) = 3$. Solve each equation for k. k equals 7 or 13. Now try each answer in the bottom equation. 7 doesn't work. 13 does. Voila!

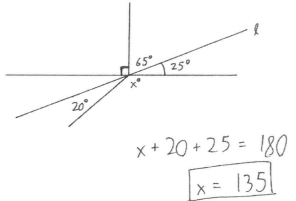

$$x + 20 + 25 = 180$$
$$\boxed{x = 135}$$

Question 11: 135
See diagram. First up, the little angle under 65. Those guys have to add up to 90, so it's 25 degrees. Now you've got three angles on the underside of line l: x, 20 and 25. Subtract the other two from 180 and you'll find x.

Question 12: 46
The median is the middle number. In a set of 9 integers, there must be 4 numbers below the middle number and 4 numbers above. From 42, count up 4 more to get to 46.

Question 13: 28
If $2f(p) = 20$, then $f(p) = 10$. Substitute p for x in the function $x + 1$. $p + 1 = 10$. $p = 9$. So we're done, right? Nope. They're not asking for p. They want f(3p). f(3p) means f(3 x 9) which is f(27). Plug 27 into $x + 1$. 27 plus 1 is equal to… umm… uhh… 28. I knew that.

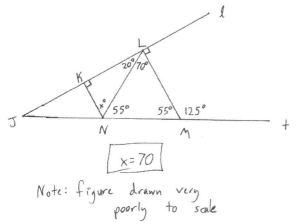

$$\boxed{x = 70}$$

Note: figure drawn very poorly to scale

Question 14: 70
See diagram. Start with the angle we are given: 125 degrees, and start working towards angle x. The 125

degree angle forms a straight line with angle NML (they are supplementary). So NML = 55. Since sides LN and LM are equal, triangle NLM is isosceles, making angle LNM also a 55 degree angle. Since the three angles in a triangle add up to 180, the top angle, angle NLM, must be 70. That angle is complementary (adds up to 90) with angle KLN. So angle KLN is 20 degrees. At last, we're getting close to x! x is in a triangle with a 90 degree angle and a 20 degree angle. x must be 70.

Question 15: 7/15, .466, .467
The mixture that is poured in takes up 4/5 of the cup. One third of that 4/5 is orange juice. 1/3 x 4/5 = 4/15. Add that to the 1/5 cup of OJ that was already there. 1/5 + 4/15 = 3/15 + 4/15 = 7/15.

Question 16: 3
Let's turn these words into some math! $a + 2b = 1.25$ x $4b$. 1.25 x $4b = 5b$. $a + 2b = 5b$. $a = 3b$. We want a/b, so divide both sides by b. $a/b = 3$.

Question 17: 4/9, .444
If we have 9 equal intervals, then each tick mark represents 1/9. Counting from zero, we see that the spot we want is 6 intervals, so it has a value of 6/9. $\sqrt{x} = 6/9 = 2/3$. Square both sides. $x = 4/9$.

Question 18: 2 or 18
Use the distance formula:
$$D = \sqrt{(x_1 - x_2)^2 + (y_2 - y_1)^2}$$
$$17 = \sqrt{(x - 10)^2 + (3 - 18)^2}$$ Next, square both sides:
$$289 = (x - 10)^2 + (-15)^2$$
$$289 = (x - 10)^2 + 225$$
$$64 = (x - 10)^2$$ Now, square root both sides:
$x - 10$ equals positive or negative 8. Add ten and the answers are 18 or 2.

Section 6: Writing

Question 1: (C)
The only good answer starts with "having." This goes against our rule that usually only bad answers start with "having" (or "being"). Fortunately, this is the first question in the section so it's pretty straightforward.

Question 2: (D)
"As soaked as" makes this a hypothetical situation. So "as if they had marched" is correct. (E) is also a hypothetical, but it's too wordy.

Question 3: (C)
There are many many many harmful effects of smoking (you shouldn't smoke, ever). SO: these thousands of harmful effects ARE well documented. Only two answer choices start with "are" and (D) uses the phrase

"in better documentation" which is as wrong as smoking is bad.

Question 4: (E)

Kind of a hidden parallel construction test here. We know the sentence ends in "increase profits" so which first half goes with that? "IMPROVE" housing.

Question 5: (D)

Run-on sentences are running all over the place in this question. Too many words in all of the answer choices but the winner. (C) looks good until you stop to ask what "it" is. There is no clear singular antecedent for it. Now, can we take a moment to congratulate Harriet Quimby for her incredible feat?

Question 6: (D)

Another tricky one – this is a tricky section. Again, get rid of what's wrong to get to what's right. You may not like (D) because "contest, for their work" sounds not great, but the other ones are much worse. Cross out the bad ones as you go along and the correct answer will become clear.

Question 7: (A)

Nothing wrong here. The color images and verbal wit give the reader pleasure. Why mess up a good thing?

Question 8: (C)

A nice twist on the trusty misplaced modifier. Here, WE get to choose the first part. "Being" is bad so that rules out (A) and (B). Which answer is simplest? Which answer is shortest? The correct answer. Also, "giftedly" is a nominee in the category of Worst Adverb in the Book.

Question 9: (E)

So many options thrown around here and your old friend "because" is the best way to connect the two halves of this sentence. Simple cause and effect: "because he regarded them as mechanical reproductions, William never painted portraits." Sometimes it helps to move the sentence around on your own and come up with a version you like before reading the answer choices. Remember: the answer choices are there to confuse you. After awhile, they all start looking good.

Question 10: (D)

Transition question! What's the best way to make this transition? Hate to sound like a broken record here, but the shortest and simplest answer is correct. Also notice the pieces of the other answer choices that make them wrong: "which duration" (A), "because of lasting" (B), "by lasting a week, making it seem" (E).

Question 11: (B)

This is a tricky one. Proves that the shortest answer doesn't always win, for one thing. The problem with a lot of these answers is that we don't know what "it" or "them" or "their" is referring to. Could be the writers or the novels. It must be specified and (B) is the best choice that does so.

Question 12: (A)

"Telling" is the wrong verb. The musical either "tells" (if it's still running) or "told" (if it has closed).

Question 13: (B)

Many unnecessary words here. All you need is "or." Or, if you listen to John Lennon, all you need is love.

Question 14: (A)

People are not things, people are human beings. "People WHO need."

Question 15: (D)

"Having been" is pretty much always horrible. Should be "had."

Question 16: (A)

Incorrect verb tense. One challenge she faced was "how to preserve" her ethnic identity.

Question 17: (D)

"When" does not connect the two parts of this correctly. People still like to have this guy around, even though he makes insulting remarks, BECAUSE he is a remarkably witty man.

Question 18: (D)

Redundancy. You just need "clearer" here.

Question 19: (B)

Subject/verb agreement. Reforms "have not managed" is correct.

Question 20: (C)

Subject/verb AND pronoun agreement. Yes, this is tricky because "it feeds" comes so much later in the passage than the "crabs" it is referring to. Still, that doesn't change the fact that we are talking about number "crabs" so "THEY feed."

Question 21: (B)

"In the catching of" is unnecessarily complicated. Just make it "to catch" are you're good to go.

Question 22: (B)

"Be criticized" is a verb and we're looking for a noun. The politician was very sensitive to "criticism."

Question 23: (E)

There are no problems with this sentence. Now, for extra credit, please draw a Pre-Raphaelite sketch of the night sky.

Question 24: (D)
We are only comparing two animals here: lions and tigers. So the lion is the "strongER" of the two. If we added a third (say, bears), then you could say the lion is the strongest.

Question 25: (C)
Parallel construction. The first part tells us that the decline in science education has two causes. What are they? 1) "Less funding for scientific research" and 2) "A decrease in jobs related to space and defense." The word "with" throws the logic of this sentence off.

Question 26: (B)
Subject/verb agreement, albeit a pretty evil one. We are not talking about the awards given out to biochemists, but the NUMBER of awards. That is only one thing. So: the number "accentuates." SINGULAR subject ("number"), singular verb ("accentuates"). Very mean.

Question 27: (D)
Faulty comparison. We cannot compare a novel to a person. We need to specify which Charlotte Bronte novel we are talking about here.

Question 28: (A)
Pronoun agreement. "Until THEY can be replaced… trucks will carry…" This is tricky because trucks comes so much later than the pronoun. Be careful. Read critically even though this is not the critical reading section.

Question 29: (E)
This sentence is fine. So we beat on, boats against the current, born back ceaselessly into the past.

Passage Revision: Letters from the Middle Ages

Question 30: (A)
Perfect example of the process of elimination. Let's do it: (B) is supposed to be a trick so don't fall for it, it's not "historical background." (C) = no, it's not repeating an "idea." (D) = no, it's not a "contrasting view." (E) = the author didn't REALLY think she had a microphone to the Middle Ages—it's a metaphor, not an "inaccuracy." So it's gotta be (A), which makes sense when you look at it again. Baby steps. Cross 'em off one at a time. Get rid of what's wrong to get to what's right.

Question 31: (A)
Well, sentence 4 starts with "a book I found…" (A) & (D) are the ones that might work. (D) is true, a library is a wonderful place and can indeed "open the door to

mystery," but it makes no sense here.

Question 32: (D)
(D) is so nice and so clean. The others are all over the map.

Question 33: (E)
The problem with this sentence is the thing about an earl rebelling in London, right? The main idea is about a messenger riding for days. The right answer correctly makes the earl piece of the sentence an appositive. Take it out and you have the only answer choice with a clear main sentence: "Once… a messenger rode for days to tell the distant head of Paston family of a feared civil war."

Question 34: (B)
Most of the questions in this passage say to look at the sentences "in context." Sometimes this is necessary and sometimes it's not. When in doubt, go back to the passage and read the sentence before and after. The problem with this sentence as it is written is that we don't know who "their" is referring to. Could be anyone, right? Or maybe we're talking about the letters' anxieties? Read the sentence before and you'll see we're talking about the Paston family. So there you go.

Question 35: (C)
This is straightforward. If you don't know what a rhetorical question is, that's cool. You DO know what the other answer choices are and you can clearly see that the writer uses them in the passage. So it's gotta be (C). Now, what is a rhetorical question? A stylistic device employed by writers. Often ends up being a question that does not require an answer. Are you psyched that this is the last question in this section and you can take a break now?

Section 7: Critical Reading

Question 1: (E)
To exchange goods directly for good is to "barter."

Question 2: (E)
If everyone agrees, then there is no more "dispute."

Question 3: (C)
"Intuition" is the ability to perceive without conscious reasoning. This is the answer. Other vocab:
Autonomy is "independence."
Sophistry is a "dishonest form of argumentation."

Question 4: (A)
This one is probably easiest by process of elimination. Answer (A) makes sense and is probably the answer,

but let's check the others. "Undermines" is weird in answer (B) and "Remedy" is weird is answer (C). So is "disparage" in (D) and "Curtails" is weird in (E). All of these are negative words and we need both words in this construction to be positive.

Question 5: (A)
Put in your own words. I might put in "critics" and "prime example." The first word has to be negative because these people "detest" this style of painting. And "exemplify" means that the second blank has to show that Duchamp's painting is an example of this style.

Question 6: (C)
"Acumen" means keen judgement and insight.

Question 7: (B)
The relationship here is easy but the vocab is hard. "Arcane" means difficult to understand, and "abstruse" means basically the same thing. This links up perfectly with "obscure and baffling digressions." If you don't know these other words, see if you can rule out any of the words that you do know (i.e. concise, definitive, spare…). If you guessed answer (A), then you're allowed to quietly curse the College Board at this time.

Question 8: (C)
The first word has to mean "open-handed." The only word that fits is "magnanimity," which means generosity. If you don't know this, you can whittle things down by seeing the second blank must be negative (because "open-handed" is positive).

Question 9: (D)
Answer (D) is the only one that really makes sense. Answer (B) is wrong because these car buyers don't truly wish to live in mountainous regions (too many bugs).

Question 10: (A)
P1 spends a good deal of effort detailing the size ("bumpers as big as battering rams") of the SUV. Not so in P2.

Question 11: (D)
This one is a bit tricky. The "subtleties" of the SUV's names lie in the fact that they "connote" certain things. This connotation is the fantasy that we are perhaps buying in to when we buy an SUV.

Question 12: (C)
Look to the phrase "rugged individualism, mastery of the wilderness, cowboy endurance."

Passage: Different perspectives on WWI
Main Idea Passage 1: Inaccurate reports from the battlefield created a divide between civilians and soldiers in WWI
Main Idea Passage 2: The War gave English women new freedoms and responsibilities, which created a divide between men and women.

Question 13: (C)
They tell you this in the intro before the passages.

Question 14: (A)
Soldiers didn't speak candidly, letters were edited, and press was biased. Civilians didn't have any real way to know.

Question 15: (C)
The report of the battle is positive and heroic and doesn't state the truth contained in the footnote, which shows what a horrifying loss the British had just endured.

Question 16: (E)
This is contained in the paragraph that highlights a biased description by the English press.

Question 17: (B)
Put these choices into the sentence and see which makes sense in the context of the passage.

Question 18: (A)
This quote is being used to support the author's opening argument.

Question 19: (E)
This passage is about women assuming more power and authority. The reference to wives and mothers is meant to show that this change was occurring even in the home.

Question 20: (B)
This is the only answer that seems at all relevant. Everything else is somehow off-topic.

Question 21: (E)
"Morbid gloating…" Their celebration could be seen as being "morbid" because it came at the cost of so many British lives.

Question 22: (B)
The point is that woman would prefer to do things that one might consider unpleasant simply because it allowed them to leave their house and their roles in the home.

Question 23: (E)
Nothing else makes sense here. The process of elimination is your friend. Use it often and respect its power.

Question 24: (C)
In P1, soldiers choose to lie about the war because the loved ones back home would not understand and reports from the press are misleading. In P2, the author says that "young men became increasingly alienated." It's not answer (D) because in P2, no one is trying to describe the atrocities of war.

Section 8: Math

Question 1: (B)
4 is the only answer given that is an even integer, a positive integer, and also less than five.

Question 2: (B)
Subtract eight from both sides, then square both sides to find that k = 49.

Question 3: (A)
We need the "number in favor" divided by the "total number of people polled". The total is 35 + 14 + 1 = 50. The fraction we want is 35/50 which reduces to 7/10. Cool? Cool.

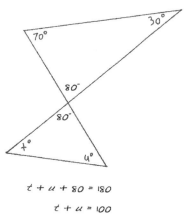

$$t + u + 80 = 180$$
$$t + u = 100$$

Question 4: (C)
See diagram. The SAT loves to make it look like there's not enough information. In fact, it's impossible to find t and u individually in this problem. But we know that in the top triangle, we have a 70 degree and 30 degree angle. The other angle therefore must be 80 degrees. That's a vertical angle with the top angle in the bottom triangle, which also equals 80. There's 100 degrees left in the bottom triangle, which is what t and u must add up to!

Question 5: (D)
Note that the problem asks for the greatest CHANGE, not saying whether that change is an increase or decrease. This is as much a reading question as a math question! Turns out the biggest change is a decrease

from the price of $4.75 to $3.75.

Question 6: (B)
The question is really just asking "for what x-value does the graph have a height of one?" Too bad the question had to be all uppity about the way it was asking it. The graph has a height of one when the x-values are between -1 and 0, so the answer choice of -0.5 is in that correct range. Are you happy now, Mr. SAT Question? Now who looks foolish?

Question 7: (A)
First, since the only base given is 2, what power does 2 need to be raised to, to get to 64? 2 ^ 6 = 64. Since the first equation involves multiplying the bases, that means the powers must be added (one of those rules of exponents!). The first equation can be rewritten as 2 ^ (a + b + c) = 64. So (a + b + c) equal 6. We are told they are DIFFERENT, POSITIVE integers that add up to 6. Trial and error quickly shows that the only options are 1, 2 and 3 for a, b, and c (order doesn't matter). Then, we have to separately evaluate 2 ^ 1 (which equals 2), 2 ^ 2 (which equals 4), and 2 ^ 3 (which equals 8). Add 2 plus 4 plus 8 to get 14. The math isn't too tricky, but the TRICKS are tricky!

Question 8: (E)
The two endpoints of a diameter must be symmetrical around the center of the circle (i.e. the center is also their average). So the x-coordinate of the endpoint we're given (-2), plus the one we don't know, must average to 3... (-2 + x)/2 = 3... x = 8. The y-coordinate is even simpler. -7 must be averaged with -7 to give a result of -7. So the coordinates are (8, -7).

Question 9: (D)
The unglamorous-but-effective way to solve this one: plug in a bunch of numbers for h into each answer and see which answer always gives the correct result. Plug in things like 31 and 49, to make sure they work, but also plug in numbers outside of the correct range, like 29 and 51, to make sure they DON'T work! They shouldn't!

The fancy-pants way to solve this one: absolute value is related to the idea of distance. The absolute value of the difference between two numbers is the same thing as the distance between those two numbers on a number line. So basically a fancy way of writing our range of values from 30 to 50 is to say that starting from the middle, 40, we don't want our child's height, h, to be more than 10 units away from 40 either to the left or to the right on the number line. (D) is saying that in math terms.

Question 10: (B)

The height of the second cylinder is the only dimension that changes from the first, and the height exactly doubles. Imagine having one soup can, and then doubling the height by stacking a second soup can on top of it. How is the volume of your pile of two soup cans related to the volume of your first soup can? It's also double.

Question 11: (A)
Pay close attention to the order of the inequality! n < k < r. Plug in the numbers they provide: n < -2 < 0. Basically, n just has to be less than -2, so the answer of -3 is the only one that works. That whole weird diamond function was a total red herring!

Question 12: (B)
.20(x) = .80(y)
Solve for y, dividing both sides by .80. Then y = (.20/.80)x which reduces to (1/4)x, which equals .25x.

Question 13: (C)
If x + y is even, then $(x + y)^2$ also must be even (Any even number squared is still even. Seriously. Try it). So $(x + y)^2$, which is an even number, plus x plus z gives us an odd result. The only way we could have gotten from an even number to an odd number was to add one odd number. If you add two odd numbers, those two odds make an even and you've gone nowhere. That means either x or z must be odd, but they can't both be odd. PS: The fact that x + y is even doesn't tell you whether x and y are odd or even: they could both be odd or both be even.

Question 14: (E)
The SAT loves testing your knowledge of what happens to small fractions when they are raised to a power. The rule for positive fractions smaller than one: the higher the power they are raised to, the more they shrink! Try plugging in x = ½ to verify this:
I. True: 1/4 > 1/8
II. True: 1/2 > 1/4
III. True: 1/2 > 1>8

Question 15: (A)
Basically, they want to know what kind of line best fits those data points? If you draw in a line that kinda sorta fits the points, turns out it's basically a horizontal line with a height of about 44. The equation for that would be y = 44. In terms of the variables they are using, it would be t(p) = 44.

Question 16: (E)
The first thing to do is to notice the relationship between L and W. The height of the pattern on the left side is 2L but on the right side is 3W. That means that 2L=3W. The easiest move to make now is to pick a value for L and W based on that relationship. Let's say

that L is 6 and W is 4. That satisfies the relationship 2L=3W, so we're good to go. Using those numbers, the 12L by 10L area would really be 12(6) by 10(6), or 72 by 60. 72x60=4320. The area of each small rectangle is 6x4=24. Divide the total area by the area of each individual tile and you'll have your answer: 4320/24=180

Section 9: Critical Reading

Question 1: (B)
Put in your own words. I would go with "diving" and "escalating."

Question 2: (B)
"Habitual boasting" links up with "egotistical."

Question 3: (D)
The first one has to mean "steadfast" and the second one has to mean "tactful." This is resolute and diplomatic.

Question 4: (C)
Autonomy means "freedom." Because of the way the sentence is constructed, the word in the blank has to mean the opposite of "having little control."

Question 5: (C)
The trick here is that the word in the first blank has to relate to the word in the second blank in a certain way, so that if the first word is "evil," the second word would have to be "evil-doers." See? One is about the acts, and one about the people that do them. All the other choices other than answer (C) has these two words in conflict.

Question 6: (A)
If you aren't sure about "Corrective," then use the process of elimination. Clearly, what he's doing is in conflict with the "theater's tendency." So the others don't make sense.
Corollary means "a natural consequence of or accompaniment to something else."

Passage: The story of Virginia and Clayton (or, is it just me or did the SAT just get a little racy?)
Main Idea: Virginia has a thing for the cello-obsessed Clayton.

Question 7: (D)
The incorrect answers here, like (A) and (B), are much broader than what is actually in the passage. It's not about ALL college orchestras...it's about one guy and and one girl in one orchestra.

though he is not built for it.

Question 8: (C)
Virginia is taking a real close look at this dude. It's a little creepy if you ask me.

Question 9: (A)
Shades swirled beneath the surface, eh? It's as if he is constantly changing. The best match for that idea is "his complicated nature."

Question 10: (A)
The first paragraph is very descriptive and figurative. Then her friends make this very SAT-inappropriate remark. It definitely changes the mood.

Question 11: (D)
The words in this part include "novitiates," (and please don't say you don't know what this word means -- it has a footnote), reverence, serenity… all of these suggest sacredness and "sanctity."

Question 12: (B)
A surprisingly tricky question! You have to look back a few lines to remember where they are when this is taking place. Line 33 mentions the "five-till-four pandemonium." That's all of the students rushing to get their instruments and themselves in place for rehearsal. So even though Virginia DOES have a crush on Clayton, the crush he is negotiating is the crush of people--the crowd.

Question 13: (E)
He's humming classical musical amid a noisy mob? Seems a little lost in his own world.

Question 14: (C)
It's gotta be (C), because we've only seen him so far playing or practicing music. He hasn't once spoken but to hum, and now he wants to go practice, even though he could probably go hang out with doting Virginia.

Question 15: (C)
The wind is whipping her blue? It's real cold, dude.

Question 16: (A)
She "felt sated BEFORE lifting the first spoonful." She was happy without any food. Must be answer (A).

Question 17: (D)
To Virginia, he even looks like his cello. Notice how many of these right answers get at the main idea of this passage, that Clayton is just really into his music.

Question 18: (D)
Clayton says he is like the bee, who flies even though he is not built for flying. Clayton plays cello even

Question 19: (E)
"Fidgety" and "awkward" on the one hand and "irresistibly beautiful" on the other. The best match for that pair is "clumsiness and gracefulness."

Section 10: Writing

Question 1: (B)
Verb tense. The Allies believed this treaty WOULD ENSURE permanent peace then and forever. They were wrong about that.

Question 2: (C)
Main sentence = "the new bird sanctuary…is protected by the state." The correct answer puts the additional information in the middle in a neat and tidy clause.

Question 3: (E)
Parallel construction = "lose weight" and "keep it off." (A) may be tempting, but in that choice "permanently" refers to losing weight, not "keeping it off", so (A) is wrong.

Question 4: (E)
No sooner had THIS happened THAN this happened. "But" doesn't work here. The other "than" answer choice is in the passive voice and has the incorrect tense usage: "he will return."

Question 5: (E)
Read this one carefully and cut through the fat to see the main, simple sentence: "one reason WAS." Only (E) does this correctly.

Question 6: (C)
A bit confusing, so use the process of elimination. Who is "they"? No one. That gets rid of (A) and (D). "No more" is grammatically incorrect so (E) is out. "As will Wayne not" is incorrect. So it has to be (C), which makes the point nicely with "any more than" AND has parallel construction: "Chaplin will not be remembered" with "Wayne will be remembered."

Question 7: (E)
Ask yourself: what, exactly, did W.E.B. Du Bois believe? That "representing historical events on stage could have a lasting effect." That's (E). REPRESENTING is the important piece. The other choices focus on the EVENTS or use "you" or "they" incorrectly.

Question 8: (A)
There is a lot wrong with (B), (C) and (E) – incorrect verb usage ("offers" instead of "offer") is just the beginning.

(D) is wrong because subject/verb agreement is wrong between "it" and "work-study programs." (A) gets it right across the board. Why mess with a good thing?

Question 9: (D)
This one is tough. Don't be afraid of too many commas if they are used correctly. (A) has the wrong verb tense ("publishing"), (B) is not a complete sentence, (C) incorrectly refers to Crisis magazine as a who (a magazine is not a person) and (E) uses the weird, incorrect idiom "published at."

Question 10: (D)
The word "walruses" is plural so (A) and (B) are immediately out for using "its." The other two get the tenses messed up (E) and use the incorrect phrase "up to them" (C). (D) is correct. Again, getting rid of wrong answers is the best strategy here. Learn to look for what is WRONG.

Question 11: (A)
The simplest and clearest way to express this sentiment is (A). The others get increasingly and unnecessarily complex. (E) is wrong for a very picky reason: even though you might assume that "there" refers to California, the first part of the sentence refers not to a PLACE but to a TEST: the California bar examination.

Question 12: (B)
Only TWO of these answers are even possible because RICHARD CONNIFF was the one who was "persuading...readers to spend hours learning..." The subject needs to follow the comma when a sentence starts like this, no matter how confusing they try to make it. (D) is wrong because "has had the effect of" is unnecessary.

Question 13: (A)
What do most drivers know? That "excessive speeding on highways wastes gasoline." That's a clear statement. The other choices make this simple idea increasingly convoluted and complex. Just like "either/or" and "neither/nor" go together, "not only/but also" come as a pair. You can use that fact to eliminate (B).

Question 14: (E)
Simple parallel construction = "produced a cartoon with sound" and "made Mickey talk."

Test 6
Section 2: Math

Question 1: (C)
One package of 12 rolls plus 4 packages of 8 rolls equals 12 + 32 = 44.

Question 2: (D)
BC is 20 MORE than AB, so BC is 50. AC = 30 + 50 = 80.

Question 3: (C)
x + 3 = a. Double both sides: 2(x + 3) = 2a. Distribute: 2x + 6 = 2a.

Question 4: (A)
This graph is in the most confusing format possible. Things are much clearer if you make your own list of scores:

	TEST 1	TEST 2
STUDENT A:	40	70
STUDENT B:	40	60
STUDENT C:	60	70
STUDENT D:	80	80
STUDENT E:	80	60

Ahh, much better. Now it's clear that student A improved the most.

Question 5: (C)
Using the scores from the Test 2 in the above answer: (70 + 60 + 70 + 80 + 60)/5 = 340/5 = 68

Question 6: (D)
The easiest way to do this is to plug in estimates for the values of u and v. It looks like u is around -.75 and v is around -.5, so u + v = -1.25. The absolute value of that is positive 1.25. y matches that answer just about perfectly. Hooray!

Question 7: (B)
When there's a fraction in the denominator, multiply by the reciprocal. Let's evaluate the two parts separately:
$1/x = 1/(1/2) = (1)(2/1) = 2$.
$1/(x-1) = 1/(1/2 - 1) = 1/(-1/2) = (1)(-2/1) = -2$.
2 + -2 = 0.

Question 8: (A)
We have enough info to know that the shape is a square (three right angles, including the origin, plus two adjacent sides are equal). Since point S has a height of 3, each side of the square must equal 3. The value of k, three units to the left of the origin, is -3.

Question 9: (A)
This one is totally straightforward if you just plug in some values from the table and see which answer they work in. The bigger numbers from the table are where it's easiest to see that the equation in (A) works and the others don't. Plug in 3 for x and try it in each answer to see if f(x) equals what it's supposed to. (A) gives the correct answer, 10. (B) gives 11, (C) gives 16, (D) gives 17, and (E) gives 19.

Question 10: (E)
Plug in for x and y to make things easy. Let's say 5 years ago a person was 8 years old. Now they are 13. How old was this person 1 year ago? 12, right? Plug in 5 for x and 8 for y into each answer to see which one gives you the same result, 12. Only (E) works!

Question 11: (B)
If you forget what the correct order of the alphabet is, it's okay to quietly hum your ABC's to yourself: W X Y Z. It's possible to get there in 3 steps from Z W Y X. Step one: reverse the entire sequence to get X Y W Z. Step two, switch Y and W to get X W Y Z. Step three: switch X and W to get W X Y Z.

Question 12: (D)
Basically, the trick is just to divide each of the box's dimensions by 4, and then multiply those new dimensions together. Let's say the bottom of the box is 20 cm x 24 cm. To fill it the bottom with one layer of these little blocks that are 4 cm on each side, you would need 5 blocks x 6 blocks = 30 blocks. That flat layer covering the bottom is 4 cm high. The box's height is 32, so you need 8 layers (of 30 blocks each) to reach the proper height. That's 240 blocks.

Question 13: (E)
Plug in a fraction for n. Let's say n = 1/4. n^2 = 1/16. $\sqrt{n}$ = 1/2. So n^2 is the smallest, then n, then $\sqrt{n}$ is the biggest.

Question 14: (C)
By looking at the line segments, it's clear that OA has the steepest (largest) slope and OE has the smallest slope. The median slope is just the slope of OC, which is 3 units up and 4 units over. Rise/run = 3/4.

Question 15: (A)
Agh! Figuring this stuff out is the worst part of traveling! The flight that left New York at noon arrived at 7PM in NEW YORK time. It was a 7 hour flight. The next flight is also 7 hours. It leaves at noon in San Fran, which is 3PM in New York. 7 hours later, it touches down in NYC, which will be at 10PM NYC time.

Question 16: (B)

The areas of weird shaded regions always involve finding the bigger shape's area and then subtracting what's NOT shaded. The bigger shape is the rectangle. Side QP has a length of 1, because it's also the size of the radius of circle P. The distance from P to S is equal to the radius of two of these circles, so that's 2. The area of the rectangle = 1 x 2 = 2. We then need to find the area of the two quarter circles. Two quarter circles are the same as half of one circle… with a radius of 1. So we use πr^2, plugging in 1 for r, and half of that is $\pi/2$. The shaded region is $2 - \pi/2$.

Question 17: (C)
When you add or subtract a number from x in a function, f(x), it shifts the function in the opposite direction. So the function f(x + 2) will be shifted -2 units, that is two units to the left.

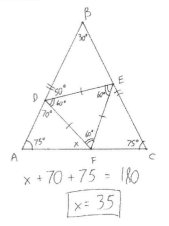

$$x + 70 + 75 = 180$$
$$\boxed{x = 35}$$

Question 18: (B)
See diagram. Triangle ABC is isosceles, so we know that the two base angles of the big triangle must be congruent. Since the top angle is 30 degrees, each base angle equals (180 – 30)/2 = 75. So angle BAC equals 75 degrees. The middle triangle has three equal sides, so it must have three sixty-degree angles. Angle EDF is 60, we are told angle BDE is 50, so angle FDA must be 70 so that those three angles add up to a straight line. Now, in the bottom left triangle, one angle is 75 and one is 70, so the third one, the one we're looking for, must be 35 degrees.

Question 19: (A)
This is a tough question…until you cross multiply each answer. For answers (B), (C), (D), and (E), you get the same statement: af = bc. However, for (A), you get a slightly different statement when you cross multiply: ac = bf. That's not the same as the others, so it's the odd one out.

Question 20: (E)
This is kinda ugly. Here's a helpful way to look at it. The

original function is xy – y. We want that to be equal to zero, so we can write xy – y = 0. We can factor the left hand side into y(x – 1) = 0. The possible solutions to that equation are y = 0 and x = 1. Don't worry too much about the different combinations of a's and b's to plug in for x and y, just keep in mind that whatever is in front of the box symbol in the answers goes in for x, and whatever comes after goes in for y. Well, since we're only plugging in positive integers, NOTHING we can plug in for y can equal zero. So the only possible solutions are when whatever is plugged in for x can equal 1. Roman numerals I and III can work, because a could equal 1. Roman numeral II can't work because (a + b) can't equal one. If a and b are positive integers, they must add up to at least two.

Section 3: Critical Reading

Question 1: (D)
The statue represents the regime, and so they topple it.

Question 2: (A)
Put in your own word. I might choose "skilled." Adept means skilled.

Question 3: (B)
I would use process of elimination here. From the first blank, it could be (A), (B), or (D). (A) is wrong because we can tell that the bird is stealing the stuff, not just assessing it. Same thing for (D) (the bird is stealing it, not just disturbing it).
Pilfer means "steal."

Question 4: (A)
This one is pretty hard. She was a scientist and also someone who experienced religious visions, so it has to be either (A), (C) or (D) because of the first blank (religion and science were related in some way for her). Because of the second blank, we can rule out (D) (religious visions don't lend scientific accuracy). Deciding between the last two is tricky. It makes more sense in this context that the church is lending legitimacy than profundity.

Question 5: (A)
Tough one here. You can get rid of (C) and (E) because opponents of the institutes are going to call it something negative in the first blank. "Perquisites" means "perks." If you don't know this, it might help to guess that pre-revolutionary French nobility are known more for their privileges and luxuries than for "tribulations" or "afflictions," which are both negative.

Question 6: (C)
The first sentence in P1 talks about how great Linnaeus

was. The second says he doesn't appreciate Linnaeus' contribution.

Question 7: (D)
The first paragraph maintains a critical distance from the topic, while the second begins with the word "I."

Question 8: (A)
Both would agree that Linnaeus was a monumental force in the history of biology. See the first sentence of P1 and the second sentence of P2 for specific clues.

Question 9: (D)
Look carefully: the author of P1 does not blame Linnaeus but rather the people who came immediately after him.

Passage: The introduction of new inventions to the village of Macondo.
Main idea: The nature of reality is challenged for the villagers of Macondo as modern inventions are introduced.

Question 10: (B)
Plug these choices in to the sentence and see which one makes the most sense.

Question 11: (C)
They were upset because the actor in one movie had died, but was alive and well in the next movie. The villagers didn't realize that it was just a story, not reality.

Question 12: (A)
It could never compare to something so "moving… human… and full of everyday truth…" as a real band of musicians.

Question 13: (D)
The telephone blew their mind, people. And wouldn't it have blown yours?

Question 14: (C)
In each instance, the villagers are expecting the inventions to be something which they are not. The phonograph is not an "enchanted mill," the actor in the movie is not a real person, and the telephone is not a rudimentary phonograph.

Question 15: (D)
Answer (D) is the only one that really fits. It's not about (A) other citizens; it's not about (B) the inventions (it's about how the villagers react); it's not about a magical performance; it's not about the idea of nature versus technology. It's just a description of villagers' reactions.

Passage: The universality of gesture.

Main Idea: The choreographer Martha Graham made use of the power and universality of gesture.

Question 16: (A)
The author is saying "listen, I'm not expert, but this is what I think."

Question 17: (B)
In this sentence the author is giving an example of her assertion about Martha Graham's use of mathematics mentioned in the previous sentence.

Question 18: (E)
The author is saying that the physical event is just the beginning of the whole event. Just like Martha Graham is taking simply physical relationships (mathematical, physical relationships) and investing in them emotional relationships.

Question 19: (D)
Every gesture has a vast range of connotation. The discussion of Jung is all about how common symbols have universal meaning. The artist believes that gestures have this same kind of universality.

Question 20: (D)
Basically, the author is saying that making eye contact holds as much of a shock or charge as any kind of "electricity."

Question 21: (D)
The author is saying that these painting have emotional cues in the same way that dance and gestures do, and that these cues are as recognizable to modern viewers as they are to viewers of that age.

Question 22: (A)
The author is talking about the elements of dance here. None of the other choices are things that fit the list along with space relations and rhythms, and "sounds" doesn't mean "stresses."

Question 23: (E)
Plug these puppies in. The author is talking about symbols that all humanity can understand.

Question 24: (B)
First off, be warned that in the first printing of the 2nd edition of the College Board's book, the editors GAVE A WRONG ANSWER IN THE BACK OF THE BOOK. This question was in the 1st edition too, and the answer then was (B), which it still should be. People sitting on the side of a restaurant have a wall to one side, which means they are only exposed to others on one side.

That's "relative privacy." If they had been seeking "reclusive isolation," they probably would not have gone to a restaurant in the first place, now would they?

Section 4: Math

Question 1: (E)
Start with the right hand equation, plug in 2 into the middle equation to find y = 6, and then plug 6 into the left equation to find x = 14.

Question 2: (A)
Todd is younger than Susan, so Susan is oldest, Todd is in the middle, and Marta is the youngest.

Question 3: (B)
To average the two areas, we need to add them up and divide by 2. But the SAT has generously told us already that they add up to 5, so we just divide by 2 to get 5/2.

Question 4: (E)
Basically, this question is asking for a number that is one more than a perfect square. The first few perfect squares are 1, 4, 9, 16, 25, 36, 49, 64. The answer that works is 50: one more than 49.

Question 5: (D)
Two sides of the triangle are radii, so they must be the same length and the triangle must be isosceles. That means that the non-labeled angle is equal to angle y. The sum of the angles in the triangle is 40 + y + y = 180. 2y = 140. y = 70.

Question 6: (A)
Keep in mind that when you see unusual stuff like this "simple square" thing the test will give you the definition of the term. Here we're looking for a number that has ONLY three factors: 1 and itself (every integer has those factors) plus its square root. Factor the answer choices. Only 121 works, because it doesn't have any factors except for 1, 11, and 121.

Question 7: (B)
Area is (1/2)bh. The base can be rewritten as (6/7)h. So the triangle's area is (1/2)(6/7)h*h which simplifies to (3/7)h².

Question 8: (B)
This is kinda tricky. First distribute the 6 exponent to a and b, to simplify it as: (a^3)(b^2) = 432. But now what? Since a and b are positive integers, the best thing is to do a factor tree for 432 and break it down into all of its prime factors. 432 factors into 2 x 2 x 2 x 2 x 3 x 3 = 2^4 x 3^3. So a^3 could equal 3^3. But we need to turn 2^4 into something to the second

power. 2^4 equals 16, which is also 4^2. So a = 3 and b = 4. a x b = 12.

Question 9: 990
Any number that has a factor of ten must end in a 0. The biggest three-digit integer is 999, but the first one below that that ends in 0 is 990.

Question 10: 30
Set up a proportion: 4 pounds / 20 people = x pounds / 150 people. Cross multiply to get 600 = 20x, so x = 30 pounds of beans. I wouldn't want to be anywhere near a room where people are eating 30 pounds of beans!

Question 11: 8, 10 or 12
If n is increased by 50 percent of itself, that means 150% of n is what we're looking for, which is the same as 1.5n. If you use trial and error with some even integers and multiply them by 1.5, it turns out that 8, 10, and 12 each work. Trial and error is awesome!

Question 12: 3400
Perimeter = 2L + 2W. So 250 = 2(40) + 2W. Thus, W equals 85. The area is L x W, which is 40 x 85 = 3400.

Question 13: 450
There are two unknowns so we need two equations. Let's say a is the quantity of $1 bulbs and b is the quantity of $2 bulbs.
1a + 2b = 600
a = 2b
Solve the two equations using substitution to find that a = 300 and b = 150. a + b = 450.

Question 14: 1/2 or .5
Don't FOIL the left equation. Just divide both sides by 4 to get (x + y)(x − y) = 10. Plug in 20 for (x − y), so (x + y)(20) = 10. Divide both sides by 20. x + y equals 1/2.

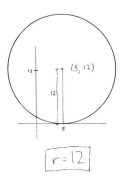

Question 15: 12
The circle touches the x-axis at a single point, which means it is tangent to the x-axis. A tangent line is perpendicular to the circle's radius at that point, so, since the x-axis is horizontal, the radius to the circle's center

is exactly vertical. The coordinates tell us that circle's center is 12 units above the x axis, so the length of the radius must be 12.

Question 16: 5/11 or .454 or .455
Quickest way to do this is add up the men and women in the voting age population to get 2500. We need the number who actually voted, which is .40 x 2500 = 1000. The bottom of our fraction is 2200, which comes from adding up the number of registered voters (men plus women). 1000/2200 reduces to 5/11.

Question 17: 8
It's not necessary to make a mess and try to draw in all 11 line segments! All of the edges of the figure are already drawn in the picture (every line segment is an edge). Since V has three lines coming out of it in different directions (each to another vertex), that means three of the eleven possible segments going to other vertices are along the edges. The other eight segments all must not be on the edges.

Question 18: 16
First, focus on the rectangle. The x-coordinates of B and C go from -1/2 to 1/2, so the distance between them is 1, and the width of the rectangle is 1. Since the area is 4, the height of the rectangle must be 4. We can assume it is symmetrical around the origin (because it overlaps a function involving x^3, which is always symmetrical), so the height of point C must be 2. We now know the coordinates of C are (1/2, 2). We plug them in for x and y into the equation $y = px^3$. $2 = p(1/2)^3$. Solve for p, which equals 16.

Section 6: Writing

Question 1: (D)
We're only talking about one car (so the verb should be "was"). Done and done.

Question 2: (C)
Parallel construction. The last part of the list ("snapping power lines") needs to match the first two: "toppling small buildings" & "uprooting trees."

Question 3: (B)
"As I entered" implies past tense. Everything but (B) is in the present or future tense.

Question 4: (B)
Yes, "sorrier than I" does not SOUND right, but it's right. Think about it as "sorrier than I (am)" and it's all good.

Question 5: (C)

"Were alarmed" matches best with "should be closed." This is a good one for the ol' get-rid-of-what's-wrong-to-get-to-what's-right rule. Nothing else comes close.

Question 6: (D)
"Having been," "being," and "having reached" are all bad so (A), (B) & (E) are out. And (C) is redundant and clunky. (D) is nice, though. OH! And that's the right answer.

Question 7: (D)
A lot of students get this one wrong. "Actuality" is weird, so those are out. Same with "their actual sailing." So you're temped to choose (A), but it's incomplete as is. It would have to include the full phrase "or did not sail." It doesn't, so you're left with (D). Don't be afraid to choose a sentence that starts with the word "that." It's weird but okay.

Question 8: (E)
The key here is the 1969 vs. 1983 comparison that is the crux of the sentence's content. The "but" is nice and gets the point across. Also, Baldwin High School is only one thing so (A), (B) & (C) are out for the word "they." Bad pronoun! The real question here is: what happened to the Baldwin High School quiz bowl team in the 70s? Why the losing streak?

Question 9: (A)
This one is about time. Since this happened BEFORE the arrival of Europeans, they "HAD developed" a unique culture. (B) has the "had" but is poorly constructed.

Question 10: (D)
Gotta be (D) or (E) because of the modifier (Who was "criticized"?) and (E) is not a complete sentence.

Question 11: (A)
Nothing wrong with this one. Don't be fooled by fancy words and phrases like "whereby" and "by which" – they are usually wrong and too verbose.

Question 12: (D)
The proper expression is "not nearly as expensive AS."

Question 13: (E)
This is fine, even though the sentence would be better if it read "Ponce de Leon who would later seek." It's your job to find concrete errors, not re-write poor wording. In fact, a lot of these sentences are deliberately quirky to trick you.

Question 14: (D)
Faulty comparison. 19th century American artists differed from ARTISTS from earlier times, not just earlier times.

Question 15: (C)
Plurality. There are numerous issues, so that = those.

Question 16: (E)
This one is fine. "Each" is a little tricky here, because it turns the plural subject fish into a singular one. What's not fine is how much these young fish are eating. Obesity is an epidemic and we need to confront it.

Question 17: (C)
Idiom. Should be "not a condition necessary TO the enjoyment of medieval literature."

Question 18: (B)
Parallel construction. Needs to match "driving less frequently" so it should be "turning off all appliances."

Question 19: (A)
You could fix this in two ways: either get rid of "had" or change "swam" to "swum." Didn't know that SWUM was a word, did ya? And that's really awesome, Gertrude. The English Channel is very wide.

Question 20: (B)
"A government agency" is only one thing. So "they" should be "it."

Question 21: (C)
Idiom. It is still a threat "to travelers," not "of travelers."

Question 22: (B)
Here's your token adverb question. You didn't fall for it, did you? Correct needs to be correct-LY.

Question 23: (E)
This is great. Also great are those baskets… they are really something.

Question 24: (A)
"The record" is only one thing so the verb "provide" does not agree. It should be "provides."

Question 25: (C)
It's not "results as," it's "results WHEN."

Question 26: (C)
Subject/verb agreement. Should be "who expectS" since we're only talking about one tourist.

Question 27: (A)
"For we students" is wrong. The correct (though bad sounding) idiom is "for us students." Take the word "students" out and it should be clearer.

Question 28: (D)

Neither/nor. "Or" is no good.

Question 29: (A)
Two things ARE available through the school's guidance office: a job directory and a list.

Passage Revision: Skunk Sniffin'

Question 30: (B)
It's not a complete sentence as written. "Having been" and "without being" are not good ever. (B) is best.

Question 31: (E)
This one is mean because it's easy if you read it in context, but the question doesn't ask you to read it in context. It's always a good idea to read the sentence before and after the sentence in question on this section.

Question 32: (D)
(D) fits the personal, story-telling tone of this essay. The author spends the first paragraph telling you this CRAZY story from his/her own life. The most tempting wrong answer is (B), I think, but the problem with it is that the author doesn't really provide multiple examples—he or she is just tellling one story.

Question 33: (B)
Ugly sentences. The colons and semi-colons are all used incorrectly – that leaves (A) and (B) and only one of them works.

Question 34: (B)
This is tricky because there seems to be some subjectivity involved. What should be done with sentence 11? Think of these questions as if you were a newspaper editor. Cut the fluff and get to the point. It's superfluous everywhere you try to put it.

Question 35: (A)
Really? This essay has a tone of playful humor? I mean, I guess it does? That doesn't mean it's funny (it's not), but it is casual and "fun." Get specific and do some critical reading here to eliminate answer choices. (B) is out because it doesn't "summarize ideas," (C) is out because it does not provide an "example," (D) is out because it does not "use persuasion and (E) is out because it doesn't "explain contradictions." Again, getting rid of answer choices you know are wrong is VERY helpful on this section. The correct answer will eventually emerge.

Section 7: Critical Reading

Question 1: (D)
A "phobia" is an exaggerated fear.

Question 2: (E)
The first blank has to be either (B) or (E). Of those two, the second blank has to be "ensure."

Question 3: (B)
You need a word that means "general merriment." That is gaiety if ever anything was.

Question 4: (C)
Put in your own word. The demagogues used the mood, but they didn't …begin… it? Create works nicely.

Question 5: (E)
Tough vocab here. "Arboreal" means "living in trees," which is obviously what we need.
"indigenous" means "native to the region."
"pliant" means "bending easily."

Question 6: (B)
Steadfast and constant means "unswerving."

Question 7: (C)
The author changed the work to appease critics, so the critics must have criticized the work. So this second blank needs a negative word. Since the critics complained about the works brevity (shortness), she must have expanded it in order to appease them.

Question 8: (A)
Tough vocab again. A lack of worldly wisdom is a way of saying "naïveté." "Furtive" means "done in a way that is intended to escape notice." "Venality," is the condition of being open to being persuaded by corrupt means such as bribery.

Question 9: (C)
The author is describing how, at certain times, the sea would be reflected on the front of the house and in the windows.

Question 10: (D)
This is close reading and attention to word-choice. For instance, the author says "so solid" instead of just "solid." A phrase like "so miraculously real," is probably your biggest indicator.

Question 11: (B)
This one is really hard. Answers (B) and (D) are both really tempting. Look to the sentence "Much less is known… recovered objects" for the answer. This is the assumption of the paragraph: If the script had been deciphered, we would know much more. Answer (D) is about ARCHAEOLOGISTS but answer (B) is about UNDERSTANDING A CIVILIZATION, which is what the paragraph is really about.

Question 12: (D)
The College Board loves these kinds of answers. They are always drawn to things like "somewhat encouraged" or "moderately amused." Things that are QUALIFIED. Here, the other choices are all too simple or strong.

Passage: The Environmental Movement's use of extreme rhetoric.
Main idea, Passage 1: Those who popularize environmental concerns often exaggerate and use fear in order to provoke a strong response.
Main idea, Passage 2: The work of the environmental movement has been largely successful, which has made its extreme rhetoric irrelevant.

Question 13: (E)
As with all of these questions, come up with your own word to replace the word, match to the answer choices, plug your choice in, and see if it makes sense.

Question 14: (C)
He's suggesting that these things had been predicted at one time but never came to pass.

Question 15: (D)
The easiest way to solve this is to replace the word "rigors" with a word of your own. Chances are, you'll pick the word "consequences," in which case you'll be good to go.

Question 16: (D)
The author is saying that people are not moved by the idea of far-away impersonal consequences, but by the near and the personal. The passage doesn't directly say "psychological" but talks a lot about "arousing fear," which is an emotional reaction. We can draw the connection to psychology that way.

Question 17: (B)
"Beginning in 1962," "(1970)," "(1972)," "(1973)." All of these facts…it's like I'm reading a history textbook!

Question 18: (C)
This one is a little tricky. It's hard to see exactly what that sentence is saying. Take your time to understand the sentence thoroughly before you look at the answers. Essentially, this is the catch-22 of the environmental movement. Because they successfully mobilized to fix the problems they were warning about in the 1960s, their pronouncements of impending doom now seem like they were wild exaggerations.

Question 19: (B)

The author is making fun of right-wing politicians who think that laws and government are a part of the problem, not a part of the solution. This question is much easier when you're a little older. Feel free to write that on your scantron.

Question 20: (B)
In the first passage, the author is critical of the environmentalist movement. That takes away answers (C) and (E). To decide between the other three choices, look to the second passage, which takes a relatively positive stance. This takes out answers (D) and (A), leaving (B).

Question 21: (D)
The reason that this passage (in particular questions 18-22) is so difficult is that these authors offer a different perspective on environmentalism than we're used to. This question exemplifies that. P2's point is that the warnings of Rachel Carson and others in the '60s led to legislation that successfully stopped ongoing harm to the environment. That's right: P2 thinks that the environment is NOT in danger BECAUSE of the laws of the early 1970s. Extreme reports about Lake Erie dying were useful in that they led to effective legislation.

Question 22: (E)
Both authors agree that this extreme line of thought (see Al Gore's quote in 73-74) is exaggerated. The difference between the two authors is that P1 thinks that those warnings were NEVER valid.

Question 23: (A)
Look to the last line (and paragraph) in P1. Fear mobilizes, compassion doesn't.

Question 24: (E)
The author of P1 clearly believes this. Look at the first sentence of P2 to confirm that this author also agrees.

Section 8: Math

Question 1: (D)
Distribute to get $3n - 12 = 18$. Add 12 to get $3n = 30$. $n = 10$.

Question 2: (D)
Multiply the options for stones times the options for metals. $4 \times 3 = 12$.

Question 3: (B)
3a is being added to the square root of b (only b is square-rooted, so you can cross off answers (D) and (E)). The right hand side of the equation should have the square (not square root) of the sum of a and b, so a and b need to be added first, then squared.

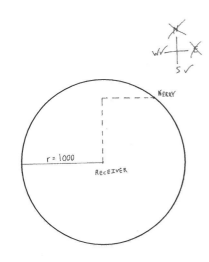

Question 4: (E)
See diagram. Visualize Kerry as being within a giant circle with radius 1000 feet. She walks north and then east to the edge of the circle. If she goes any further north or east, she'll be outside the circle, but she can go south or west and stay within the circle, because she'll be heading back towards the center.

Question 5: (A)
Cross multiply to get $ax = 8x$. Divide by x. $a = 8$.

Question 6: (A)
Angle u is a corresponding angle to r, so u = 50 degrees. And s is a vertical angle to u, so s also equals 50 degrees. Angle t is supplementary to u, so it equals $180 - 50 = 130$ degrees. $s + t + u = 50 + 130 + 50 = 230$.

Question 7: (C)
If line L is perpendicular to the y-axis, then it's a horizontal line. All equations for horizontal lines take the form "y = some number". Since it passes through (5, -3), the height of the horizontal line is -3, so the equation is $y = -3$.

Question 8: (E)
First distribute the negative and simplify the equation to get $p(x) = 7x - b$. Don't forget to distribute the minus sign to the b! Plug in 1900 for p(x) and 300 for x. Thus, $1900 = 7(300) - b$. Turns out $b = 200$.

Question 9: (E)
This one is interesting! It's helpful to think of the results when you square the first twelve integers: 1, 4, 9, 16, 25, 36, 49, 64, 81, 100, 121, 144. Those numbers end in the following digits: 1, 4, 9, 6, 5, 6, 9, 4, 1, 0, 1, 4... After the first ten numbers, the pattern repeats,

and just keeps on repeating The answer choice that is not seen on our list is (E), the number 8. No perfect square ends in 8.

Question 10: (B)
Assuming the bag doesn't contain any broken, jagged shards of marbles (because that would be dangerous), we need a whole number of marbles that divides evenly by 4 and 6. The number 12 fits the bill!

Question 11: (D)
Let's say I have three prices: $10, $12, and $14. Their sum is $36. Their average is $12. Their sum divided by their average is k, which in this case equals 3. 3 is the number of prices on the original list. It always works that way!

Question 12: (D)
The area of the square is 81, so each side of the square is 9. The top triangle has a perimeter of 30, including one side which we now know is 9. The two remaining sides must add up to 21. Those two sides are part of the figure outlined by the solid line. The situation is the same for each of the four triangles, so the total perimeter of the figure is 21 x 4 = 84.

Question 13: (B)
When it says g(2) = k, what the problem is really asking is "What is the height of the function when 2 is the x value?" The height is 5, so k = 5. Next, what is the height of the function when 5 is the x value? Somewhere in between 2 and 3, so about 2.5.

Question 14: (E)
This is a little sneaky. You can't just multiply the two inequalities together. The way to make sure you get the right answer is to multiply each endpoint times each other one. In other words, multiply 0 x -1 and 0 x 3, and 8 x -1 and 8 x 3. Out of those four, take the smallest and biggest answers, which are -8 and 24. The set of all possible values for xy is within that range.

Question 15: (B)
Life is good for those people that remember a slightly obscure Geometry theorem called the Exterior Angle Theorem which says that an exterior angle in a triangle equals the sum of the two interior angles not touching it. Angle n is an exterior angle of both the left and right triangles. That means that in the left triangle, the two angles marked with arrows add up to n, and in the right triangle, the two angles marked with arrows add up to n. So the sum of all four angles is n + n = 2n. Thanks, Geometry!
Alternatively, you could plug in a number for n, and then plug in values that work for all of the other angles, and see which answer fits those numbers.

Question 16: (C)
The first term of the sequence is t, and the second term is (1/3)t + 3. The ratio of the second term to the first is ((1/3)t + 3) / t. To make the whole thing a little less ugly, multiply it by 3/3 and simplify to get (t + 9) / 3t. You can always plug in a number here too. Try t = 6. The second term would be 5, because (1/3)*6 + 3 = 5. Plug t = 6 into the answer choices to find the one that gives you the ratio 5/6.

Section 9: Critical Reading

Question 1: (B)
The best way to see this one is to look at the second blank first. At this time, people became interested in black culture. That interest must have inspired them. The other choices don't make sense.

Question 2: (A)
Look to the first blank here. What do employers do with resumes? The only choice that makes any sense is evaluating. "Supplement" fits in nicely.

Question 3: (E)
Easy question with some tricky vocab here. Docile means "easy to control", which is the opposite of "hard to control."
Adroit means "skillful"
Gluttonous means "excessive"
Supple means "flexible and adaptable"

Question 4: (C)
This word leads to describe how much of a range she showed. Scope means "breadth or range."

Question 5: (E)
"Elucidate" means to explain of clarify. If you know this, then you know that our word must be positive in nature. Another clue here is the time element. They are comparing ancient with relatively modern, so "Foreshadows" looks good.

Question 6: (E)
Look to the second blank first. What kind of discourse would "Denunciations" and "accusations" preclude (prevent)? "Meaningful" or "Orderly" discourse. Now you have some vocab to contend with. "Cacophony" means "an unpleasant combination of loud, jarring sounds," and "paucity" means "an inadequacy or lack." Gotta be E.

Passage: Frederick Douglass and the women's movement
Main Idea: Frederick Douglass had a long and

ever-changing relationship with the Women's Rights movement.

Question 7: (D)
This passage is primarily about Douglass's work as an activist.

Question 8: (E)
Whatever you choose, make sure you plug it in to the original sentence to make sure it sounds good. Praising is clearly the best choice.

Question 9: (D)
Douglass made this choice in order to include ALL movements struggling for equal rights: "All rights for all."

Question 10: (D)
When the author says that the movement accepted "The logic of this position," they are accepting the POLITICAL logic of the position. You can see evidence of this in lines 25-26. If they're concerned about losing supporters, that is a political concern

Question 11: (B)
He went from "entertaining serious doubts" about a particular idea to being a hardworking and active supporter of the idea.

Question 12: (C)
This one is a bit tricky. The phrase must be something intrinsically related to "ownership." What is ownership of property if you don't control it? The reason safeguarding is wrong is because it isn't broad enough. Having control of something allows that you also are able to safeguard it.

Question 13: (A)
She was willing to "advance women's rights on the back of the 'defenseless slave woman.'" She was more committed to the one cause than to the other.

Question 14: (E)
When the Women's Rights movement endorsed Stephen Douglas, were they not endorsing his racist legislation?

Question 15: (C)
Douglass's own political style was direct action: Organizing citizens with the goal of passing legislation. There is a hint in the phrase "words and 'moral suasion." If Douglass is not primarily for the use of words, then he must be for action.

Question 16: (B)
The simplest answer is the best here. If Douglasss

disagreed with Garrison, and women's rights leading didn't like that, then they must have been more closely in agreement with Garrison.

Question 17: (E)
In the passage, he's usually on Susan B. Anthony's side (two out of three times she is mentioned.)

Question 18: (A)
This is a tough call between A and E. Look to the last sentence, which says that Douglass helped broaden the scope of the women's movement to make the final decision.

Question 19: (D)
Answer D is the only answer that is both on topic and sufficiently broad.

Section 10: Writing

Question 1: (E)
Shortest answer wins! Simple, clear & mellow.

Question 2: (B)
Faulty comparison. We're comparing the duties of firefights to the duties of police officers (or "those of a police officer").

Question 3: (D)
Take out the aside "one of the most popular writers of her day" and the answer becomes clear: "Pearl Buck… won the Novel Prize."

Question 4: (B)
Ugh. All these are ugly. (B) makes this horrible sentence work most efficiently, though.

Question 5: (D)
Only the correct answer contains the parallel construction necessary to make this sentence fly.

Question 6: (A)
Parallel construction again. 1. He does not speak Spanish & 2. He has never visited Mexico. All the other choices try to get too fancy.

Question 7: (B)
Since "our" is part of the second half, "we" is the only right choice for the first half.

Question 8: (E)
Starting a sentence with "having" is rarely good and almost never good on the SAT. Two things, beautifully parallel in their construction, brought about the establishment of these standards: a) A growing awareness &

b) The leadership of Florence Nightingale.

Question 9: (B)
The expedition was sent to check "the report," not the villager. That part comes first. (E) might tempt you at first, but doesn't it seem like it's creating a weird noun called "a Turkish villager report"? As in, "hey, have you seen the latest Turkish villager report? Best one yet!"

Question 10: (C)
(C) is so nice and short and simple and clean. It's tricky because it's comma-less and some students are afraid of it, but read it aloud and you'll get it.

Question 11: (E)
He was fired from his job BECAUSE of something, so it's (C) or (E). (C) is tempting, but ultimately does not express the content of the sentence as directly as (E).

Question 12: (D)
Another sentence that needs a "because" like the last one. (E) is the only other contender and it's far too wordy and clunky. So we beat on, boats against the current...

Question 13: (D)
Again, don't be afraid to get rid of the comma. Lots of pronoun weirdness in these answer choices too. "They" is correct for "computers," not "it."

Question 14: (E)
"Of all the states represented in the conference" COMMA... This modifying (adjective) clause must be followed by the subject it is talking about: the great state of Missouri (the Show Me state). Have you noticed the trend of questions testing this specific grammatical rule? They LOVE to test this one. Understand it, look for it and get it right!

Test 7
Section 2: Critical Reading

Question 1: (A)
What do equal rights laws do? They guarantee equal rights. The other words don't make sense. To "lobby" is to persuade an political representative or influential person.

Question 2: (A)
The word in the blank must be a synonym of "heterogeneous," which means consisting of diverse elements. "Motley" means the same. "Motley Cru," on the other hand, means endless nights of alcohol-soaked rock and roll!

Question 3: (C)
In this question, the word in the first blank has to be in relation to the word in the second. If the book has a lot of footnotes, then the editors must have added a lot of info. If the book has few footnotes, then the editors must have gotten rid of some info. (C) is the only one that works in this way.

Question 4: (A)
The professor believes that the actions of the government were contrary to humanitarianism. To be humanitarian is to be concerned with improving the lives of others. So the opposite would be self-serving. "Dubious" means "skeptical."

Question 5: (E)
Hard vocab here.
Conflagration means "a large fire."
Concordance means "a similarity or agreement between things."
Distillation means "Something that consists of only the essential aspects." This one is tempting, but composite is actually the opposite of distillation.
Aberration means "departure from the norm."
Amalgamation means "a combination of things."

Question 6: (E)
This is about the struggle of a Hispanic writers to find an adequate mode of expression. It's not about getting published or celebrating so (A) and (B) are out. It's not about the writer's mastery of language (C) and it's not about new artistic approaches (D).

Question 7: (D)
Answer (D) is almost identical to the situation in the passage. The point is that it's hard to express yourself in a language that is not your native tongue.

Question 8: (B)

The author calls the work a "masterpiece" and the portrait "finely honed." "Awe" (D) is much too strong a sentiment.

Question 9: (A)
This is one way in which modern computers have surpassed HAL.

Passage: The Founding Fathers' Gender Blindspot
Main Idea: The Founding Fathers felt no need to consider women in the drafting of the New Constitution.

Question 10: (A)
The point is that, while the drafters of the constitution called woman "free people," they never really even thought to include them in the political system. The irony!

Question 11: (E)
"They had found ways of exerting influence of political events." These are some of them.

Question 12: (B)
The fact that these women were "loyalists" is important because it broadens our view of women's political activities.

Question 13: (C)
The author is illustrating the irony that, at this time, a couple could be happily married even though the man wouldn't really even consider the woman as being his political equal.

Question 14: (D)
It's in their natures. This is "innately."

Question 15: (C)
In context, we see that John Adams isn't really taking his wife's ideas seriously. And yet, if only for a moment, Adams is able to see outside his own cultural bias. This passage is about the cultural bias of the founding fathers. This is the small moment when we see someone begin to overcome it.

Question 16: (D)
One "ridicules" something "ludicrous" and "fears" something "threatening."

Passage: Animal Play
Main Idea: Scientists have several theories as to why animals play.

Question 17: (C)
Try these options out. "Nearly equal" is the one that makes sense.

Question 18: (E)
Variety. This paragraph shows that many animals play and that they all play in different ways.

Question 19: (E)
"Muscle Fiber"... "movement." This is about the physical body and it's development. In case you didn't really know, that's what "physiological" means.

Question 20: (D)
The principle illustrated in the lines is that animals play at doing things that will be important in their adult years. Adult monkeys need to be good at climbing trees.

Question 21: (B)
The essential lesson being learned is how to function as a group. A soccer team is the clearest example of a functioning group.

Question 22: (D)
Theory: Play socializes group members. Opinion: Play is simply for fun. The theory suggests that play is functional. The opinion is that is has no useful function.

Question 23: (E)
This paragraph introduces another theory about play (that it is just for fun).

Question 24: (A)
Fagen's point about bears playing is that it serves no useful function. What useful function does dance serve?
You've finished this section. Now would be a good time to dance.

Section 3: Math

Question 1: (A)
Set up a proportion: 25 pounds of flour / 300 rolls = x pounds of flour / 12 rolls. Cross multiply to get: (25)(12) = 300x. Solve for x, which equals 1.

Question 2: (E)
In the expression $2(x/y)(y^2)$, one of the y's can cancel, simplifying it to $2xy$. Since $xy = 10$, $2xy = 20$.

Question 3: (B)
If x were equal to 8, then y would be equal to 22 to make them add up to 30. But since x is greater than 8 (for example, x could equal 11), then y has to be a number less than 22 (for example, 19) to make the equation still add up to 30.

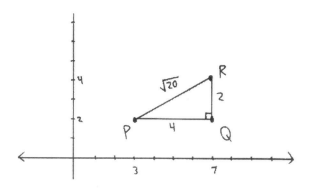

Question 4: (C)
See diagram. Since the y-coordinates between P and Q don't change, the distance between P and Q is the change in x-coordinates, which is 4. The distance between Q and R is 2. The third side of the triangle is the distance between R and P, and for that you need to use either the distance formula or Pythagorean theorem. The two legs of the triangle are 2 and 4, so $2^2 + 4^2 = c^2$. c equals $\sqrt{20}$. The three sides add up to $6 + \sqrt{20}$.

Question 5: (D)
The weird expression they write, $8 + (26 - 1)9$, is actually the textbook formula for finding the nth term of a sequence. It's a clue! 8 is the first term, and the difference between each term is 9. That expression will give you the 26th term. Even though it says $26 - 1$, it gives us the 26th term, not the 25th. There are 25 intervals BETWEEN the first and 26th terms.

Question 6: (A)
This problem is not going to give us any numbers at all? Seriously? Well, the one thing we can cling to amidst this stormy sea of confusion is that there are three pairs of vertical angles in the figure. So the following pairs of angles are equal to each other: (r and x), (s and y), and (t and z). We can think of them as three unknown values instead of six. The trick is that we need to know the value of at least two of those three DIFFERENT unknown values to figure out all the angles. For example, if we know the value of r and s, then we also know the value of x and y. Then we could find the value of t because r + s + t form a straight line and must add up to 180, and same thing for z. So the answer that is NOT sufficient is answer (A) because t and z are the same value, and we would still have two unknown pairs (four unknown angles), which we couldn't figure out.

Question 7: (C)
Let's say the two numbers that differ by 1 are 7 and 8. Their sum is 15, so t = 15. Now we plug 15 into each answer for t, and we want to see which one gives us the value we are looking for, which is 8.
To solve algebraically, for the two numbers that add up

to t, let's call the BIGGER one x and the SMALLER one x − 1. Then x + x − 1 = t. Solve for x, which equals (t + 1)/2.

Question 8: (A)

First, it's helpful to turn the chart into a list. Let's forget about the new kid in class – no one likes him anyway. The first three students all have 0 siblings, so we can start there and make a list of the 12 current students' siblings like this:
0, 0, 0, 1, 1, 1, 1, 1, 1, 2, 2, 3
The current median (middle) number is 1. The current average of the list is the sum of that whole list (13) divided by the number of terms (12), which is 13/12. Now we need to add in that darn new kid in class. Let's say our new kid has 0 siblings. The median of our list is still 1. Or let's say our new kid has 3 siblings. The median of our list is STILL 1. The median doesn't change. Now we need the new average of the list to equal 1. If the new kid has x siblings, the new average is the sum of the list (13 + x) divided by the total kids in the class now (13). So (13 + x)/13 = 1. Solve for x, which is 0.

Question 9: 2/5 or .4

Divide the first equation by 2 and solve for x, which equals 7. (x − 3)/(x + 3) equals 4/10 which reduces to 2/5.

Question 10: 128

$2x - 3 = 253$. $2x = 256$. $x = 128$.

Question 11: 2400

We need the total black sneakers manufactured. Let's start with the column of "Low-tops." The top entry must be 4,000 to add up with 1,500 to get 5,500. Then from left to right across the top, the white high-tops are 3,600 and white low-tops are 4,000 for a total for white sneakers of 7,600. In the right-hand column, the total of black sneakers must be added to 7,600 to get to 10,000 total sneakers, so the total of black sneakers is 2,400.

Question 12: 3

The width of the rectangle, from P to S is 2 units long. Perimeter = 2w + 2L. So 10 = 2(2) + 2(L). L = 3. That means the height of point R is 3, so the coordinates of R are (1,3). Since R is also on the parabola, plug those coordinates into x and y in the equation $y = ax^2$. $3 = a(1)^2$. $a = 3$.

Question 13: 8/3 or 2.66 or 2.67

Plug in the values for a and c into the equation. $2b + b = 2 + 6$. Solve for b. $3b = 8$, so $b = 8/3$.

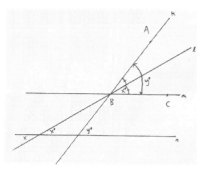

Question 14: 22.5 < x < 27.5, 45/2 < x < 55/2

See diagram. Angle y is a corresponding angle to ABC, so it must equal angle ABC. The vertical angle from x is a corresponding angle to one of the halves of ABC. So basically, x is half the value of y. Pick any value for y that is between 45 and 55 and divide it by 2, and that answer is correct.

Question 15: 24

Deal with the plumbers and trainees separately. One experienced plumber out of 4 is on the team, so there are 4 options. For the trainees, two out of four are chosen for the team. We can write out the options by labeling the four trainees A, B, C, and D. The options for picking two trainees are: AB, AC, AD, BC, BD, and CD. Six options. Multiply the options for experienced plumbers (4) times options for trainees (6) to get 24.

Question 16: 10

We need to find the area of the big circle. The area of the small circle with radius 6 is πr^2 which equals 36π. The shaded area is 64π, so the big circle has a total area of 100π. Now we can find the radius of the large circle by writing $100\pi = \pi r^2$ and solving for r, which is 10.

Question 17: 8

This one is really mean! Plug in some prime numbers for p, r and s. Let's say 3, 5, and 7. Then 3 x 5 x 7 = 105. It seems like there would be 5 factors: 1, 3, 5, 7 and 105. BUT, there are three more hidden factors that come from combining TWO of the prime numbers. Specifically, 3 x 5 is a factor, as is 5 x 7, and 3 x 7. So there are a total of 8 factors.

Question 18: 70

This question is very difficult. Very. Here we go:
We can write an equation based on what we know at time t = 0… $6 = c - (d - 4(0))^2$ which simplifies to:
 $6 = c - d^2$
We can write another equation for the ball at its maximum height… $106 = c - (d - 4(2.5))^2$ which simplifies to:
$106 = c - (d - 10)^2$

Now we have two equations and two variables, c and d. With a little algebra, we can solve for those variables. Rewrite the first equation as $6 + d^2 = c$, and then substitute that into the second equation for c... $106 = (6 + d^2) - (d - 10)^2$. FOIL and simplify to get $106 = 6 + 20d - 100$. It turns out that $d = 10$. We plug d into the first equation ($6 = c - d^2$) to find that $c = 106$. Now we can finally find the height at time 1 by putting c and d into the original formula and solving the equation $h = 106 - (10 - 4(1))^2$. It turns out that $h = 70$.

Section 4: Writing

Question 1: (B)
Poor Mr. Chung. The correct answer is direct and simple. The others are passive and icky.

Question 2: (E)
We know we're talking about tigers so there's no need for "of them." The best way to combine these two aspects of this fascinating tiger is with the word "yet," which points out how amazing it is that this tiger is both strong and peaceful.

Question 3: (C)
Who or what is "like most residents?" The Curtis Family, of course. Only two answers get this right and (D) is not a complete sentence.

Question 4: (B)
Isn't it interesting that Houston is a foreign-trade port, even though it is sixty miles inland? That's what is notable about this statement and sentence, so "although" is needed to point that out. Did you know that the city slogan for Houston, TX was once: "Houston: It's Worth It."

Question 5: (C)
Take out the aside so you have a simple sentence: "Great literature... endures." Great literature is only one thing, so "it" is the only option.

Question 6: (C)
Don't fall for "considering" because it sounds so pretty and special. "Because" is the simplest way to complete this sentence. (D) uses it, but is also clunky and too wordy. (E) is no good because "being that" is evil.

Question 7: (C)
It's always good to get rid of what's clearly wrong first, particularly when the whole sentence is underlined. "Having been" and "beings" are bad, which only leaves the correct answer and (D). (D) is not a complete sentence. There you go!

Question 8: (D)
There is a lot of information about C.G. Jung to fit into this one, right? The correct answer does so in a way that is actually a complete sentence.

Question 9: (C)
"Consequently" and "therefore" are tricky; semicolons are trickier. Remember, in order for a semicolon to be correct both pieces need to be complete sentences. These answer choices are messy, but there's no reason to repeat "people," which gets you to the right answer.

Question 10: (A)
Don't let the "so" throw you. It's definitely strange, but it's also correct because "has provided" is parallel with "has produced."

Question 11: (E)
Take out the "becauses" and you have a simple sentence: "the writer's recent book is at once FRUSTRATING...and DELIGHTFUL." That's parallelism.

Question 12: (B)
Frank Capra and George Stevens are two people so it must be "as directors."

Question 13: (D)
Adverb alert! "Calmly." The lack of parallel construction with "thoughtfully" should be a big clue.

Question 14: (A)
Take out "my colleague" and how does it sound? Does "I" sound better? Yes, it does.

Question 15: (D)
Parallel construction. "To remain" with "to move."

Question 16: (E)
This one is fine. Also true. Seems like everyone is running a marathon these days.

Question 17: (E)
This one is so mean because it sounds so bad and yet there is nothing wrong with it. It's cool if you tried to find something. Just remember: it has to be WRONG. Do you know why it's WRONG? If not, it just may be no error. Don't be afraid of no error.

Question 18: (C)
"Whereby" sounds so fancy and is so wrong. A simple "so" would do.

Question 19: (A)
Subject/verb agreement. We're talking about the numerous SOURCES of a river, so "are" is needed.

Question 20: (C)
It's the 21st century and this happened in 1850! So Jim found a pass "that soon became…"

Question 21: (C)
Tense. The flood "has made" the bridge inaccessible, so this is happening now. "We rented" a small boat.

Question 22: (C)
"Plus being?" No no no. Keep it simple. "And" would be fine.

Question 23: (C)
"Your own" is out of step with the two uses of "one" in the passage.

Question 24: (E)
This is fine. Plan and write an essay in which you agree or disagree with the warning in the plays.

Question 25: (B)
The sentence starts specifically with "a student," so "one" is no good.

Question 26: (A)
Idiom. John Edgar Wideman is regarded AS one of the most talented writers. That's how we say that. Why? Good question.

Question 27: (B)
Mastery is one thing. "Are" should be "is."

Question 28: (D)
Faulty comparison. We cannot compare the industrial use of plastics to steel. Rather, it should be "is greater than THAT OF steel, aluminum, and copper combined."

Question 29: (E)
This is okay. So…who gets the dolls now?

Passage Revision: Meeting Nancy Prince

Question 30: (B)
The correct answer delivers on this very dramatic moment in which the writer finally reveals what person from the past he or she would like to meet. It says "in context," so read a couple sentences before and before answering.

Question 31: (A)
Oooooh, tricky! Which of these revisions would NOT improve the sentence. Meaning that four of them would. This is a terrible sentence so at least four changes are needed. The only answer choice that does not help is the first one, "I should explain." We know the writer is the person explaining so adding this does

nothing for us.

Question 32: (C)
The sentence in question is very simple: "Nancy was right there in Saint Petersburg." The only thing this accomplishes is to emphasize the major point that she was in the thick of it while all this big stuff was happening.

Question 33: (D)
The best way to handle these is to try each one and see which one blows your mind the most by making this bad sentence suddenly okay. (D) is the clear winner here.

Question 34: (E)
Well, if we're going to insert something at the beginning of a paragraph, it had better be a good topic sentence or introduction. Browse the paragraph and you'll see that it's all about Nancy and how she learned all this stuff and did all this stuff and was in the middle of all this stuff. In other words, it's all about HER. (E) is the only answer that's all about her.

Question 35: (E)
This again! So four of these help and one does not. Some of these are up for debate, maybe, but "tons of things" is not a good thing to add to an essay in any situation. "Tons of things?" Not good.

Section 5: Critical Reading

Question 1: (C)
These words are going to be opposites. The second word is easier. What kind of creatures like to run in packs? Social creatures. Social is the opposite of "lone."

Question 2: (E)
The word in the blank is going to be related to "renowned." Noteworthy.

Question 3: (D)
Working first on the first blank we can narrow the choice down to (C) and (D), since his hunch was correct. The second word relates to "hunch." Intuition.

Question 4: (A)
It has a pretty good effect, even though it can't completely get rid of pain. "alleviate" means "to make something more bearable."

Question 5: (C)
If you feel someone's suffering, then you are "empathetic." That's what empathetic means.

Question 6: (A)
Working on the first blank first, you can eliminate choice (B) and probably (E). The second blank has to mean something like "got in the way of." "Interfered with" is the closest to this meaning.

Question 7: (E)
The word is going to be the opposite of "lighthearted and even-tempered." "Truculence" means "aggressive, or sullen, or angry." If you don't know this word, you can maybe get rid of some of the others.
"Resilence" is "the ability to recover quickly."
"Affluence" is "wealth."
"Affability" means "being good-natured."
"Equanimity" means "even-temperedness."

Question 8: (C)
Hard vocab here. Working with the first blank, you can eliminate everything but (B) and (C). "Accessible" means "understandable," "lucid" means "clear," and "hackneyed" means "commonplace." The second blank has to mean something like "dense" or "not-understandable." This is "impenetrable."

Question 9: (B)
Most simply, these passages are about children and toys.

Question 10: (E)
The author of P2 thinks that toys are for fun and that kids would do fine without them. So words and phrases like "furnish a playground" or "rehearsals for reality," would probably make him or her sick with annoyance. As in, "gimme a frickin' break, hombre!"

Question 11: (B)
One word: "hogwash." Or, as a wise man once paraphrased: "gimme a frickin' break, hombre!"

Question 12: (D)
The author of P2 thinks the author of P1 should stop talking about "rehearsals for reality" and pick up some play-doh. Let's get real, hombre.

Passage: The experience of listening to books on tape, pros and cons.
Main idea, Passage 1: Audio books impose the voice of the reader on the text and rob the listener of the intimate experience of reading alone.
Main idea, Passage 2: Audio books create a shared and valuable experience between the listener and the reader.

Question 13: (E)
Author two makes no mention of genders.

Question 14: (C)
The author is making the point that this kind of active participation isn't possible when listening to a book on tape.

Question 15: (D)
The author thinks that gender has an effect on the language used. If it didn't, the author would not hear the language as being sexed.

Question 16: (E)
This is about what happens when a person of one gender "performs" (even if, when reading, the performance is taking place in the reader's head) the work of a person of another gender.

Question 17: (A)
The voice of the audio book speaker is somehow neutral, and so does not get in the way of the listener's ability to hear the writer's voice.

Question 18: (B)
This idea is an exception to the rule, an instance in which it is more enjoyable for the reader to hear the work read aloud.

Question 19: (B)
Refer to the anecdote about the daughter in P1. This is what frustrates the author of passage one... that there is no real dialogue going on.

Question 20: (E)
The author likes hearing books read aloud because she feels that she is in dialogue with the reader of the book. A dialogue is an exchange of opinions. So these little things allow her to gauge the opinions of the readers.

Question 21: (B)
Pragmatic because the author is legally blind. And "pedagogical" (related to teaching), because the author thinks it's a good lesson to have her students read to her.

Question 22: (D)
The moments that the author of the passage chooses to include are moments where her students are correcting themselves.

Question 23: (C)
She's admitting that, yes, her kids might be putting on a little performance in order to gain her sympathy.

Question 24: (C)
We've talked about the child thing. This anecdote is set

in opposition to the passive nature of listening to books on tape. The husband anecdote shows how being read to can be a shared experience, which is the main thrust of this passage.

Section 7: Math

Question 1: (C)
60 is divisible by 3, so the next largest number less than 60 that works is three less.

Question 2: (D)
X is symmetric around a vertical and a horizontal line. And possibly diagonal lines, depending on how picky you are and what sort of font you use.

Question 3: (D)
Bobby always gets $10, plus $2 per chore. So 10 + 2n. Bobby's got a pretty sweet racket going on.

Question 4: (C)
Count the boxes in Figure A. It has 13 boxes, and its area is 26 square centimeters, so each little box has an area of 2. Figure B has 8 boxes, so its area is 16.

Question 5: (B)
Albert went down 150. Goldberg went up 100. Patel went up maybe 25. Smith went down 50. Wang went up 50. Goldberg increased the most.

Question 6: (D)
If we count up that there are 5 things being averaged, we can turn this into an equation: (6+ 6 + 12 + 16 + x)/5 = x. Simplify to get (40 + x)/5 = x. Solve for x, which equals 10.

Question 7: (C)
Let's start with what we know, 40 degrees, and work from right to left. In the right hand triangle, 40 + 90 + 2y must equal 180, so 2y equals 50. The next angle, y, equals 25. Angle z is in a right triangle where z + 25 + 90 must add up to 180, so z = 65.

Question 8: (C)
Odd numbers are doubled and even numbers are printed the way they are. Therefore, 26 could be printed if the number 13 were selected and then doubled, or it could have been printed if 26 were selected and then left the way it is.

Question 9: (A)
The best way to avoid a mistake is plug in numbers. Let's say m = 2 and s = 10. Then in 2 minutes and 10 seconds, there are a total of 130 seconds. Plug in m = 2 and s = 10 into each answer, and the one that gives the

correct answer of 130 is (A).

Question 10: (D)
Take the contents of each parentheses and set them equal to zero one at a time. If 2x − 2 = 0, then solve for x, which equals 1. If 2 − x = 0, then x = 2.

Question 11: (C)
Take the cube root (third root) of both sides. $x = y^3$.

Question 12: (E)
We're looking for a segment with a negative slope, so we can focus on the ones that slope down to the right. Out of those, the slope from D (1, 3) to C (3, 1) is -2/2 = -1.

Question 13: (A)
Aha, some logic! Each number satisfies exactly one of the conditions and one of the numbers is odd, so the other two numbers must both be even. One number must be an EVEN multiple of 5, like 10, 20, or 30. The fact about Kyle's birthday is utterly stupid and pointless. Out of the answers, only (A) contains one odd number and one even multiple of 5.

Question 14: (C)
Square both sides of the equation and FOIL the right hand side to get $x + 9 = x^2 − 6x + 9$. Subtract 9 from both sides to get $x = x^2 − 6x$.

Question 15: (E)
The first ten perfect squares would all be in the range we're looking for: 1, 4, 9, 16, 25, 36, 49, 64, 81, 100. So the number of integers up to 100 that are NOT perfect squares is 90.

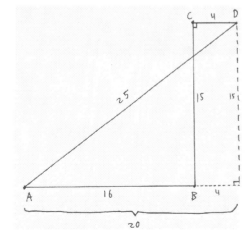

Question 16: (C)
See diagram. Connect point A to D with a straight line. That line can be the hypotenuse of a right triangle where the bottom leg is 20 and the side leg is 15. By Pythagorean Theorem, the straight distance from A to

D is 25 miles. Now we add up the segments they gave for Diane's original route: 16 + 15 + 4 = 35. So the 25 mile trip would be 10 miles shorter.

Question 17: (D)
The circle with radius of 1/2 has an area (using πr^2) of $(1/4)\pi$. The circle with a radius of 1 has an area of 1π. The ratio of larger area to smaller is $1\pi / (1/4)\pi$, which simplifies to 4 : 1.

Question 18: (B)
The list of consecutive integers starts with -22, -21, -20… and will add up to very negative values until the list starts getting into positive numbers that cancel out the negatives. When the list goes from negative -22 all the way to positive 22, the sum of the whole thing will cancel out to zero. So we don't even have to worry about anything before 22. If we look at the positive numbers 23, 24, and 25, it turns out that they add up to exactly 72. So the list must start at -22 and end at positive 25.

Question 19: (A)
This one looks more painful than it really is. Solve the first equation for x by raising both sides of the equation to the (-3/4) power. The exponent above x cancels out and we get $x = k^{(6/4)} = k^{(3/2)}$. Next, solve the second equation by raising both sides to the (3/4) power to get $y = n^{(6/4)} = n^{(3/2)}$. So $xy = [k^{(3/2)}][n^{(3/2)}]$, which can be rewritten as $xy = (nk)^{(3/2)}$. Now we raise both sides to the (-2/3) power to find the answer that $(xy)^{(-2/3)} = (kn)^{(-1)}$, which equals 1/nk.

Question 20: (E)
That equation for f(x) doesn't really matter at all. What we need to do is look at how the first graph is shifted to become the second graph. The point on the first graph at (-1,3) has shifted to the corresponding point (2,1), which is three units to the right and two units down. The constants h and k are the regular notation for a shifted graph, where h is the amount of shift left or right (but with the opposite sign of the shift), and k is the shift up and down (with the same sign). So the shift 3 units to the right means that h = -3, and the shift 2 units down means k = -2. hk = 6.

Section 8: Critical Reading

Question 1: (E)
How would YOU feel if the editorial you had written contained several errors? Dismayed? Embarrassed? Certainly not overjoyed, intrigued or prepared. (A) doesn't work because "authenticated" makes no sense in the second blank. (E) is correct.

Question 2: (D)

Wetland refuges are set up by conservationists when natural wetlands have been lost or are threatened. "Established" is the only word that works here and "compensate for" is good for the first blank so (D) is great!

Question 3: (D)
If ginger is used to treat coughs, colds and upset stomachs it must also be like a medicine right? "Curative" = "able to restore health." Well, there you go!

Question 4: (C)
These two answer choices need to go together. Either the scientific organization is stoked because the newspaper reported all about the major research conference or the organization is mad because the newspaper didn't. Both words work in (C).

Question 5: (C)
"Merely" is key #1 and "enabling them to attract mates and to hide from predators" is key #2. So the wings are not only pretty, but they have some serious practical use. (C) is correct. "Beautiful" works for (D), but the wings are not a "result of" the survival of the insects.

Question 6: (D)
Straight-up vocab challenge here. Which word works with "separating the good from the bad." Guess what "winnow" means? "To examine something in order to remove the bad, undesirable parts." YEAH! (D). This is an example of a question you can skip if you have no clue about any of the words.

Passage: Henry Mulcahy gets fired!
Main idea: A professor gets dismissed for openly challenging the President of the college and broods about it.

Question 7: (D)
Tricky. It's not first person, it's third person, but it's definitely an observer who knows a lot about Mulcahy. Like, ALL about him. (D).

Question 8: (A)
The sentence after line 22 gives this one away when it talks about how Mulcahy openly challenged President Hoar in meetings and made him angry. Firing him would certainly be a vindictive move and would probably not be very wise since everyone witnessed their dispute. All signs point to (A).

Question 9: (E)
Whoa. This seems like a good time to mention that this is a difficult and meandering passage. Stay focused on what the question is specifically asking. Basically, the lines in question list all the things he fought for. Nothing more, nothing less. Possibly, a "wide range of

topics?" (E) is perfectly general and open and perfectly correct.

Question 10: (C)
You just knew they were going to ask about the eggs, right? I mean, what is going on here? He's being cute, asking a dietician to unscramble eggs. Get it? Scrambled eggs? This part of the passage is followed by him smiling, so he's being "funny." Very funny. Simply (C).

Question 11: (E)
In context, the smile is followed by "the letter... elicited a kind of pity, mingled with contempt and dry amusement. Finally, a straightforward answer on this section. (E).

Question 12: (A)
This is what the second paragraph is all about. He thinks he's being fired because he's critical of so much of the college's practices. (A) is this. The rest of the answer choices here are unrelated to the passage.

Question 13: (B)
This is a very difficult question and many students get it wrong. The key is in line 37, which describes the attempt at "trite" and "tedious" and goes on to say these are qualities that would not be associated with a "progressive college." So what answer choice is most closely the opposite of these ideas? (B). Is this a mean question? Yes. Don't feel bad if you chose (A).

Question 14: (B)
Same deal as #13. Dudley and Wilkins State are implied to be the opposite of a progressive college in context. So (B) is right. Now move on from this annoying set of questions. This is a hard passage, isn't it?

Question 15: (D)
In other words, keep your business and your personal life separate. He is hurt by the firing because he thinks what he did should be considered separately from who he is. (D) is correct.

Question 16: (E)
Another hard one. In context, the sentence means that the president simply DIDN'T LIKE HIM; there was nothing complex or nuanced about his dislike, it was flat and clear. "Unequivocally" = without hesitation or ambiguity. This is the best answer. (E).

Question 17: (A)
Another semi-tricky one. Mulcahy seems to think pretty highly of himself, wouldn't you say? He thinks he's pretty great. So the "irony of his biography" is that he hasn't garnered the recognition he thinks he deserves. (A).

Question 18: (E)
If the answer is not clear (which is probably the case here), go with the process of elimination. In fact, always go with it because it works great. There's nothing about his devotion to literature (A), he is obviously not intimidated by his peers (B), not anything specifically about his dedication to teaching and research (C) and nothing about arrogance toward students (D). The only choice you cannot confidently eliminate is (E). He's definitely an intelligent guy and he seems to have trouble with the administration.

Question 19: (D)
One more hard one and this very difficult section is over. The key is the last sentence: he sees himself as the victim "of that ferocious envy of mediocrity for excellence that is the ruling passion of all systems of jobholders." In other words, he thinks he's excellent and everyone else is mediocre. (D). Mmmmmm. Time for a rest. Go watch YouTube for a bit.

Section 9: Math

Question 1: (B)
6 red cars out of 10 gives a probability of 6/10 or 3/5.

Question 2: (A)
The fact that AB = BC makes the triangle isosceles, and isosceles triangles are always symmetrical around their bisector (BD in this case). So we can conclude that anything on the left hand side of the triangle IS equal to the corresponding part on the right hand side. So that rules out answers (B), (C), and (D). Also, there's a Geometry theorem that says that the bisector of an isosceles triangle is also perpendicular to the opposite side, so that rules out (E).

Question 3: (B)
Before you touch your calculator, notice that we're given what 30 percent of m is and we are asked for 15 percent, which is just half of the earlier value, meaning half of 40.

Question 4: (E)
If we multiply or divide a negative number by 2, it will still be negative. Same thing is true for adding or subtracting 2 from almost any negative number. But $2 - n$ must turn n positive. For example, if n = -10, then $2 - (-10) = 2 + 10 = 12$.

Question 5: (D)
Since all the answers are whole numbers, we should get rid of the decimal in our ratio by multiplying everything by 10. Now our ratio is 12 to 10. That doesn't

match anything yet, but it does reduce to "6 to 5." Cool, dude!

Question 6: (D)
These crappy pictographs don't look much like homes, but at least we can see that there are 3 and a half crappy pictographs. Since each one equals 5 million, 3.5 x 5 million = 17.5 million.

Question 7: (B)
There's nothing better for this one than good old guess and check. The difference between two perfect squares is 7. Let's start thinking about the first few perfect squares: 1, 4, 9, 16, 25, 36, 49... (The SAT loooooves perfect squares). As the perfect squares get bigger, the differences between them quickly get much bigger than 7. So the answer we're looking for is pretty early on, between 16 and 9, which means $4^2 - 3^2$.

Question 8: (C)
Let's use the highly scientific technique of guessing the values of these points. u looks to be about -0.8 and w is about -0.5. Then the absolute value of u – w is roughly positive 0.3, which corresponds to x.

Question 9: (D)
First we get n + 5. Then we get 5(n + 5). Then we get 5(n+5) – 5. Before the last step, let's simply what we have, which is 5n + 25 – 5, which is 5n + 20. Now we divide by 5 to get n + 4.

Question 10: (B)
Each poster uses four pieces of six inch tape. That's 24 inches of tape per poster. We need to convert to feet, so that's 2 feet of tape per poster. Since our buddy Philip started with 300 feet, the amount he has left is 300 – 2n.

Question 11: (B)
Reflecting a line about the x-axis changes the slope from negative to positive (or vice versa), but doesn't change the numbers in the slope. So the slope of line L must be 4/5.

Question 12: (A)
Try each answer. If n and p both equal zero, then sure, n can equal 3p.

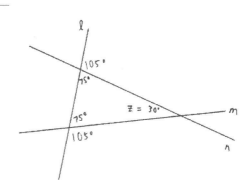

Question 13: (D)
See diagram. First, looking at the triangle that z is in, the two other angles plus z must add up to 180, so the two other angles must add up to 150. Let's pretend that they're each 75 (those are possible values, so it's not cheating to pretend). Angle y forms a straight line with one of those angles, so y must equal 105. And by the same logic, x would equal 105. So x + y = 210. We'd get the same answer if earlier we had picked two different angles that added up to 150... 210 is always the final answer. Pretending is good.

Question 14: (E)
For parabolas, if the x^2 term is positive, which it is in this case, the parabola opens upwards. So the answer isn't (A) or (B). And if the constant term c is positive, which it is in this case, then the parabola's vertex is above the x-axis, which means that only (E) can be the answer.

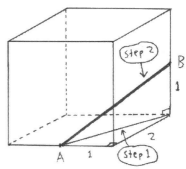

Question 15: (D)
See diagram. We need to draw in some segments and do double Pythagorean Theorem to find the answer. First, we can find the distance from A to the point on the base directly below B. One leg of the triangle is 1, and the other is 2, so $c^2 = a^2 + b^2 = 1^2 + 2^2 = 5$. So c = $\sqrt{5}$. Now that length of $\sqrt{5}$ becomes one of the legs of a new right triangle, and the other leg is the half edge going straight up to B, with length 1. The hypotenuse is the length we're looking for, AB, which can be found by calculating a new hypotenuse, h, where $h^2 = (\sqrt{5})^2 + 1^2 = 5 + 1$ which means the new hypotenuse is $\sqrt{6}$.

Question 16: (C)
We need to plug a into the function x² – x, to get a² – a, and then we plug in (a – 2) into the same function to get (a – 2) ² – (a – 2). Then we set both results equal to each other and solve algebraically:

$a^2 - a = (a - 2)^2 - (a - 2)$
$a^2 - a = (a^2 - 4a + 4) - (a - 2)$
$a^2 - a = (a^2 - 4a + 4) - a + 2$
$a^2 - a = a^2 - 5a + 6$
$4a = 6$
$a = 6/4 = 3/2$

Section 10: Writing

Question 1: (B)
THE STUDENTS are signing up for next year's courses, so it can only be (B). (A) looks like it COULD be right, but the noun at the beginning of that clause is "the students' schedules". The schedules themselves are not signing up for next year's courses.

Question 2: (B)
The correct answer is simple and quick, the others are too complicated, use "being," or use the unnecessary "whereas."

Question 3: (C)
Whoa. Great one for process of elimination. See how wordy they can make these answers?

Question 4: (D)
Another one with too many convoluted words and unneeded syntax switches. Is Syntax Switches a good name for a band? Discuss.

Question 5: (B)
This one is hard. They all seem too wordy and are. "They" and "them" are plural and don't match the singular "department" in three of the incorrect answers. The only one that is grammatically correct in this sense and has proper subject/verb agreement is (B).

Question 6: (B)
"Of which" and "fascination" are no good. The semicolon works nicely here, dividing the sentence into two complete, but separate parts.

Question 7: (A)
"Having" and "being" make all of them wrong but the sentence we started with: she "allowed very little of her work to be published BECAUSE her exacting standards…" That's fine.

Question 8: (D)
This one can be hard to see, especially because the correct answer doesn't have a comma, which seems wrong at first. Read them all the way through and you'll see that (D) is the only choice that makes it clear that the COLLEGES have since become coeducational and not the women or young people.

Question 9: (B)
This is a good one for the trick of taking out the additional clause. Really, the main sentence is: "The Navajo…speak an Apachean language." All the stuff in the middle is additional information, best separated from the main sentence by two commas.

Question 10: (E)
For one thing, we need the parallel construction that "to please" and "to influence" provide in the correct answer. Also, all the other answer choices are redundant by using "work of art" after the first part of the sentence specifies "an art form." We know we're talking about art.

Question 11: (E)
Here we have parallel construction that may be difficult to see. Which answer choice matches with "continued inflation" most directly and efficiently? The correct answer, of course.

Question 12: (A)
Parallel construction cloaked in confusion. "Able to stay alive" matches with "able to pass." None of the incorrect choices keep this intact and all of them put the information in a confusing and unclear order.

Question 13: (E)
This one is mean. First off, the whole sentence is up for correction, which is annoying. Secondly, they all sound clunky. The key here is that we have to compare the NUMBER of alligators to the NUMBER of Gila monsters. The only answer choice that does this is (E).

Question 14: (D)
The problem piece of information here is how to fit in the heliograph, right? Most of the answer choices have too many commas and dangling phrases and unclear syntax. (D) is nice because it includes the bit about the heliograph as a nice aside in the middle of a fairly simple sentence. Great! Pick that one.

Test 8
Section 2: Critical Reading

Question 1: (D)
The residents "fear" that "commercial development" will NEGATIVELY affect a "secluded" and "quiet" island. So (D).

Question 2: (E)
This deals with the misconception that the Amazon is only related to Brazil. Remember, work with one blank at a time on questions with two answers. Best choice is (E).

Question 3: (C)
The clue here is clear: "providing far more information." Surfeit, (C), is correct.
Modicum means "a small amount"

Question 4: (B)
This one is about understanding that the two words must contain opposite ideas to fit the context of the sentence. On this one, you have to look at both words in each answer choice at the same time to see if they are good solid antonyms. The only one that makes sense is (B). "Conciliatory" is positive and means "to appease or get along with," "confrontational" is negative and means "to confront or not get along with." Problem is that the other words are really tough. If you don't know most of them, maybe skip this one. For the record, "phlegmatic" means "lack or emotion." "Penurious" means "having very little money."

Question 5: (C)
The word "humdrum" is the key here. It means "dull because of being too familiar." In other words, consumers are not impressed with amazing new technology because they've had cell phones and the internet for awhile now and have become used to magical electronics. (C) is correct because "jaded" means "no longer interested in something." The other words don't fit this idea correctly.

Question 6: (D)
The adverbs in the answer choices are clutch here. Both passages address the fact that science fiction is "socially useful" (D). The other answers only apply to one of the passages or to aneither of them.

Question 7: (E)
Both passages make it clear that the "science" in science fiction is unrealistic and not based on fact. (E).

Question 8: (C)
Passage 2 has more respect for the science element in science fiction than Passage 1 does: "there is a general respect for science and some appreciation of its methodology." The lines referenced in Passage 1 pretty much trash talk the science. So (C) is good.

Question 9: (B)
They both think it's fun and kinda cool, right? So they "appreciate" it. (B) is best. "Qualified" means "with some reservation," (remember that...they LOVE that definition of "qualified") which is true in both cases.

Passage: Human vs. Animal Perception
Main idea: Humans, who perceive the world mainly through sight, perceive the world very differently than animals do.

Question 10: (B)
"Ancillary" means "of lesser importance." So sight is king, the others are second best. (B) is the answer and contains a central idea of the passage.

Question 11: (C)
Don't be scared by the word "phenomenology." This one is simpler than it seems. The whole passage is about how we use our senses to know about something. (C) is basically the same idea, restated. The other choices all contain key words that point in the wrong direction: (A) has "memorable," (B) has "behaviors," (D) has "rules," and (E) has "effects."

Question 12: (C)
Stick with the main idea. (C).

Question 13: (D)
This is tough because the answer choices are overly verbose. The question is simple enough: you know THAT Fido is aware of the kitty but not HOW. Does he see it, smell it, feel it or beam it into his mind? Of these unnecessarily complex answers, (D) is best.

Question 14: (A)
Pretty straightforward here, just stick to the main idea. It's all about dog vs. human perception. (A).

Passage: W.E.B. Du Bois and Marcus Garvey
Main idea: Du Bois and Garvey adopted different approaches in their roles as leaders of the Black community, and these differences led to friction between them.

Question 15: (D)
Just looking for the main idea restated here. Don't be tempted by (B), the passage is not about their "charismatic appeal," it's about the difference in their philosophies.

Question 16: (C)
This paragraph is all about racial identity versus national identity. (C) hits that exactly. Look for wrong words in the other answers. (B) "practical demands," (D) "literary and political ambitions," (E) this passage has nothing to do with Germans.

Question 17: (A)
Read the whole bit about line 12 in context. Du Bois could be seen as saying "forget about our repression and help your country win the war!" It's more complicated that that, of course, but some Black Americans could see it that way. (A). Note that (D) is the exact opposite idea.

Question 18: (E)
Basically, American racism is bad, but Nazis are much much worse. (E).

Question 19: (D)
The end of the paragraph says he is most loyal to the "United States of the World." (D) is the closest to that.

Question 20: (B)
The quote from Du Bois is that Garvey thinks having black skin is a "patent to nobility." "Patent" in this sense means "right." That's (B), baby.

Question 21: (C)
Same idea as question 20 so stick with it. (C).

Question 22: (E)
Gotta get specific here. It's clear that Garvey was initially down with Du Bois so (A), (B) and (C) are out. Now we're down to the two positive choices. Did we read that Garvey SPECIFICALLY "admire his writings?" No, so go with the more neutral "appreciate his influence" = (E).

Question 23: (A)
The passage says Du Bois grew to appreciate Africa, but didn't view it as the answer to all racial problems as Garvey seemed to believe. (A).

Question 24: (A)
At first they were hanging out and it was cool. By the end of the passage, they don't like each other very much and Du Bois implies that Garvey will "inflame, lie and steal." Pretty negative. (A) is the only answer that has a clearly negative second word.

Section 3: Math

Question 1: (D)
Convert the fractions to decimals. $1/5 = .20$, and $1/4 = .25$.

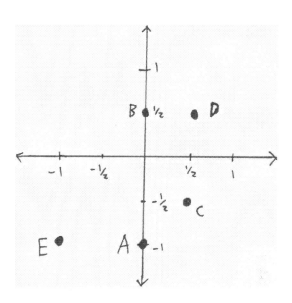

Question 2: (B)
See diagram. Draw it! Answer (B) is 1/2 unit from the origin. Is anything closer than that? (A) and (E) are both at least one unit away. (C) and (D) both involve going a half unit to the right and a half unit up or down. The straight distance to the origin from (C) and (D) can be found by drawing a right triangle, where the hypotenuse is what we want. The hypotenuse is $\sqrt{2}/2$, which equals more than 1/2.

Question 3: (A)
Underneath line AB, there are 5 angles labeled "x" degrees which must add up to 180. $5x = 180$. $x = 36$. On the top side of line AB, two x angles plus a y angle must add up to 180. $2(36) + y = 180$. $72 + y = 180$. $y = 108$.

Question 4: (C)
Distribute: $6565 = 65x + 65$. Subtract 65 from both sides. $6500 = 65x$. $x = 100$.

Question 5: (D)
The SAT loves to test those wacky exponent rules! When you multiply the bases, you add the exponents. So $(m^x)(m^7) = 28$ means that $x + 7 = 28$. $x = 21$. When you raise a power to another power, you multiply them together. So $m^{5y} = m^{15}$. $5y = 15$. $y = 3$. $x + y = 24$.

Question 6: (C)
The TOTAL decrease from 1987 to 1990 was approximately $156,000 - 114,000 = 42,000$. To find the

decrease per year, divide by the number of years (three). 42,000/3 = 14,000.

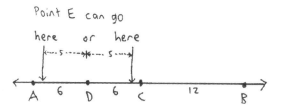

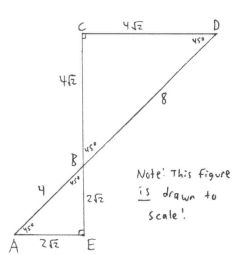

Question 7: (B)
Tough one. Since angle x equals angle y, Triangle ABE is an isosceles 45-45-90 right triangle. Angle y is a vertical angle with angle CBD, so Triangle BCD has a 45 degree angle and a 90 degree angle, and therefore must also be an isosceles right triangle. Too bad the SAT "forgot" to draw the triangles to look isosceles. The hypotenuse of an isosceles right triangle is $\sqrt{2}$ times bigger than the length of the legs. Since AB is 4, BE is $4/\sqrt{2}$, which equals $2\sqrt{2}$. Length BD is 8, so leg CB is $8/\sqrt{2}$, which equals $4\sqrt{2}$. The total distance from C to E is $2\sqrt{2} + 4\sqrt{2} = 6\sqrt{2}$.

Question 8: (A)
Plug in numbers to make things easy! Let's say it costs d = 10 dollars for 8 ounces of coffee beans and each ounce makes c = 2 cups of brewed coffee. Then for $10, you get 16 cups of coffee. Set up a proportion: 10 dollars / 16 cups = x dollars / 1 cup. Cross multiply and solve to find x = 5/8. Now try each answer by plugging in 10 for d and 2 for c. Answer (A) works and gives us the value we want: 5/8.

Question 9: 120
Cross multiply. 120 = ab.

Question 10: 6/25 or .24
The fourth term is (6)(1/5) = 6/5. The fifth term is (6/5)(1/5) = 6/25.

Question 11: 1 or 11
See diagram. Since C is the midpoint of AB, C is 12 units away from A. D is the midpoint of AC, which makes D 6 units away from point A. To get to point E from point D, we need to go 5 units, either left or right. If we go towards A, then AE = 1. Or, if we go 5 units away from A, then AE = 11.

Question 12: 39
We can make our Algebra teachers happy and write an expression for five consecutive integers that add up to 185:
x + (x + 1) + (x + 2) + (x + 3) + (x + 4) = 185.
5x + 10 = 185.
x = 35. But x was the FIRST integer in our list. The GREATEST integer is x + 4, which equals 39.

Question 13: 6500
Out of $2500, $1200 was standard pay, so $1300 was from sales. 20 percent of the dude's sales was $1300, so .20x = 1300, where x was his total sales. x = 6500.

Question 14: 5/18, .277, or .278
Since a circle has 360 degrees, if we divide it into 40 degree wedges, it will produce 360/40 = 9 wedges. Each wedge is 1/9th of the total disk, so the weight of a wedge is 1/9th the total weight. (1/9)(2.5) = 2.5/9 = 5/18.

Question 15: 2
$x^2 - y^2$ is the difference of two squares, and equals (x + y)(x - y). So (x + y)(x - y) = 10. We are told that (x + y) = 5. So (5)(x - y) = 10. (x - y) = 2.

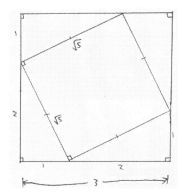

Question 16: 5
See diagram. Since squares have equal sides, the four white triangles in the corners of the big square are all the same size. Each triangle has a leg of length 2 and a leg of length 1. The hypotenuse of each triangle can be found by using $c^2 = a^2 + b^2$. $c^2 = 2^2 + 1^2$. $c = \sqrt{5}$. The triangle's hypotenuse is also the side of the shaded square, so the sides of the shaded square are $\sqrt{5}$, and the area is $(\sqrt{5})^2 = 5$.

Question 17: 11
What this crazy function is saying is that 2 is the remainder when 13 is divided by k. The number 11 goes once into 13 with 2 left over, so k = 11. We can't use a number like 5.5, because when it comes to remainder problems, we're only working with the set of integers.

Question 18: 3/8, .375
The number 86 is a weighted average, which can be calculated by multiplying the various numbers of students by the scores they got, and then dividing by the total number of students (p + n). In math terms:
$(70p + 92n) / (p + n) = 86$
$70p + 92n = 86(p + n)$
$70p + 92n = 86p + 86n$
$6n = 16p$
$p/n = 6/16 = 3/8$

Section 4: Writing

Question 1: (D)
"The problem IS compounded in countries WHERE…" Strip away the fat to see the main pieces of the sentence and the correct answer becomes clear.

Question 2: (C)
A rare instance where "having" is okay. The others use the wrong verb tense or are just plain dumb (B). You should be able to get rid of the incorrect answers here to see that (C) is the only option, even though you are afraid of picking an answer with "having" and you should be!

Question 3: (D)
Simplest and shortest answer wins. Use the process of elimination to get rid of answer choices that are too wordy and confusing and you'll be left with (D).

Question 4: (B)
Look for the parallel structure: "exposing faulty household products" and successfully "demanding their recall" is correct.

Question 5: (B)
Think about this simply: what have feminist critics emphasized? Correct answer = "that every woman reads from her own unique perspective." The other choices have incorrect pronouns ("their") and verb usage ("reading").

Question 6: (B)
Two parts to this one: 1) Subject/Verb agreement = "The spirit…REQUIRES" and 2) Parallel construction = "academic honesty, respectful behavior, and responsible action."

Question 7: (A)
"Finding financial services" is one thing, so "it" is correct.

Question 8: (B)
First get the subject/verb agreement clear here. "Television's programming difficulties THREATEN." Only (B) and (C) work and "acuter" is not necessary so (C) is out.

Question 9: (E)
Parallel construction. "To appeal and persuade" matches with "to educate and inform." That's it!

Question 10: (A)
Paul Robeson has to follow the comma since he is the undergraduate in question. The only possible answers are (A) and (D) and (D) uses the ugly "having led him eventually."

Question 11: (E)
This is a difficult question. The only answer choice that has correct verb tense, subject/verb agreement and pronoun usage is (E). Even though starts with the ugly: "often by questionable means…" Sorry. Very mean question.

Question 12: (C)
Adverb! How did the canoe float? "Serenely."

Question 13: (A)
"She had taken" lets us know that this happened in the

past. So: "would have voted" is correct.

Question 14: (E)
This is okay. Really, it is. Something has to be 100% grammatically incorrect to be wrong.

Question 15: (D)
Another adverb. "Calmly." The additional adverb "competently" is a nice clue here.

Question 16: (C)
"In the early days?" You mean way back when? Oh, so engineers would sometimes THROW.

Question 17: (A)
Workers are people, not things (even in the eyes of store managers). So which = who.

Question 18: (B)
"More" is about quantity, as in: he has MORE soda than Mike does. You can't prefer something more than something else, but you can prefer is OVER or prefer it TO something else.

Question 19: (D)
"Your" = bad. "To improve one's standing of living" = correct.

Question 20: (C)
"The use" is one thing, so it HAS increased.

Question 21: (C)
"Would be" is conditional, but this delay is going to happen and it's going to happen now. It "will be" delayed. That's really too bad because a new library complex sounds exciting (and a good use of public funds).

Question 22: (E)
This one is fine, isn't it? Yes. A better question = will the workers really feel uncomfortable if they acquire their demanded independence? They'll probably love it.

Question 23: (C)
One can jump over a fence, but one cannot protest over a party's failure. "Vehemently protested" is the way to do it.

Question 24: (A)
Take out the older sister and which sounds better: "the friendly competition between me" or "the friendly competition between I?" Okay, they both sound dumb, but "I" sounds dumber. Keep this in mind: after the word "between", you'll ALWAYS say "me" and never say "I".

Question 25: (A)

All people are going to be one model? Nope. "People who wish to be models."

Question 26: (D)
What is "it" referring to? Relive the moment, yes, but that's not a specific "it." So: "the hero…would choose to do so" is correct.

Question 27: (A)
"The professor's insistence" is one thing. It "IS" not part of the plan.

Question 28: (E)
This one is fine fine fine.

Question 29: (D)
Oooh tricky. The professor is making a choice between two things, right? Not BETWEEN one thing OR another thing, BETWEEN one thing AND another thing. Mean one. Good idiom to memorize.

Passage Revision: Mom's interest in historical maladies

Question 30: (D)
"Them" is unclear in context. Specifying that we're talking about "her theories" is a good call.

Question 31: (D)
Technically, none of these should be added to sentence 7 because they are all kind of stupid, but if you HAVE to insert something go with (D). The process of elimination helps again here (as it always does). (A), (B) & (E) all connect this sentence to the previous one incorrectly or confusingly. And "you should" (C) is not good because "you" is not good for an essay. "I" (D) is okay because the essay is from the first person perspective.

Question 32: (C)
(C) fixes this the best. Remember how much they love to start sentences with "Because," and again, get rid of the wrong ones. (D) contains "you," (B) and (E) are too wordy, and (A) needs a connecting word somewhere around that comma.

Question 33: (B)
"In context" is clutch here. Sentence 8 talks about how the writer has become an authority among his peers because of his mom's unusual interest. Sentence 9 & 10 offer an example of that. So (B) is nice.

Question 34: (A)
HA! (B) is funny. (A) keeps the flow going and brings it back to what the essay is about: his mom and her thing for the psychology of famous dead people.

Question 35: (D)
After Sentence 7 is the best place to do this because the focus of the passage changes from background about the writer's mom and her weird fetish to the writer and how he brought the fetish to school. Kinda creepy.

Section 5: Critical Reading

Question 1: (B)
"Warped mirror" is the key here. So the language is used to "distort" (B).

Question 2: (D)
This about how these three different cultures ABSORBED one another's customs. (D).

Question 3: (E)
This is about the idea that Anna's impact arose over time, not all at once. "Cumulative" is the right idea: (E).

Question 4: (B)
The key here is that Francis does the opposite of "openly defying adversaries." Avoiding "conflict" is a good way of doing that. (B).

Question 5: (E)
This is interesting, isn't it? If sleep is signaled for several minutes before it actually happens, that means it ACTUALLY occurs "instantaneously." Surprising? Yes. Correct? Also yes. (E).

Question 6: (B)
Okay, a little harder now. If Ellen campaigned for practices that came to be known as ecology, she is most likely positively related to environmental preservation. Both words in (B) point to this and that's the right answer.

Question 7: (A)
The vocab is what's tricky here because the sentence gives us the definition: "to complete quickly." In fact, in RECORD TIME. Guess what? That's what "alacrity" means: "promptness or speedy readiness." (A).

Question 8: (A)
This is a difficult question. The key word here is "yet." It celebrates YET criticizes or doesn't celebrate. "Censures," (A), is correct. In congress, when someone is "censured," they get a slap on the wrist that means you did something wrong and we are not celebrating you.

Question 9: (D)
Well, sounds like Stephens succeeded as a professional artist, despite the social restrictions of her time. (D)

is correct. The only word that justifies the part about "maintain social respectability" is "improper." Tough one. Don't be tempted by the other choices that might sound like they're headed in the right direction. (A), for example, might seem right but "exclusively" makes it too extreme and wrong.

Question 10: (C)
She's practical and she makes it happen. (C). (B) "Perfectionist" and (D) "Dreamer" are examples of choices that are too strong. The passage suggests might possess some of these qualities, but nothing that intense.

Question 11: (B)
The middle part of the passage contains the answer. It says the Native Americans altered their practices and began competing with one another. Sounds like "distorted relationships," right? (B).

Question 12: (C)
The key word is "strangeness."(C), "exotic," is correct.

Passage: J. Paul Getty's museum
Main idea, Passage 1: The museum is ugly, in bad taste and horribly designed.
Main idea, Passage 2: First person account from Getty himself denouncing the critics and defending the museum's design.

Question 13: (B)
Definitely has a negative connotation in the context of the first paragraph, which says the museum is in "aggressive bad taste." The only truly negative and appropriate answer is (B).

Question 14: (D)
DESIGN is the main beef the critics have. Knowing the word "garish" is also important here: "crudely showy and excessively ornate or elaborate." (D) is great.

Question 15: (A)
This is a tricky one because the lines referenced seem straightforward enough, but the answer choices are odd. Make sure you specifically pinpoint the main point of the section in question. In this case, the main point comes at the very end: "the details… have been combined and executed in a manner that… creates an incongruous appearance." So even though it sounds weird, (A) is the right answer.

Question 16: (E)
It's all about the FLOOR PLAN and it's laid out specifically in the passage. Can you dig it? (E).

Question 17: (C)
Remember, it's always a good idea to get rid of the

wrong answers to get to the right one. In this case, most of the answer choices are clearly off track and unrelated to the bulk of the passage. The second paragraph talks about how the building is a re-creation of the Villa dei Papyri and the third paragraph says the details are all based on "known Roman examples." So (C) is looking pretty great.

Question 18: (C)
They "beamed" because they were happy. The question is WHY? (D) and (E) both reference the financial aspect of the situation, but their agreement is more focused on Getty's artistic idea for the building. Or, his "preferences." (C) is right!

Question 19: (A)
What aspect of the museum is most often discussed in there passages? The design. The design. The design. And in context, this line is also talking about the design. (A).

Question 20: (A)
Oooh. Another question about the design! And boy, isn't Getty proud of his brave design choices in the face of criticism? He's a cocky dude, it seems, and very proud of his "courageous defiance."

Question 21: (D)
P2 makes it clear that Getty knew a lot of critics wouldn't like his ideas and he went ahead with them anyway because he believed in their merit. (D) is correct. (B) might be tempting, but he never felt his "intentions" had been "misunderstood – he knew they understood and didn't like them anyway.

Question 22: (C)
P1 focuses a lot on how the building was modeled on an ancient building and is not a faithful representation. Getty doesn't even mention that aspect of the design. (C).

Question 23: (D)
Again, only a few of these answers actually address the main point of the passages which is what again? Oh yeah, the design. Which idea is shared? That the building should itself be carefully and artistically designed is assumed in both passages. Choose (D) and you shall be FREE!

Question 24: (E)
This answer is in the last sentence of Passage 2. "The very shrillness of their cries and howls very quickly exhausts their wind." In other words, his building will remain standing long after their criticism is forgotten. (E).

Section 7: Math

Question 1: (B)
Wow, the SAT makers are actually aware of fun things, like games?! The value of the letters in "exquisite", in order, is "155111111". The total is 17.

Question 2: (B)
$2x = 30$. $x = 15$. $x - 5 = 10$.

Question 3: (E)
Answer (E) always works because an odd times an odd (5) is still an odd, but then add 1 and you have an even! For example, if $t = 7$, then $5t + 1 = 36$.

Question 4: (C)
The perimeter of DEF is $4 + 8 + 9 = 21$, which is also ABC's perimeter. ABC's three equal sides much each be $21/3 = 7$ units long.

Question 5: (E)
The Other Brands category had 900 pairs of jeans and was 20% of the total sales. If the total sales were x, then $.20x = 900$. $x = 4500$. Over. Done. Next.

Question 6: (C)
We have to convert feet to yards before we multiply! 12 feet = 4 yards. 18 feet = 6 yards. So the area that needs to be carpeted is 4 yards x 6 yards = 24 square yards.

Question 7: (D)
This wins the prize for Weirdest Word Problem Ever Written. Who has EVER found themselves in this situation?! Please email us if you have.
Anyhoo, the kitten and bunny weigh 7 pounds. If you keep the kitten on the scale and swap the bunny for the puppy, the weight becomes 8 pounds, so the puppy must be 1 pound heavier than the bunny. We can call the bunny's weight b and the puppy's weight b + 1. Together, those two weigh 9 pounds, so $b + b + 1 = 9$. $b = 4$. The puppy's weight must be 5.

Question 8: (B)
Set up a proportion! .25 inches / 16 feet = x / 40 feet. Cross multiply: $10 = 16x$. $x = 5/8$ of an inch.

Question 9: (A)
The point must be on both graphs, so plug the coordinates (p, 0) into either of the equations for x and y. For example, $0 = -p^2 + 9$. $p^2 = 9$. $p = +3$ or -3. The answer they're looking for is positive 3.

Question 10: (B)
The shortcut way to do this one is to calculate that after 1 hour, the machines together will have made 750

bolts, and after 2 hours, they'll have made 1500 bolts. They'll have made 900 bolts sometime between 1 and 2 hours. Out of the answer choices, the only one that is even in that range is 72 minutes.
The more "formal" way to do it is to call "t" the time needed to make 900 bolts. Then $300t + 450t = 900$. $750t = 900$. $t = 900/750 = 6/5$ of an HOUR, which in minutes is $(6/5)(60) = 72$.

Question 11: (E)
The table tells us that when $t = 0$, $g(t) = 2$. If you plug those values into the answers, they only work in answers (D) and (E). Now we can plug in 1 for t in answers (D) and (E), and the correct choice should give us a value for $g(t)$ that equals 0. (E) works.

Question 12: (C)
This question is a little annoying. You have to check each answer carefully. (C) works because three 12th graders travel 6 or more miles, but only two 11th graders do.

Question 13: (A)
All of the possible answers take the form 3 _ 4. The blank in the middle could hold any digit from 0 through 9 (304, 314, 324, etc.), which means there are 10 distinct options.

Question 14: (D)
Oh, $y = mx + b$, will you ever leave us alone? In the graph they give us of $y = mx + b$, the y-intercept (b) is -1. The slope (m) is rise/run = -1/3. So, to find the graph of $y = -3mx + b$, we can plug in our m and b. $y = (-3)(-1/3)x + (-1)$, which simplifies to $y = x - 1$. The correct answer should still have a y-intercept of -1, but a slope of positive 1. That is true of (D).

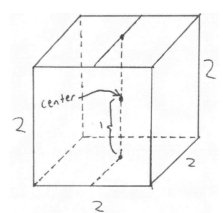

Question 15: (A)
See diagram. If the volume of a cube is 8, then each side is 2 ($V = s^3$). The height of the cube is 2. The center must be halfway in between the top and bottom, so it must be 1 unit from the bottom.

Question 16: (E)
Plug in (2x) for x and (2z) for z.
$5(2x)^3/2z = 5(8x^3)/2z = 40x^3/2z = 20x^3/z$. The new answer of $20x^3/z$ is four times bigger than the original value of $5x^3/z$. You could also pick a set of values for x and z, let that determine y, then try it again with twice the x and twice the z values.

Question 17: (B)
We don't really need to evaluate the function they give us using exponents and logs and all that stuff. Reducing a price by 20% is the same thing as multiplying it by 4/5 (because 80% of the price remains, and 80% = 80/100 = 4/5). So we can just use that fact to adjust the car's value. After 1 year, the car's value is 5000(4/5) = 4000. After another year, the value is 4000(4/5) = 3200.

Question 18: (D)
Here is the order of the braids after each step:
Start: ABC
Step 1: BAC
Step 2: BCA
Step 3: CBA
Step 4: CAB
Step 5: ACB
Step 6: ABC

Question 19: (E)
The problem mentions a set of 11 numbers, but the same principles about the median apply to smaller sets as well. To make things easier, let's say we have a set of just five numbers: 2, 4, 6, 8, 10. Our median (middle number) is 6. Let's try OUR set with each answer choice:
(A) Doubling each number gives 4, 8, 12, 16, 20. The median has changed to 12.
(B) 12, 14, 16, 18, 20. The median has changed to 16.
(C) Increasing the smallest number COULD change the median. If we change 2 to 9, then we have to rearrange the order and the new set is 4, 6, 8, 9, 10. The new median is 8.
(D) Same idea as (C). If we change 10 to 1, our set is 1, 2, 4, 6, 8. Our median has changed to 4.
(E) 2, 4, 6, 8, 15. Aha! Our median is still 6! Making the largest number even bigger will not affect the order of the rest of the list, so it can't affect the median.

Question 20: (B)
This problem is really, really tough. It might be the hardest problem in the book. To find the perimeter of the shaded region, we need to add up 4 lengths: SA, AC, CT, and arc SBT. Arc SBT is one quarter of the circumference of a circle with radius 6. The full circumference would be 12π, so arc SBT is 3π. Next,

we can find AC by using the fact that the diagonals in rectangles are the same length, so AC = BR. BR is also a radius of the circle, meaning that BR = 6, so AC = 6. Lastly, we can find SA and CT at the same time. The total distance going from point S straight down to R and then across from R to T equals 12 (two radii, 6 plus 6). That distance from S to R to T can also be broken down into four line segments: SA + AR + RC + CT = 12. Because we're told that the length plus width of the rectangle is 8, that means AR + RC = 8. SA + 8 + CT = 12. SA + CT = 4. The perimeter of our shaded region is $3\pi + 6 + 4 = 10 + 3\pi$. Ay carumba!

Section 8: Critical Reading

Question 1: (B)
They liked Harlem, but they weren't FROM Harlem. Three of the answer choices are negative and only one works: (B).

Question 2: (A)
Contact lenses fix vision, right? "Corrected," (A), is correct.

Question 3: (C)
This one hinges on knowing that "raze" means to tear down a building. If Roberta likes to rehabilitate older buildings, why would she tear them down? (C), baby, see?

Question 4: (C)
The auditors neither spoke nor smiled. Sounds like they were pretty cold. Not very warm. Get it? (C), "glacial," is correct. Even if you don't see this, the other answer choices don't work with the key idea that they were mean so they must be eliminated. "Nondescript" means "unremarkable," not "cold."

Question 5: (D)
Straight-up vocab question. What means flexibility and grace? If you chose (D), you are correct!
Tremulous = shaking, trembling or quavering
Fickle = Likely to change

Question 6: (A)
Might be tough to get the content right here. The museum was on the verge of financial collapse and it got a much needed INFUSION of cash. This is the only word that works here. (A) is correct. Reprieve = to halt or delay somebody's punishment. (C) might be tempting because "advance" seems to work, but "rebate" does not. Rebate = money that is paid back.

Passage: Imagining Grandma (or Susan Ward in winter)

Main idea: The author imagines his grandmother's life via her letters and reflects on how the sense of "home" has changed over time.

Question 7: (B)
She's far from home as this passage gets started so "parental burrow" must mean the comfort and safely of home. "Burrow" means "a snug place." Nice? (B).

Question 8: (C)
She doesn't need a time machine because she's living a version of it! Her life is just like theirs in so many ways. It resembles theirs. (C) is right.

Question 9: (D)
Same idea as question 8 = she's living like her grandparents lived, seeing what they probably saw. (D) says this exactly.

Question 10: (C)
You know the phrase to be "bogged down?" It means slowed down. The town of Milton is dim and gentle. The pace of life, that's what we're getting at here. "Deliberate" has about 12 meanings, one of which is "slow." (C).

Question 11: (E)
You have to read beyond line 11 to get this one right. Always read in context, a sentence or two before and after. Right after talking about the San Francisco ladies, she talks about her husband's job security and that "the comfortable past asserted itself unchanged." (E) does it right.

Question 12: (D)
This is tricky. "Sunk" sounds bad, but everything else in the passage at this point is positive. She likes her life and her mellow new existence. (A), (B) and (C) are all negative and there's nothing about letting down her defenses so (E) is out. (D) sounds too general to be correct, but it is.

Question 13: (D)
The key is in the sentence before the line in question: "we have lived to shallowly in too many places." The paragraph starts off with wondering whether Americans can ever again have that experience of returning to a home to intimately known. All signs point to (D).

Question 14: (D)
The narrator implies that frontier historians have theories about the type of people who immigrated to the West that do not apply to his grammy. Pretty mellow here, just "introducing a viewpoint" that he does agree with. (D).

Question 15: (A)
They key here is the line "the West was not a new country being created, but an old one being REPRODUCED." Bingo = (A).

Question 16: (B)
The important piece here is that they carry little baggage of the "cultural kind." So (B) is the winner with "values of the past."

Question 17: (E)
What is all this weird space imagery all of a sudden? That's exactly the point (kind of dumb, yes). Modern generations are in a brave new foreign world that makes little sense and is disconnected from anything previously known. (E) is the best answer for this.

Question 18: (D)
The whole last part of the passage focuses on "new pioneers," the modern generation and its lack of an attachment to home. Don't be tempted by (A). There's nothing that says they "long to achieve their own sense of place," just that they are unable to experience a true sense of home. It's (D).

Question 19: (C)
Here it is, a HARD question. When you have no idea, the best strategy is to get rid of answers that aren't right. Step by step, one at a time. They recognize change, but they don't resent it = (A) is out. We don't know where the narrator has lived and Susan lived in two places, not "many parts of the country" so (B) is out. (D) and (E) are untrue. So it's (C)! Don't believe that this is true? Go back and read the italics and lines 8-9. Isn't that CUTE! They are both writing about grandparents. That's so CUTE. Go get a snack. You are done, forever, thinking about Susan Ward.

Section 9: Math

Question 1: (A)
$3(4) - 1 = 12 - 1 = 11$

Question 2: (D)
Any number multiplied times one results in the original number.

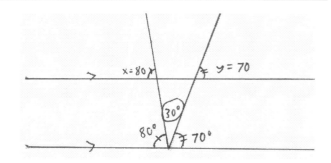

Question 3: (A)
See diagram. The angle directly to the left of z corresponds to x, so that angle is 80. The angle to the right of z corresponds to y, so it equals 70. These three angles, 80, z, and 70, form a straight line, so $80 + z + 70 = 180$. $z = 30$,

Question 4: (C)
If the direct route has length x, then the scenic route is $x + 5$. $(x + 5) + x = 35$. $x = 15$.

Question 5: (B)
Who in the world says that traffic lights are amber?! Us normal people call it "yellow". We need to add up the times the light is not red and divide by the total. $(40 + 10) / 80 = 5/8$.

Question 6: (B)
Since things are directly proportional, we can set the problem up like this:
24 dollars / 20 degrees = x dollars / 15 degrees.
$360 = 20x$. $x = 18$.

Question 7: (E)
To average them, first we have to figure out what all the angles add up to. $u + v + w = 180$, and $x + y = 90$. Our total for the five angles is 270. $270/5 = 54$.

Question 8: (C)
x can't be negative or else x^2 would be positive and would be to the right of x. The correct answer must be a positive fraction between 0 and 1, because those fractions get smaller in value when they are raised to a higher power.

Question 9: (A)
The slope of this line (rise/run) = 3/1. The equation of the line is simply $y = 3x$ (note: the y-intercept is zero). We can plug in the coordinates h and k into the equation: $k = 3h$. Now, if we pick a value for h, like -2, we can find the corresponding value for k. $k = 3(-2) = -6$. We are looking for $k/h = -6/-2 = 3$.

Question 10: (E)
To get rid of absolute value signs, add a plus or minus

sign to the other side of the equation and solve both versions. m – 3 = 5 or m – 3 = -5. m = 8 or -2. We want the negative value, m = -2. k + 7 = 15 or k + 7 = -15. k = 8 or k = -22. Again, we want the negative answer, k = -22. Finally, we carefully evaluate m – k = (-2) – (-22) = -2 + 22 = 20. Ugh!.

Question 11: (C)
Each time the rating increases by 5, the flow speed is cut in half. Starting from 5w, we go to 10w, 15w, then 20w, increasing by five 3 times. So the flow speed is cut in half three times. 1/2 x 1/2 x 1/2 = 1/8. 5w is 8 times faster than 20w.

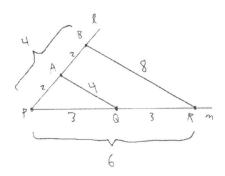

Question 12: (E)
See diagram. Triangle PAQ and Triangle PBR are similar triangles, so the sides are proportional.
PA / PB = AQ / BR.
2 / 4 = 4 / BR
BR = 8.
The perimeter of QABR = 4 + 2 + 8 + 3 = 17.

Question 13: (D)
g(5) = 5^2 + 5 = 30.
h(4) = 4^2 – 4 = 12.
30 – 12 = 18.

Question 14: (A)
Plug (m + 1) into the function and evaluate.
h(m + 1) = $(m + 1)^2$ – (m + 1)
= $(m^2 + 2m + 1)$ – (m + 1)
= m^2 + 2m + 1 – m – 1
= m^2 + m
The result, m^2 + m, looks similar to the definition of function g. A little trial and error with the answers verifies that it's equal to g(m).
Even easier than that is to pick a number for m and plug it in. Get a value, then compare it to what you get from the answer choices.

Question 15: (B)
The $28 price is a 40 percent markup from the store's cost; in other words, it's 140 percent of the cost. 28 = 1.40c, where c is the store's cost. c = 20. Now, em-

ployees get 30 percent off. .30(20) = 6. 6 dollars is the amount the employees save, so they pay 20 – 6 = 14.

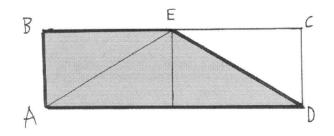

Question 16: (C)
See diagram. Let's draw a picture! Since E is a midpoint, if a line is drawn straight across the rectangle from E, it will divide the rectangle in half. Next, drawing lines from E to A and from E to D will divide each half in half again. The rectangle has been divided into four equal quarters, and the quadrilateral we are looking for, ABED, is exactly three quarters of the rectangle's area. Since ABED's area is 2/3, we can write 2/3 = (3/4)X, where X is the rectangle's area. Multiply both sides by 4/3 to solve for X. X = 8/9.

Section 10: Writing

Question 1: (B)
Good ol' parallel construction. "Has been driven" = "has taken refuge."

Question 2: (D)
First off, notice the modifying clause at the front of the sentence. "Computers" must come immediately after that. Most of these answer choices use "computers" and "they" (redundant) or just "they" (what?) – (D) is specific and clear and efficient and good and CORRECT!

Question 3: (B)
It's short, it's concise and all the other one's are clearly wrong. Get rid of what's wrong and you will find what's right = (B).

Question 4: (E)
First of all, parallel construction with "finding political support" and "designing a campaign" is necessary. Secondly, three things are listed so all of these things ARE faced by candidates.

Question 5: (A)
It's important to include "only" because it's amazing that this tiny animal is a relative of such huge animals. "Although" is the best way to write this ("whereas" stinks). Side note = don't be swayed by the answers

that contain the word "size." It's redundant and the sentences are bad.

Question 6: (C)
Three bad sentences with "beings" and "havings." Of the two remaining, "but" is a better word than "and" because of the content of the sentence. It's sad (BUT true) that many actors audition for a role BUT only a few are selected.

Question 7: (E)
Since "combining" is not underlined, we know this sentence is going to be in the present tense. Also, starting with "the author" is best since the author (not the reader) is the main focus of the action. Starting with the reader puts the sentence in the passive voice and the passive voice is BAD.

Question 8: (D)
"Adopted by" is the correct phrase. You wouldn't write: "many orphans have been adopted through Madonna." Or, "many foreign children have been adopted in Brad Pitt." Then it's about verb form and "to honor" is much better than "in honoring."

Question 9: (B)
The "it" (referring to the income gap) is nice and needed. "And" is also needed after the comma to connect the two parts of the sentence. (B)!

Question 10: (D)
Oh man, this one is all over the map. Okay, pick the sentence apart. What is the main subject of the sentence? Something is being hotly debated, right? Is it the Basque language itself? No, it's the ORIGINS of the Basque language. Only (D) makes the origins the focus of the sentence. Also, take out the side track about it being Europe's oldest language, and that answer choice reads: "The origins of the Basque language…are hotly debated." Perfect!

Question 11: (A)
Well, since we're talking about the workers, it's best to follow the comma with what we're specifically talking ABOUT: "their productivity." That brings us to (A) and (E). And only (A) properly gets the point across that it's not surprising that their productivity was very low. (E) seems to say that the productivity ITSELF was not surprising. It might seem like a slight distinction and it is, but it makes all the difference.

Question 12: (E)
This is an example of a hard question. Welcome! When there's so much information to get across, semicolons tend to get the job done better than commas. Also, it's necessary to specify "these changes" in the second part

of the sentence – "they" is unclear. So you probably get down to (D) and (E) and might choose (D) because (E) seems too wordy and "of the college" seems redundant. But both pieces of a sentence separated by a semicolon need to be complete sentences and we don't know what "its" is referring to in (D). Ugh. Yeah, it's (E). Thank you for participating this hard question.

Question 13: (A)
Kindly, they followed a hard one with a relatively straightforward one to give your brain a break. Wordy words like "nevertheless," "notwithstanding" and "being" get rid of three and (D) uses the incorrect "had been." Whew.

Question 14: (C)
OH NO! Another hard question -- very similar to question #12, actually. So much going on here, it's a good bet that a semicolon will hold it all together better than a comma and it surely does. Between the two semicolon answers, (C) is the better choice because (D) does not have an independent clause after the semicolon.

Test 9

Section 2: Math

Question 1: (A)
The numbers 32 and 33 are in both sets.

Question 2: (C)
Linda traveled twice as far (20 miles) in half the time (one hour). So her rate in miles per hour is 20 miles / 1 hour = 20.

Question 3: (C)
Distribute to get: $x = k^2 - 2k$. Now we want $x + 1$, so add 1 to both sides. $x + 1 = k^2 - 2k + 1$.

Question 4: (B)
They give the equation $y = ax + b$ just to be difficult; there's no reason why we can't just call it $y = mx + b$, which we're more familiar with. So let's rename variable "a" as "m" for this problem. And m is the slope. In the original figure, the y-intercept is 1, which means b is 1. Now we're looking for the graph of $y = 2mx + b$. b hasn't changed, so the correct answer must still have a y-intercept of 1. The slope has been multiplied by 2, which means it will be steeper than the original. Answer (B) still has a y-intercept of 1 and has a steeper slope.

Question 5: (A)
Since this is an isosceles right triangle, we know that the hypotenuse is $\sqrt{2}$ times the side length. This hypotenuse is therefore $x\sqrt{2}$. The perimeter of the triangle in terms of x is $x + x + x\sqrt{2}$, which simplifies to $2x + x\sqrt{2}$. This must equal the perimeter they provided. $2x + x\sqrt{2} = 4 + 2\sqrt{2}$. We can solve the equation for x or plug in the answers and check them; either way, it turns out x = 2.

Question 6: (C)
The median is the middle number of the whole list. Once Sam's score is added to the list, there are 17 scores:
60, 70, 70, 75, 75, 80, 80, 80, 85, 90, 90, 90, 90, 95, 95, 95, 100.
Out of 17 terms, the middle term will be the ninth (because there are 8 before and 8 after). The middle term in the list above is 85.

Question 7: (D)
Oh Ahmad – that guy sure loves his containers! Let's plug in and say that the total capacity x = 160. Then if he has 16 containers with a capacity of 160, they each hold 10 gallons. The other group of 8 containers also has a total capacity of 160, so the capacity of each of those is 160/8 = 20 gallons. Those turn out to be the larger containers, and they are found by dividing x by 8.

Question 8: (D)
It's not necessary to try to draw this rectangle and calculate its various slopes. The secret is that we know from Geometry that the sides of a rectangle are perpendicular to each other. And two perpendicular lines have slopes that are negative reciprocals of each other. For example, if one side has slope 2, then a side perpendicular to it has slope -1/2. A rectangle has 2 pairs of parallel sides, so in this instance, it would have 2 sides with slope 2 and 2 sides with slope -1/2. The product of all four of those slopes multiplied together is 1.

Question 9: 2/3 or .666 or .667
40 minutes out of 60 minutes were not commercials, which reduces to 2/3.

Question 10: 10/3 or 3.33
What this word problem means in math terms is $0.3x = 1$. Solve by dividing by 0.3. $x = 1 / 0.3$, which simplifies to 10/3 or .333.

Question 11: 875
We need to plug the numbers they gave us into the function: $(10 ^ 3) – (5 ^ 3)$, which simplifies to $1000 – 125 = 875$.

Question 12: 2 or 3
This is a little bit of a mind bender. The formula for the total area of rectangle PQST is our old friend base times height. The base in this situation is 5 plus some integer (the length of UT). However, because URST is a square, the height must also be equal to the length of UT. So 5 plus some number, times that same number must equal a total between 10 and 30. $(5 + x)(x)$ is a way to look at it algebraically. If we start plugging in small positive integers for x, it turns out that 2 and 3 are the only options that work. $(5 + 2)(2) = 14$, and $(5 + 3)(3) = 24$.

Question 13: 36
It's easiest to convert the fractions into sixths. 1/3 of the balloons are red, which means 2/6 are red. Half that many are green, which means 1/6 are green. So the red plus green balloons account for 3/6 of the total, leaving another 3/6 (a.k.a. 1/2) that must be blue. Since 18 balloons are blue, and the blue are half of the total, the total balloons are 36.

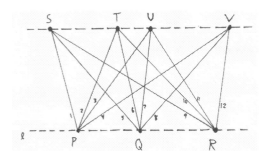

Question 14: 12
See diagram. Let's look at point P. It doesn't count to connect P to point Q or R, because all three points are on the same line, so it's impossible to draw a line that contains only 2 of them. We can only connect P to points on the other line. From point P, you can draw four separate lines: from P to S, from P to T, from P to U and from P to V. Each of the three points on line L (points P, Q, and R) can be connected to each of the four points on the other line, so the total possibilities is $3 \times 4 = 12$.

Question 15: 5
We are adding up $2 \wedge x$ four times, so we can rewrite the equation as $4(2 \wedge x) = 2 \wedge 7$. We can also rewrite the number 4 as $2 \wedge 2$ to get everything to have a base of 2. Now we have $(2 \wedge 2)(2 \wedge x) = 2 \wedge 7$. When we multiply the same base, we add the exponent, so $2 \wedge (2 + x) = 2 \wedge 7$. Now we can ignore the bases and just set the exponents equal to each other. $2 + x = 7$. $x = 5$.

Question 16: 71
This is an interesting question. We have five integers whose average is 15. We don't know any of the numbers, but we can write an equation for the average: SUM / 5 = 15, where "SUM" is the sum of the unknown integers. If we multiply both sides by 5, then the sum of the integers = 75. The way to make one integer as big as possible is to make the other four as small as possible. Since they have to be positive integers, the smallest value for four of the integers is to make each one "1." (There's nothing saying they can't repeat). If four have the value of 1, then the last integer would have the value of 71 to make them all add up to 75.

Question 17: 10/7 or 1.42 or 1.43
Of Alice's 17 steps, the first 10 just get her back to where she started, so the last 7 steps are when Alice covered the ground Corinne covered in 10 steps. If a is the length of each of Alice's steps and c is the length of each of Corinne's, then $7a = 10c$. We solve that equation for a, which equals $10/7c$.

Question 18: 3
If we plug in (2m) for x in $x^2 + 18$, then $f(2m) = (2m)^2$

+ 18. The other side of the equation is $2f(m)$, which means $2(m^2 + 18)$. Set those equal to each other and simplify:
$(2m)^2 + 18 = 2(m^2 + 18)$
$4m^2 + 18 = 2m^2 + 36$
$2m^2 + 18 = 36$
$2m^2 = 18$
$m^2 = 9$
$m = 3$ (the problem only wants the positive answer).

Section 3: Writing

Question 1: (B)
Who worked as a nurse in the streets of Calcutta? Mother Teresa. Introductory phrases must be followed by the subjects to which they refer.

Question 2: (B)
First words get it down to (A) and (B). "To hold" is shorter and cleaner than "and they would hold."

Question 3: (D)
"Using" vs. "used"? Used. "To survey" vs. "surveying"? To survey. Remember that "ing" verbs are usually weaker than more active verbs.

Question 4: (D)
"Were" vs. "was"? ONE of the most popular foods "was." "Something" is also singular, so (D)'s repetition of "was" is correct.

Question 5: (E)
The strongest way to begin this phrase is with "they," which leaves us with (A), (C), and (E). (C) is out because of "having." In the battle of (A) vs. (E), (E) is more concise.

Question 6: (E)
This one is about correctly making comparisons. If we are comparing like to like, we must repeat the word "audiences" to make that comparison clear. (E) beats (D) because the verb "did" is stronger than the more passive "with."

Question 7: (A)
Comparisons again! You can't compare "the inspiration" to "Frank Lloyd Wright," "Wright's architecture" to "architects," "American architects" to "Wright's designs," or "Wright's inspirations" to "architects." Only (A) correctly compares "American architects," who are people, to "Frank Lloyd Wright," who is also a person.

Question 8: (D)
This one is tricky because the answer choices all seem so similar, but the question is one of parallel structure.

Always err on the side of over-matching. In this case, that leaves you with (A) and (D), and the question becomes whether you need the repetition of "in." Because of "in poetry" in the beginning of the sentence, you do.

Question 9: (B)
Memorize this: "because they love because"! When you see a sentence that begins with "because," a warm, comforting feeling should wash over your mind. Why? Because the makers of the SAT are testing to see if you know that, despite the fact that English teachers say that you can never ever ever begin a sentence with "because," this is only technically true if that sentence is a fragment. This leaves you with (A) and (B), and "is the reason why" in (A) is redundant.

Question 10: (A)
WTF?! This sentence is confusing in so many ways. Eliminate the really ugly (i.e. wordy) choices first: (C) and (E). Then concentrate on the meaning of the words that come after "earlier" in the remaining choices. (A)'s "even though" sets up the opposite better than either "but" or "without."

Question 11: (E)
Concentrate on the comma just before the underlined portion. You can't change the comma, so check to see if the clause in the answer choice works grammatically with that punctuation. (A), (C) and (D) don't. Even though people think "and so no more than a few" is a bit odd, (B)'s ending the sentence with "because of that" is worse.

Question 12: (C)
"Wrote." Not "had wrote."

Question 13: (C)
"More busier" is redundant, like saying "more better." You can either change it to "busier" or "more busy."

Question 14: (B)
There "are" two German shepherds.

Question 15: (B)
Memorize this! People = who/whom, places = where/ in which, things = that/ which. Students are people "who" smell chocolate.

Question 16: (E)
No problems here.

Question 17: (E)
Two E's in a row? It happens.

Question 18: (B)
Singular/Plural: There "are" no more than two species.

Question 19: (B)
Singular/Plural: (B) should refer to the "signs" plural. Drivers can react to "these" signs.

Question 20: (A)
Verb tense: "has to imitate," not "is having to imitate."

Question 21: (B)
A lot of people choose (A) because they just don't like the way it sounds, but there are bigger fish to fry here. If you "cut out the fat" and eliminate the comma-to-comma splice "and the United Nations itself," you will see that nations "have" issued, not nations "has" issued. Nations are plural.

Question 22: (C)
Parallel structure is especially crucial when the sentence contains a list. Here, we need to match the past tense verbs in the first two listed items. The programs "familiarized" young people, "taught" them traditions, and "gave" them the opportunity.

Question 23: (A)
Singular/Plural. Cut out the prepositional phrase "of diverse animal species" and you will see that observation "shows," not observation "show."

Question 24: (A)
Idiom: "Far away" means physical distance, as in, "Thank God that tsunami is far away." Here we are talking about non-physical distance, so the phrase should just be "far from."

Question 25: (B)
"Has," "have," and "had" are time traveling words when attached to verbs, meaning that they indicate that something has or had happened not just once, but over a period of time. "For the past hundred years or more" tells us that this is the case in this sentence; therefore, (B) should be changed to "has been."

Question 26: (C)
Idiom: inconsistent "with."

Question 27: (D)
Comparing two things vs. more than two! When you are comparing only two things, you may not use the superlative, or "est" form. Everything must be bett-ER, ugli-ER, etc. Therefore, Bovary has "more" spirit and determination.

Question 28: (A)
"Between" always goes with "me." Learn it. Know it. Love it.

her time'?"

Question 29: (E)
The tempting wrong answer here is probably (D) "had long been," because that phrase sounds odd. However, odd is not the same as wrong. Just because something is weird doesn't make it wrong, especially on a hard question!

Passage Revision: Lou Hoover

Question 30: (A)
Without a strong verb like "attended," some of these answer choices, like (B) and (C), turn the sentence into a fragment. (E) is wrong because that comma would need to be a semi-colon, and (D)'s "having" is weak.

Question 31: (D)
We need to link the ideas in these two sentences in a way that reflects the meaning of the original sentence while remaining grammatically concise. (D) does both of these things.

Question 32: (D)
They are asking you specifically about linking ideas here, so focus on the specific meaning of the first phrase in each answer choice. (A) is out because she didn't do anything "because" she learned things as a child, (B) loses because "since her time in China" introduces unrelated information, and (E) can be eliminated because the word "nevertheless" indicates an opposite. When judging between (C) and (D) ask yourself, "is this part of the essay more about doing things 'by this time' or doing things in addition to, or 'in the midst of' doing a lot of other things?"

Question 33: (A)
Remember how we hate "being"? Any opportunity to change "being" to something else should be embraced.

Question 34: (B)
Eliminate the worst answer choices first: (E) is out because of "being," and (C) is out because it contains wrong verb tense. Now concentrate on the meaning of words like "consequently" (D), "in addition to" (B), and "and" (A). "Consequently" indicates a cause and effect relationship, but that doesn't make sense coming out of sentence 13. (D)'s "in addition to" beats (A)'s "and" because it correctly connects the new sentence 14/15 hybrid to sentence 13.

Question 35: (B)
Remember the function of a good conclusion. A good conclusion should restate the main idea of the passage. (A) and (B) are the top two answer choices, so ask yourself, "is the passage more about Hoover being 'gracious and polished' or 'accomplished and ahead of

Section 4: Critical Reading

Question 1: (E)
Clue words "water" and "flooded" point to "drenched."

Question 2: (B)
Clue phrase "advantages and disadvantages" indicate that we are looking for something positive in the first blank and negative in the second. "Squander" is too negative for the first blank, and "resistant" and "immune" don't work for the second. Though "insure" and "maintain" both seem to work, "maintain" is a better match.

Question 3: (C)
Clue phrase "knowing every detail" points to "curiosity."

Question 4: (E)
The clue word "despite" is an opposite indicator, and "still affects up to 500 million people" tells us that the disease is still bad. Therefore we need something positive in the first blank and negative in the second. This gets rid of (B) and (D) for their first blank words, and (C) for "abate". Though "cure" and "eradicate" both work, "flourish" is a stronger match than "flag."

Question 5: (B)
The clue phrase here is "unlikely to offend," which eliminates all but (A) and (B). Even if you do not know what "innocuous" means, does "impressionable" ACTUALLY MEAN, "unlikely to offend"? No.

Question 6: (B)
The clue phrase here is "prevailed against great odds," but this one is all about whether or not you know the words. Take apart the word "indomitable." In = not. Dom = something about domination. Able = able to be. Indominable = unable to be dominated.

Question 7: (A)
Yup. This one sucks. All the words seem to work! How am I supposed to know if the business is good or bad?! "Although" and "actually" are opposite indicators, which means something bad is going on with the business. Most people get this for the first blank, which eliminates (B), (C), and (E) if you know the words. Then they think, "oooh -- bankrupt fits so perfectly!" True, but there are no positive clue words in the entire sentence, so you cannot prove something positive like "charitable."

Question 8: (B)
Ah, yes. The last vocab question. The serious vocab test. The clue phrases to focus on here are "overweening pride" and "usurp nature." This, of course, is only comforting if you know what "overweening" and "usurp" mean. Luckily, you are probably at least somewhat familiar with the lesson of Frankenstein, which deals with the idea of playing God. "Hubris" is the only logical match.

Question 9: (B)
Both authors acknowledge that Clemens had personal tragedies in his life; however, they disagree on how much these personal tragedies are responsible for what he wrote. (D) is the only other answer choice in the running with (B), but since the author of P2 never mentions Adams, you can't know if he's ever heard of the guy.

Question 10: (B)
The clue phrase here is: "slow process of incubation."

Question 11: (E)
The main idea of P2 is that the personal tragedies Clemens experienced are the most important factors in understanding his work. That gets rid of (A) and (C), since (C) is the main idea of P1, not P2. (B) and (D) both contain irrelevant information, so (E) is the best choice.

Question 12: (D)
The main idea of P1 is that while Clemens' personal issues "certainly are contributory causes," they are less important than the "growing political discords, moral conflicts, and economic problems of his age." (D) is the only answer choice that reflects the thesis of the passage.

Passage: The Neuroscientist and The Brain
Main idea: Brains are highly adaptable, and even scientists do not understand completely how brains do what they do.

Question 13: (E)
How boring is this passage?! It's overly technical, it's dry, and Ebert and Roper give it two thumbs down. But those are the breaks, so let's figure out how to get these questions right. (A), (B), and (C) are out because they get the tone wrong. As you can tell, this passage is way to dry to be "amusing," but it is also not negative, like (A) and (C) would suggest. (D) and (E) seem very similar, but because of the first person point of view, "personal account" beats "case study."

Question 14: (C)
Focus on the fact that "although" is an opposite indicator. This indicates a contrast, which gets rid of all but (B) and (C). (C) is better than (B) because the contrast

is between his old self and his current self, not himself and "other individuals."

Question 15: (A)
This question seems like it should be easy but is frequently missed. Think about what the phrase "there must be" means. For example, "This traffic is terrible! There must be an accident somewhere up the road." It means that all logical reasoning would point to a certain outcome being true, even though you may not have the actual evidence to prove it. A lot of people don't know the word "conjecture," but if you're being really picky about the other words, none of them except "inquiry" even remotely reflects this meaning. In the end, "inquiry" is also wrong because the author is not ACTUALLY phrasing his statement as a question. BTW: "Conjecture" means "educated guess."

Question 16: (D)
(C) and (E) are too extreme in tone, but you do want to match the moderately negative meaning of the author's statement. What he's saying is, "our methods are not good enough." Therefore (A) and (B) are too positive, which leaves us with (D).

Question 17: (E)
Now is when you need to start building on the main ideas of the passage. What is this passage really about, besides making you wonder if skipping college for a career in burger flipping is such a bad idea after all? The main idea is not only that the brain is doing a lot of cool stuff, but also that it is doing it unconsciously. The clue phrase is "most have occurred by themselves, unconsciously, by... of which I know nothing."

Question 18: (D)
Focus on clue phrase, "but all the particulars you will have to find out for yourself." (D) is the only match. (Also: Notice how many opposite words occur in this passage? There are almost too many althoughs, thoughs, and buts to count. Build on this idea of contrast).

Question 19: (C)
This one is tricky because they are asking you what you can assume, not what you can prove. The clue sentence here is: "you're the neurologist -- you must see this all the time." This lets us assume that because the author is a neurologist, it is logical that he would be familiar with the processes that are going on in his brain. (B) is the most popular wrong answer because it seems to build on the ideas in question 18, but (C) is a better match for the clue phrase.

Question 20: (D)
Just after the word "richness" comes the clue phrase

"endless diversity," which points to "variety."

Question 21: (A)
The author mentions his profession because it makes sense that a physician would see the world as it pertains to "health and disease." It's about the author, not his patients, which eliminates (C) and (D). With the remaining three answers, consider the tone. (B) and (E) are out because they are somewhat negative, and there is no clue word basis for a negative answer in this part of the passage. In fact, words like "marvellingly" and "richness" convey just the opposite. Therefore (A), although somewhat vague, is the only possible choice.

Question 22: (B)
The clue phrase "see them as creative too" tells us that there is a positive bent to this answer, which gets rid of (A), (C), and (D). (E) is wrong because the passage does not say anything about "spirituality." (B) works because "productive change" is a good match for "unexpected growth and evolution."

Question 23: (C)
That the author uses the phrase like "demands a view of the brain as dynamic and active rather than programmed and static" insinuates that there may be people who don't hold this view. Again, this one is tricky because we're inferring or assuming, rather than proving based on the evidence. Try to simplify and just match words: "inflexible and unchanging" matches "programmed and static."

Question 24: (E)
Main idea = the brain is awesome! How many times have you seen words like "adapt," "change," and "limitless" in the passage? Yup. A lot.

Section 5: Math

Question 1: (E)
We're told that the fourth term is 30. The fifth term is 31 multiplied by 2, which is 62. The sixth term is 63 x 2 = 126.

Question 2: (E)
$a(x + y) = 45$. Distribute the a. $ax + ay = 45$. We're told that $ax = 15$, so we plug that in. $15 + ay = 45$. $ay = 30$.

Question 3: (B)
Ignore the parts of the speedometer that aren't in "Miles per hour" (we don't need to worry about the metric system!). In terms of "Miles per hour," we can see that the needle is between 30 and 60. The distance between 30 and 60 is divided into four equal intervals.

The difference between 30 and 60 is 30. Divided by 4, that means each interval is 7.5. The needle is one interval to the right of 30, so it is at 37.5.

Question 4: (C)
The digits 4, 5 and 6 can be arranged in 6 ways: 456, 465, 546, 564, 645, 654.

Question 5: (B)
There are two triangular faces to the figure and three rectangular faces. So the total surface area is 3r + 2t.

Question 6: (C)
Solving this one algebraically is wicked hard. But multiple choice makes our life easy! Just try each answer choice and use process of elimination. It turns out that 3 works for n. $(3 + 1) / (2 \wedge 3) = 1/2$. $4/8 = 1/2$.

Question 7: (E)
The average of a set of numbers is the sum total divided by the number of things. So in this case, $p = $ TOTAL / 14. Multiply both sides by 14 to get the total. So $14p = $ TOTAL.

Question 8: (C)
The coordinates of the midpoint are the averages of the coordinates of the endpoints. We're looking for t, which is the y-coordinate of the midpoint. The y-coordinate of point A is -1, and the y-coordinate of point C is 5. The average of those y-coordinates is $(-1 + 5) / 2 = 4 / 2 = 2$.

Question 9: (B)
Trick question! The answer is just zero. There are three "chunks" multiplied together that equal zero. One chunk is just the number k, one chunk is $(2x + 3)$, and one chunk is $(x - 1)$. For the equation to equal zero, any of those three chunks must equal zero. k is the one we care about, so the quick way to solve this is to realize that if k equals zero, then that will work and our equation equals zero.
(The values for x that would make the equation equal zero are $x = -3/2$ and $x = 1$, but we're told x must be bigger than 1. So, those don't matter. k must be zero).

Question 10: (A)
We have information about all of the men in the Williams family. Answers (B) and (C) involve men who might not be members of the Williams family, and we don't know anything about them, so those answers don't work. Answer (D) doesn't work because there could be a tall woman in the Williams family (or a bunch of tall women) – we don't know for sure. And answer (E) directly contradicts what we know. So (A) is the only one that must be true.

Question 11: (B)
Let's use that good ol' formula: Circumference = $2\pi r$. If the circumference is π, then $\pi = 2\pi r$. Divide both sides by π to get $1 = 2r$. Solve for r. $r = 1/2$. That looked harder than it really was!

Question 12: (D)
The general formula for direct proportions is $y = kx$. In this case, $y = kx^2$, where k is some constant. We can plug in the values for y and x that we're given. $1/8 = k(1/2)^2$, and now we can solve for k. $1/8 = k(1/4)$. Multiply both sides by 4/1. $1/2 = k$. Now we use that to find the new value of x when $y = 9/2$...
$9/2 = (1/2)x^2$
$9 = x^2$
$x = 3$ or -3. They want the positive value.

Question 13: (D)
This is a cool concept. An everyday example is that if, on a given day, three US dollars are equal in value to 2 Euros, then that means the Euro has more value than the dollar on that day (because it takes fewer Euros to get the same value). Applying that logic to our variables, it takes 7 times w to get to a value that is equal to four times x. That means that each x has a greater value than each w. If you list them all in order using that same logic, w has the least value, then u, then v, then x.

Question 14: (B)
Let's plug in -60 for h(t) on the left side of our equation. $-60 = 2(t^3 - 3)$. Now solve for t. Divide both sides by 2.
$-30 = t^3 - 3$. Add 3 to both sides.
$-27 = t^3$. Cube root both sides.
$-3 = t$.
They're looking for the value of $2 - 3t$, so we plug in -3 for t.
$2 - 3(-3) = 2 + 9 = 11$.

Question 15: (D)
Let's say $x = 6$ and $y = 10$. Then answer I is 60, which is divisible by 15. Answer II is $18 + 50 = 68$, which is NOT divisible by 15. And Answer III is $(30 + 30) = 60$, which is divisible by 15.
Answers I

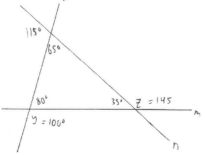

Question 16: (E)
See diagram. We know that in the triangle, the top angle must be 65 to form a straight line with the 115 degree angle. We can plug in any numbers we want for the other two angles in the triangle, as long as they add up to 180 when we include the 65 degree angle. One option would be 80 degrees and 35 degrees. Angle y forms a straight line with the 80 degree angle, so y = 100. Angle z forms a straight line with the 35 degree angle, so z = 145. $y + z = 245$. They will always add up to 245, even if we had picked different numbers in the triangle.

Question 17: (D)
One way to algebraically refer to three consecutive odd integers is n, n + 2, and n + 4 (increasing by twos because every other integer is odd). This problem is saying that $n + (n + 2) + (n + 4) = 111$. If we simplify the left side, $3n + 6 = 111$.

Question 18: (A)
There are 18 arcs of length 2 and 18 arcs of length b, and together, they all add up to the total circumference of 45. So $18(2) + 18b = 45$. We can solve for b. $36 + 18b = 45$. $18b = 9$. $b = 1/2$. But we need to find the pesky DEGREE measure of b. Well, the ratio of little arc b to the whole circle's circumference is equal to the ratio of the degree measure of b out of the whole circle's degrees (360). Let's math-ify that idea:
$(1/2) / 45 = x / 360$. Cross multiply to get $(1/2)(360) = 45x$. $180 = 45x$. $x = 4$ degrees.

Question 19: (C)
This problem is much easier to solve if that formula looks kinda familiar to you (you might have seen similar formulas in math class when talking about interest compounded annually. Fun fun fun!). In the formula they give us, $c(n) = 300x^n$, the number 300 is the maintenance this year, n is the number of years from now, and x is the amount the maintenance cost increases each year. If the cost of maintenance increases each year by 10 percent, that means that next year it will be 110 percent of this year. And the year after that, it will be 110 percent of 110 percent of this year. Basically, each year the cost is multiplied by 110 percent, and that is what should be the value of x. But we have to remember to turn a percent into a decimal by dividing by 100, so $x = 1.1$.

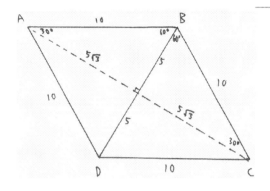

Question 20: (B)
See diagram. If all the segments are congruent, then the two triangles in the original figure are both equilateral. When we draw segment AC, we divide each equilateral triangle in half, dividing each one into two 30-60-90 right triangles. (Oh no! Not THOSE again!) Let's say that each of the original segments is length 10. Then, using the cool ratios of 30-60-90 right triangles, if the hypotenuse is 10, we know the short leg is 5, and the longer leg (the one we want) is 5√3. The total length of AC is two of those 5√3 legs, so AC is 10√3. The ratio of AC to BD is 10√3 / 10, which is √3 / 1.

Section 6: Critical Reading

Question 1: (D)
1929 to 1994 is a long time when you're talking about human careers. (D) is the only answer that reflects this.

Question 2: (C)
You may be thinking, "I'm not a marine biologist! Is 4,700 feet a long way to dive or not? Does this evidence confirm or refute that whales are among the deepest divers?" Think about the wording of "over" 4,700 feet versus something like "merely 4,700 feet." Regardless of the number, we can assume "over" means a lot and "merely" means not a lot. Therefore, the dive "confirms" earlier "speculations."

Question 3: (D)
The clue phrase "wild" is the key to the second blank, which means (C) is out. Since no one indulged in said "wild" behavior, the first blank needs an opposite. What is the opposite of "wild"? Not (A), (B), or (E) for sure. However, does "secluded" ACTUALLY MEAN "not wild"? No. Can you be secluded in a cabin by yourself for 20 years and still do crazy stuff? Yes.

Question 4: (E)
This one is a lot like question 2 because it is difficult to tell whether the new evidence confirms or refutes the old evidence. Memorize this: New = different.

Question 5: (E)
The clue phrases here are "complained," which indicates a negative, and "short-term profits," which makes it specific. This one comes down to the words, and if you can take apart any of the words based on roots and prefixes, you may realize that "opic" is in some way related to sight: think "optomotrist," or "optic nerve." "Myopic" means "short-sighted."

Question 6: (C)
This passage is short but not sweet. Since question 6 acts as a vocab question, try the words in the sentence. (B) and (C) are the only ones that seem to work, so the question becomes: are you literally "portraying" Flaubert, as in drawing a picture of him? Or are you merely "imagining" him in your mind?

Question 7: (A)
The clue phrase here is the very stylized "oh-so-exquisitely bored," which points to (A). Most of the wrong answers are wrong because you don't have the evidence to prove them. All we can know from the last sentence is what he is wearing, that he is reading, and that he is seeming, not necessarily being, "oh-so-exquisitely bored."

Question 8: (A)
This passage is even worse than the last one! It's so full of technical jargon that it's difficult to know what's going on. Focus on the clue phrases "visual minimalism" and "easy on the eyes," which indicate that a lot of information is getting broken down into easy pieces. Most people get it down to (A) and (B), but if you think specifically about (B), aren't details already small? Wouldn't we want to accentuate the important details rather than make them smaller?

Question 9: (C)
Beware of the literal! Are these maps literally "drawings," "illustrations," or "representations of a specific place"? No. Now you're left with (B) and (C). If you can untangle the main idea of the passage, it's more about how humans "process" information than it is about how the world looks to the eye.

Passage: Black Women
Main idea: Black women are different from both white women and black men, though not everybody wants to admit it.

Question 10: (E)
The key word in this entire passage is different, different, different!

Question 11: (A)
The tone in this statement is one of confidence, which

eliminates all but (A) and (C). However, the author is not exactly making a "decision" about anything.

Question 12: (D)
The clue phrases here are "a combination, not just a mixture" and "transformed." (D) is the only answer choice that matches these ideas.

Question 13: (B)
The first question to ask yourself is, "is the tone generally positive or generally negative"? Based on the main idea: black women = good, black men and white women = not so good, we can infer that the tone is generally negative. This gets rid of (C) and (D). (E) is out because it is an extreme, not a general negative. The proof for (B) can be found in lines 29-31. Black men and white women want black women to join their club because strength lies in numbers; therefore, it's about "self-interest" rather than "affection."

Question 14: (D)
The clue phrase is "denial of difference is not the road to harmony." (D) is almost an exact word match.

Question 15: (E)
Tone? Generally negative. This eliminates (A) and (D). Now the question is one of extremity. "Defiant" is too extreme. "Skeptical" is too mild. "Admonishing," which means, "chastising," works because the author is in essence saying, "tut, tut, don't do that. It won't lead to the outcome you desire."

Question 16: (A)
Focus on the clue phrases "millions of people are talking all at once," and "silencing any one of them puts in danger".

Passage: Akaky (Or: Russian literature is weird). Main idea: Akaky is a government paper-pusher who, though mocked by his colleagues, gets some sympathy from the narrator.

Question 17: (B)
You can only know what you have been specifically told, and by line 5 in the passage, that's not much. So eliminate things that you can't prove. (A) is out because the author isn't angry. (C) and (E) are too broad, and therefore impossible to prove given the information in the passage. Which leaves you with (B) and (D). Now focus on the phrase, "there is nothing in the world more readily moved to wrath than a department," and you will see that it's more about the department than it is about Akaky.

Question 18: (C)
The clue phrase here is "he was always seen in the

same place, at the very same duty." We don't know anything about his "uniform" (B), how long he had been working (D), or his age (E). Between (A) and (C), (A) loses because you cannot prove that Akaky "tried.... continually" to change his nature.

Question 19: (D)
The "simple fly" is like Akaky because the porters "took no more notice of him." The clue word "notice" matches "easily overlooked."

Question 20: (A)
Eliminate based on the rules of "generally positive" vs. "generally negative." The clue phrase "as is usually done in well-behaved offices" indicates that these quotations are something good. (A) is the only positive answer choice.

Question 21: (C)
Beware of the literal! That eliminates (A) and (B). (E) doesn't make sense in the sentence. In the battle of "fabrication" vs. "discovery," it is clear that the co-workers are making up the stories rather than "discovering" real things about Akaky's life.

Question 22: (A)
The good news is that (B), (C), and (D) are total nonsense. Once you get it down to (A) and (E), you really have to read closely for the narrator's tone here. Ask yourself, "is the way the author describes the young clerks flattering?" No. He basically makes them out to be bullies. Therefore (A) is the best choice.

Question 23: (E)
Keep thinking about positives and negatives. The new clerk thinks he hears the words, "I am your brother," which is a positive sentiment. (E) is the only answer choice that matches.

Question 24: (E)
When the boss "rewards" Akaky with more complicated work, Akaky perspires, mops his brow, and basically freaks out. That's bad, which eliminates (A), (B), and (D). Akaky's reaction to the new job shows mainly that prefers the simple job of copying to "increased responsibility," but that doesn't mean he doesn't work hard.

Section 8: Math

Question 1: (C)
Divide both sides by 100 to get $67 = 6k + 7$. Solve for k, which is 10.

Question 2: (B)
If we try each answer choice, -4 works. Three more

than -4 is -1, which is still negative, but five more than -4 is 1, which is positive. Awesome.

Question 3: (E)
Angle z is made up of one half of angle x plus one half of angle y. So z = 35 + 20 = 55.

Question 4: (C)
They like to test this concept! The probability of 2/5 means that there are two apples for every five pieces of fruit. The important number is 5. The total amount of fruit must divide evenly by 5, so 52 is the option that could NOT work.

Question 5: (C)
If the square has sides of length 3, its perimeter is 12. The triangle also must have a perimeter of 12, but it has 3 sides, so we divide 12 by 3 to get a side length of 4.

Question 6: (D)
This looks a little confusing, but the trick is that since x is negative 1, we want x to be raised to an even power, making it positive 1. Therefore, answers (B) and (D) will be positive numbers and we can ignore the others because they'll be negative. The value of (B) is four times whatever k is, and the value of (D) is 8 times whatever k is, so (D) is biggest.

Question 7: (E)
Josephine does ALL three things every day? That sounds exhausting!
If we remember that speed is distance divided by time, then speed on the graph will be represented by the SLOPE of each segment. (Slope is change in y divided by change in x, and the y-axis is distance and the x-axis is time). She swims first, and that is the slowest thing, so the first line segment (going from left to right) should have the smallest slope. Cycling comes next, so the middle segment should have the steepest slope. And running (the third segment) should have a slope in between the other two. Answer (E) has the graph that matches those slopes the best.

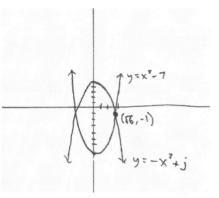

Question 8: (A)
See diagram. We need to plug $\sqrt6$ in for x in the first equation. $y = (\sqrt6)^2 - 7$, so y = 6 – 7 = -1. k represents that y-coordinate, so the coordinates of the intersection point are ($\sqrt6$, -1). We now plug those coordinates into the second equation.
$y = -x^2 + j$
$-1 = -(\sqrt6)^2 + j$
$-1 = -6 + j$
$5 = j$

Question 9: (A)
The fastest way to do this is just try the answers. If we plug in 4 for x, then 2 – 4 = -2. The absolute value of that is 2, which is less than 3. That is the only answer that works.

Question 10: (C)
Though many people only vaguely recall it from math class, there's a formula for finding the sum of the angles inside any polygon, and it is perfect for what we need in this situation. Thanks, math! The formula is: (n – 2)180, where n is the number of sides. This pentagon has 5 sides (as pentagons often do), so its interior angles must equal (5 – 2)180, which is (3)180, which is 540 degrees total. We divide 540 evenly between 5 angles, so each angle is 108. Angle x forms a straight line with one of those 108 degree angles, so 108 + x must add up to 180. x = 72.

Question 11: (C)
What the problem is saying is that the 6 inch drawing equals 3/8 of the real length. Or, in math terms, 6 = (3/8)x. Multiply both sides by 8/3 to find that x = 16.

Question 12: (E)
The important thing here is that the fraction is being divided by 2, and the result is an integer. That means the top of the fraction must be even, because only even numbers divide evenly by 2. So, the value of (x + 3) must be even. 3 is odd, so x must also be odd, because two odds add up to an even number.

Question 13: (B)
There are a lot of easy traps to fall into on this problem. Our goal is to find the slope of QS, and we can do that if we find the coordinates of point Q and the coordinates of point S. Looking at the smaller circle, Q is in the center, so it is half as high as point P. P's coordinates are (3, 6), so Q's coordinates are (3, 3). (Note: Q is lined up directly under P, so the x-coordinates are the same but the y-coordinate is half as big.)
The same logic is true for point S. It is lined up under point R (11, 10), so the coordinates for S are (11, 5). The slope between Q (3, 3) and S (11, 5) is the change in rise over change in run, or 2/8 = 1/4.

Question 14: (B)
This one is a little weird. p goes into n + 3 and also goes into n + 10. That means that n + 3 is a multiple of p, and then we added 7 and arrived at another multiple of p. If the multiples of p have a difference of 7 in between them, that means p itself is equal to 7. (Just like how if we look at some multiples of another number, like 3, the difference between them will be distances of 3: 27, 30, 33, 36, etc.).
Back to our problem: we can check our answer by making n + 3 a multiple of 7. If n + 3 = 14, then n = 11, and n + 10 = 21. Clearly, if p = 7, it goes into both 14 and 21, so our answer works.

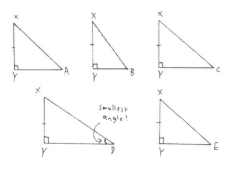

Question 15: (D)
See diagram. If you have one side of a triangle set in place, and you move the opposite corner of the triangle further away from it, the angle at that corner gets smaller (more acute). All of the answers are really asking about triangles where segment XY is set in place, and the opposite corner is either A, B, C, D, or E. The smallest angle will be the one at the point FURTHEST from XY. The correct answer is point D. D is the furthest point from XY (we can focus on the distance from Y to D, which is further than from Y to A, B, C, or E, because D is all the way diagonally across the cube from Y). No number crunching is necessary, though you can feel free to plug in numbers and use Pythagorean Theorem to verify that D is the furthest point from point Y

(and also from point X)!

Question 16: (D)
This has a trick that makes it EASY!! Take the expression $x^2y - xy^2$ and factor it. There is an x in both terms and a y in both terms, so it factors into $(xy)(x - y)$. But those two chunks are the two things they already told us the value of! We know xy is 5, and (x − y) is 7. So this is really just an ugly, weird way of asking us to multiply 5 times 7.

Section 9: Critical Reading

Question 1: (B)
It's clear that the traffic needs to be made better, which points to "alleviate."

Question 2: (D)
"Actually quite disturbed" is negative and "though" is an opposite indicator, so we want something positive in the blank. This leaves (D) and (E), but "considerate" is not the opposite of "disturbed."

Question 3: (B)
This is one of those rare questions where you actually need to assess both blanks at once. We are looking for opposite words, which eliminates (A) and (E) outright. The words in (D) are not similar, but they are also not opposites, so (D)'s out. Because most people don't know the word "dilatory," the question is whether (B) is a strong match or a weak one. Congratulations! It's strong!

Question 4: (E)
"Had been profitable" is contrasted with the opposite indicator "but," which tells us that bad practices did something bad to the land. (A) is out because of "conscientious," (B) loses because of "sustained," and (D) fails on both accounts. So. Is "shrewd" good or bad? And what the hell does "denuded" mean? If you can figure out that "shrewd" actually has a positive connotation, the answer has to be (E).

Question 5: (A)
The phrase "usually take decades" means that we're talking about time. "No one expected" indicates an opposite. What is the opposite of taking a long time? Taking a short time! Even if you do not know the meaning of "dispatch," do any of the other words mean "to take a short time"? No.

Question 6: (B)
Clue words "eclectic" and "fused" inform this word choice, but in the end it comes down to the words. Think about science class. An "amalgam" is a blend of

two or more elements.

Passage: The Merits of Free Music Downloading
Main Idea Passage 1: Free music means songwriters don't make money and that is bad.
Main Idea Passage 2: Free music makes musicians more popular and that is good.

Question 7: (E)
Both of the authors speak in the first person about their experience writing music professionally. The only other semi-reasonable answer would be (B), but the main idea is more about how the authors made rather than appreciated the music.

Question 8: (D)
You can only know what the passages ACTUALLY tell you. And if both authors have to agree, then the evidence has to be in both passages. (A) is talked about in 1 but not 2. (B) is never directly stated in either passage. (C) is an opinion espoused only by the author of P1, and (E) sounds good but is not really the point. If you're looking for evidence that (D) is right, check out lines 14-20 in P1 and lines 62-66 in P2.

Question 9: (A)
The clue words in this part of the passage are all about money: "bread and butter," "a songwriter makes nothing until....for sale to the public," "deprived of the royalty," and "earned."

Question 10: (A)
(A) is the only choice that matches the main idea of P2: downloading music makes an artist more popular, which increases sales of the artist's music, which is good.

Question 11: (C)
It's all about money for the author of P1, so you can eliminate choices (A), (B), and (D) pretty easily. The rest is about knowing the vocab. The word "pragmatic" means practical and is the closest match.

Question 12: (D)
Money money money! (C) and (D) are the choices that deal with money; however, (D) is a closer match for the ideas in the clue sentence: "I might have occasionally written some music for fun, but I would not have had the luxury to compose full time."

Question 13: (E)
Remember that every single word in an answer choice must be defensible. (A) is out because of "traditional," (B) is out because of "complex technological," and (C) is out because of "adolescent impulse." Most people get this one down to (D) and (E). (D) is too extreme -- what

is so "radical" about P1? (E) works because the author is arguing against the "particular practice" of downloading music for free.

Question 14: (D)
Any time the SAT peeps use quotation marks, it almost always indicates some kind of sarcasm or irony. That leaves (C) and (D) as the only possible answer choices in question 14. However, if you really look at (C) -- yes there may be some kind of mocking going on, but is the author mocking "practices of the music industry" itself? No.

Question 15: (C)
Again with the sarcastic tone! In this section of the P2, the author is trying to make the point that the great artists of the past did not need copyright laws to produce masterpieces. By using the phrase "pretty decent" to describe Sophocles, Dante, Shakespeare, etc. -- all people who are universally understood to have been geniuses -- the author makes this point by being ironic.

Question 16: (E)
This one is another hidden vocab quiz. But like any vocab question, you don't need to know all of the words to get the question right; you just have to know enough. Build on the ideas expressed in the answers to the previous questions. Build on what you understand about the tone! Question 14 was about skepticism and question 15 was about irony, so what's the likeliest answer in 16? Something related to sarcasm, right? If you know enough of the words, or at least the right one, you'll see that "satirical" is related to "satire." Satire is related to humor and irony.

Question 17: (A)
Is P2 the positive one or the negative one? Positive. Therefore, the answer is going to be positive. This leaves us with (A) and (B), and now the question is: is the main idea of P2 more about being "popular" or having a "sophisticated worldview"?

Question 18: (B)
Keep building on the main idea and getting rid of the fluff. (A) and (E) are way too broad for the main idea of the passage. (D) is negative, which goes against the tone of P2. And in the battle of (B) vs. (C), (C) loses because his reference to VCRs is more of an analogy than it is an anecdote about his personal experience with VCRs.

Question 19: (C)
We're talking about the author of P2 here, so positive or negative? Positive. This leaves us with (A) and (C). Even if you don't know what "renown" means, does "artistic freedom" match the main idea that free

downloading is good because it makes an artist more popular? Is popularity the same thing as freedom? No it is not.

Section 10: Writing

Question 1: (B)
Remember: because they love because! That eliminates all but (B) and (E). "It" vs. "they"? Solar energy = "it."

Question 2: (A)
We hate "having" and "being"! Once you get rid of the "havings," you are left with (A) and (D). "Stated" is shorter and more concise than "gave a statement."

Question 3: (D)
First words! The officers (plural) "maintain." Now you've got (C) and (D). Although (C) is shorter, and therefore usually the better choice, the company will be able to improve sales "by" increasing imports rather than "and" increasing imports.

Question 4: (D)
Eliminate the wordy birdies: (A), (B), and (C). (D) is clearer and the verb "are" is more active than the verb "have."

Question 5: (D)
Parallel structure is crucial when making a list. "Doctors," "lawyers," "engineers," and "chemists," are all nouns describing people who do specific jobs. (D)'s inclusion of the word "professionals," rather than "professions," is the only answer choice that matches the rest of the list.

Question 6: (C)
The questions in which the answer choices all seem very similar can be frustrating. Focus first on the comma, which you can't change, and ask yourself which answers become grammatically incorrect when placed after a comma. (A) and (E) fall into this category. (D) sounds the worst of the three remaining choices, so it comes down to (B) and (C). (C) is shorter. Voila. (C) is correct.

Question 7: (B)
Introductory phrases must be followed by the subjects to which they refer. Who believes that crossword puzzles stimulate her mind? Dolores. In the battle of "will spend" vs. "would spend," "would" wins because of the tense of the verb "stimulated."

Question 8: (C)
(D) and (E) are out because of "being." After that, it's about untangling the word knots in the remaining

choices and (C) is the least tangled of the three.

Question 9: (D)
Memorize this! People = they, A person = he or she, You = you, One = one, I = I. The subject here is "someone"; therefore, you need "he or she."

Question 10: (D)
Who was brought to the United States at the age of thirteen? Le Yan Phou. Now you're choosing between (D) and (E), and (D) is more active and concise.

Question 11: (C)
This one is about pronoun clarity. Who is running for re-election? Mayor Julia Wilson or her daughter? The only answer choices that make a decision on this issue are (B) and (C); however, (B) is a big fat mess.

Question 12: (A)
Two camps: "Although" vs. "The Superintendent." Do you need an opposite indicator like "although" in the sentence? Yes. (A) is far less wordy than (B) and uses the correct verb tense.

Question 13: (B)
The rules of parallel structure tell us that we need to match "read" with "evaluate," rather than "evaluating" or "evaluated." This leaves us with (B), (D), and (E). (E) is out because the comma should be a semicolon, but alas! (B) and (D) both sound fine. In the end, (B) wins because it connects the ideas in the sentence more simply than (D) does.

Question 14: (D)
This one is seriously maddening, but if you remember the rule of "comparing like to like," you can get it. You can either compare whales to birds or the "songs" of whales to the "songs" (or "those") of birds, but you cannot compare an animal to a song or vice versa. (D) is the only answer choice that makes a correct comparison.

Test 10
Section 2: Math

Question 1: (E)
Three pencils are $4.50, so each pencil is $1.50. If the price increases by $0.50, then each pencil now costs $2.00. Five of them will cost $10.

Question 2: (E)
The easy way to do this is plug the values from the tables into the answers and see what works. $y = 4x - 1$ works. For example, if we plug in $x = 2$ and $y = 7$, then $7 = 4(2) - 1$. Cool.

Question 3: (B)
Circumference $= 2\pi r$, so circumference is proportional to radius. If Circle A has a twice the circumference of Circle C, then Circle A also has twice the radius of Circle C. The line segment AC is made up of the radius of the big circle (AB) plus the radius of the small circle (BC). If AB is twice as big as BC, and they add up to a distance of 6, then AB is 4 and BC is 2.

Question 4: (B)
The best thing to do is write in the coordinates of each answer choice. The correct answer needs to have an x-coordinate that is 3 more than the y-coordinate (ignoring positives and negatives). The coordinates of point B are (-4, -1). That fits the bill, because the absolute value of -4 is 4, and the absolute value of -1 is 1, and $4 - 1 = 3$.

Question 5: (D)
The people that said they were less than 40 includes two slices of the pie chart: people less than 20 (30 percent of the total) plus people between 20 and 40 (20 percent of the total). We add the percents to get 50 percent. Since 1,000 people were surveyed, 50 percent of 1,000 is 500.

Question 6: (D)
Keep in mind that if a number divides evenly by 3, the remainder is zero! Let's look at some possible numbers: 9, 10, 11, 12, 13. When 9 is divided by 3, the remainder is 0. When 10 is divided by 3, the remainder is 1. When 11 is divided by 3, the remainder is 2. When 12 is divided by 3, the remainder goes back to 0. When 13 is divided by 3, the remainder is 1, and the pattern repeats. Answer (D) is the only one that fits this pattern. Another quick tip is that any answer choice that contains the number 3 must be wrong, because 3 can't be the amount left over when you divide by 3!

Question 7: (C)
The formula for inverse proportions is $y = k/x$. The SAT doesn't give you this formula, but if you don't know it, this problem really stinks. But now we have the formula, so we are happy. Let's plug in the first numbers they gave us. $15 = k/5$. $k = 75$. Now we keep that value of k and look for the new value of y when x is 25. $y = 75/25 = 3$.

Question 8: (A)
There IS enough information but we've gotta do some substituting! The second equation they give us is $2x + 2y + z = 20$. Let's change the order so it goes $2x + z + 2y = 20$. Focus on the first two terms, $2x + z$. The first equation told us that those are equal to 2y. So we can replace 'em. We take $(2x + z) + 2y = 20$ and turn it into $(2y) + 2y = 20$. Aha! Now we can solve for y. $4y = 20$, so $y = 5$.

Question 9: 13/2 or 6.5
Distribute the 2 to get $2x - 6 = 7$. Add 6 to both sides. $2x = 13$. Divide by 2. $x = 13/2$.

Question 10: 10
Since the x-coordinate is 4, we can just plug that in for x and solve for y to get the y-coordinate.
$y - 4 = 3(4 - 2)$
$y - 4 = 3(2)$
$y - 4 = 6$
$y = 10$
By the way, it's just a coincidence that the answer to question 10 is the number 10. There's no secret pattern on the SAT where sometimes the number of the question is also the value of the right answer. Or is there? No, there's not. That'd be cool, though.

Question 11: 45
Car A need a gallon of gasoline for every 20 miles, so to go 60 miles, it needed 3 gallons of gas. When Car B uses 3 gallons of gas, it will have gone $(3)(15) = 45$ miles.

Question 12: 105
The angles in a quadrilateral (4-sided figure, that is) always have to add up to 360. We know that three angles in this figure are 65, 100, and 120. Those add up to 285. To get the total up to 360, the fourth angle (the one not labeled) must be 75. That angle forms a straight line with angle x, so $75 + x = 180$. $x = 105$.

Question 13: 12.5 or 25/2
The first term is 20.
The second term is 8.
The third term is $(20 + 8) / 2 = 14$.
The fourth term is $(8 + 14) / 2 = 11$
The fifth term is $(14 + 11) / 2 = 12.5$. Aha! 12.5 is the VALUE of the first term that's not an integer.

Question 14: 3/50 or .06
We need to solve for x in terms of z. $x = (1/5)y$ and $y = (3/10)z$. We can substitute the right hand side of the second equation in for y in the first equation. $x = (1/5)(3/10)(z)$. If we multiply the fractions together we get the answer: $x = 3/50$ of z.

Question 15: 192
AE is the short leg of a 30-60-90 right triangle. That means we can find side BE, which is the long leg of that triangle. The long leg is $\sqrt{3}$ times the short leg. Since AE is 8, BE is $8\sqrt{3}$. Now we know that one side of the square is $8\sqrt{3}$, so the area of the square is $(8\sqrt{3})^2$, which is $(64)(3)$, which is 192.

Question 16: 8/7 or 1.14
Since the ratio of peanuts to cashews is 5 to 2, that means the ratio adds up to 7, and the ratio of cashews to the TOTAL mixture is 2/7. If the weight of the whole mixture is 4, we multiply 4 by 2/7 to get 8/7 pounds of cashews.

Question 17: 0 < X < .375, or 0 < X < 3/8
If line m starts at the origin and intersects somewhere BETWEEN A and B, then line m must have a slope that is greater than zero but less than the slope of line L. Since line L goes through the origin (0, 0) and the point (8, 3), we can find that its slope (rise over run) is 3/8 (or .375 as a decimal). So line m can have a slope that is ANY number you can dream up between 0 and 3/8. Go ahead, dream up a fun, wacky slope. Let your imagination run wild. Anything between 0 and .375 will work as long as you can grid it in.

Question 18: 1350
With any median question, we always should first put the numbers in order from smallest to biggest: 1238, 1351, 1459, 1552.
Now, we need to add some number X to our list, and have 1351 be the median. Since the median is the middle number, we need to have the list be balanced and have 1351 be in the middle, with two numbers on the left of it and two numbers on the right. There are already two numbers on the right, so we need to add the number X to the left of 1351. That means X could be any number less than 1351, and the biggest possible value of X is 1350.

Section 3: Writing

Question 1: (C)
It's short and sweet, and "supported" matches the verb tense of "opposed." (B) is VERY tempting, but it's missing a word. In order to be correct it would have to say "were enthusiastic TOWARD and supportive of."

Otherwise it sounds like the groups were enthusiastic OF the rules, which is idiomatically incorrect.

Question 2: (D)
The answer choices fall into two camps: comma v. "is." Do you need a verb here to make it a full sentence? Yes. Then it's a choice between "where" and "and." "Where" wins.

Question 3: (A)
Remember how much we hate "having" and "being"? Kinda goes out the window on this one. "Being" is (nearly) always bad, which eliminates (B) and (D), and (A) is the most succinct of the remaining choices. What does succinct mean? Get out your vocab. flashcards.

Question 4: (D)
Who are they? We don't know. Therefore (A), (B), and (C) contain vague pronouns. "Wherever" is shorter than "in the place where."

Question 5: (E)
Who is driving down the road? "The house", "the family's attention", or the "family"? Exactly.

Question 6: (D)
Which one is the shortest? Exactly.

Question 7: (B)
There are some real piece of …..let's say "stuff" answer choices in this one. Most of these are not even sentences. Once, you've eliminated (A) and (E) for "being," (B) is the only choice that doesn't sound like you're trying to choke down an entire sleeve of saltines all at once.

Question 8: (C)
This one is tricky because all the answers seem pretty similar, so go with first words: "Scientists" or "Seeking"? Neither sounds terrible, but in general we know that subjects are strong and "ing" verbs are weak, so "Scientists" is most likely the best way to begin the sentence. Now focus on the smaller differences. (B) is out because the comma before "they" would need to be a semicolon, which leaves you with (A) and (C). Admittedly they both sound fine, but which one is shorter? (C). Remember: in an apparent tie, the short one wins.

Question 9: (C)
"Is" v. "Are"? Are. Now you're thinking about clarity and parallel structure. With it's repetition of the word "for," (C) is the most parallel.

Question 10: (B)
Again with the vague pronouns! What is it? Who are they? Does the music draw on the experiences, or do the artists draw on the experiences? (B) and (C) are the

only choices that make a clear decision on the issue. Finally, "the reason is that" beats "the reason is because" because the word "reason" already makes clear that there is a "because." Wow, that was a mouthful.

Question 11: (D)
Who is raised in a large and noisy city? "It", "When", "Going", "Delightful", or "I"? Only "I" can be raised in a large and noisy city.

Question 12: (B)
Plans are plural. There "are" plans.

Question 13: (B)
Managed "to keep."

Question 14: (E)
No problems here. Most people who get this one wrong want to change (C) to "are;" however, the subject of this sentence is actually "Introducing," which is singular.

Question 15: (D)
The veterinarian examined the horse "calmly". Not "calm".

Question 16: (A)
Details "have," not "has."

Question 17: (D)
Verb tense. The phrase "were watching" must be matched by "was."

Question 18: (D)
Neither...nor.

Question 19: (C)
The subject is George Thornton Emmons, not "a handful of ethnographers." He is only ONE who committed "his" life. And even if it were supposed to be plural, you would need to change "their life" to "their lives."

Question 20: (A)
Verb tense. Morgan "spent."

Question 21: (A)
Memorize this! People = who/whom. Places = where/in which. Things = that/which. Technically, a world is a place. Read this one in that clichéd movie trailer voice and it'll sound right..."In a world, where the rate of technology and social change accelerates frighteningly, one man must save them all! Keanu Reeves stars in: Question 21."

Question 22: (A)
When assessing "I" v. "me," take out the other person's name and read it again. Ms. Tanaka asked I? No. Ms. Tanaka asked me.

Question 23: (E)
Both (A) and (D) sound a little funny to some people, but they're not technically wrong.

Question 24: (D)
Once you get into medium/hard question territory, it can become necessary to "cut out the fat," or eliminate the grammatical accessories in the sentence. This includes most prepositional phrases and appositive clauses. If you eliminate the phrase "rather than the state," you will see that workers "own," not workers "owns."

Question 25: (A)
Idiom: Listening to.

Question 26: (C)
Vague pronoun. Who got the raise? Ms. Andrews or her co-worker?

Question 27: (E)
Nothing wrong. The rule they seem to be testing you on here is the rule of comparing 2 things v. comparing more than 2. Since cheetahs are being compared to all other land animals, the superlative "fastest" is appropriate.

Question 28: (A)
Singular/Plural: they were successful "as candidates."

Question 29: (E)
This sentence is long, but there is a lot of fat that you can cut out. The most frequently chosen wrong answer is (C) because people want to change "is" to "are." However, "which" is singular in the same way "each" is singular. Which ONE individually is more likely to win. Some people want to change "more likely" to "most likely," but we are only comparing two things here, so you have to keep "more."

Passage Revision: Otis and The Elevator

Question 30: (C)
(A) and (C) are the best options here, so the question is: Do you need the sentence at all? Any sentence that provides relevant information which would be lost if the sentence were deleted should be kept. (C) retains the sentence, but clarifies the pronoun "they."

Question 31: (D)
This one hinges on the words after "device" in the answer choices. (D) is the only choice that is both grammatically correct and concise.

Question 32: (D)
These answer choices make no sense! Very awkwardly worded. Most people get it down to (D) and (E), but while (E) is short, and therefore tempting, it doesn't establish the cause and effect relationship that we are looking for. It lumps "people" and "freight" into the same category, but what the sentence should convey is that before Otis' development, elevators could only transport freight; however, after Otis's development, they were safe enough for people to use.

Question 33: (B)
This one also sucks, so try to pick the least stupid answer. The most important thing to consider is that this will be the first sentence of the paragraph, and therefore needs to function as a transition between the ideas in paragraph 1 and those in paragraph 2. (A) is out because "freight" is not the focus of the second paragraph. (C) is out because the word "entirely" is too extreme. (D) is irrelevant, and you can't prove it. (E) is irrelevant and doesn't function as a transition.

Question 34: (E)
At this point you may be thinking, "are they trying to purposefully drive me insane with awkwardly worded answer choices?" Yes they are. Think about how wording affects meaning. Again, we are looking for an answer that shows the cause/effect relationship. Because people had to schlep up and down many flights of stairs before Otis' elevator, it was preferable to get a room on the bottom. This leaves you with (B) and (E); however, if you really look at (B), it gets it backwards. (B) insinuates that it is because rooms on the lower floors were already considered better that people did not want to walk up the stairs. That logic doesn't make sense, unless these people are just really status-conscious when they stay in hotels.

Question 35: (D)
This one usually comes down to (B) and (D). While (B) may seem irrelevant, deleting it would push sentences 1 and 3 together, which do combine logically without something in the middle.

Section 4: Critical Reading

Question 1: (A)
Clue words "accident" and "apologized" signify the students were freed from blame, pointing to "exonerated" as the only possible second blank match.

Question 2: (C)
The clue word "although" signifies an opposite. The opposite of "exhibiting to the general public" would be

NOT showing the unwashed masses any of your brilliant writings. Unfortunately for Thurgood Marshall, the Library of Congress "disregarded" his wishes.

Question 3: (A)
The clue phrase here is "no evidence of having been mended," and the phrase "rather than" again signifies an opposite. (They love opposites!) What is the opposite of mending something? Throwing it away, or "disposal" rather than "repair." *Be careful of (D): the "you can't interpret that far" answer. Some people think, "well if you think about it a certain way…..not fixing your clothes could indicate being spiritual and not worrying about such worldly concerns as sock darning." But did the sentence SAY that? No.

Question 4: (D)
The clue word "terminal" means "end", which points to "conclude."

Question 5: (C)
The clue word "swell" points to "distension." You may not know this word, but you can probably tell that the other four choices don't mean "swelling."

Question 6: (E)
Clue words "selflessly" and "worthy of imitation" point to only positive words, which leaves you with (B) and (E). However, "emancipators," while positive, doesn't mean "worthy of imitation."

Question 7: (A)
The clue word "annoyed" tells us we're looking for a negative word, while "fawning," which means "being overly affectionate", (think Lavender Brown in the "Harry Potter" books), tells us specifically what kind of behavior is annoying. The answer, "obsequious" is a word that a lot of students don't know, so use process of elimination.

Question 8: (D)
The phrase "which might deplete them forever," indicates that unconstrained ------- of natural resources would be bad. So the second blank most likely means something like "conservation." If you're being very picky about what "conservation" means, this eliminates (A), (B), and (C). In the battle of "exploitation" v. "stockpiling," exploitation wins.

Question 9: (C)
All we know thus far is that she's traveling and she's thinking about time; therefore, there isn't enough proof for anything but (C).

Question 10: (D)
The final half of the last sentence: "but she, Camilla,

the only daughter, is supposed to shed a different light on the woman," insinuates that Camilla is expected to give people a deeper, more personal understanding of her mother than the scholars who merely "talk about Salome's poetry and her pedagogy." This points to (D).

Question 11: (A)
This one usually comes down to (A) and (D). Why is (D) wrong? Because we can only judge the opening paragraph which, while mentioning "the national media," does not compare the situation in Minnesota to a "national one."

Question 12: (E)
The clue word "misleading" tells us that the author's attitude is negative, which leaves us with (D) and (E). However, "resentful" is a very personal emotion, whereas "critical" is more academic, and therefore more appropriate to the passage.

Passage: Physicists (Or: This Joke is Not Funny) Main idea: Physicists see the world in abstractions. Details are bad and just get in the way.

Question 13: (B)
The author does not pass judgment on any of the approaches taken by the scientists. Instead, the "joke" merely describes each approach and underscores the fact that people in different fields take a different view of the problem. This passage is all about "differences" and "details."

Question 14: (E)
The engineer focuses solely on efficiency of production based on mathematical dimensions. (Oh those cold, unfeeling engineers!) This eliminates (A) and (C). (B) and (D) are about efficiency, but result in a negative outcome. Therefore (E) is the only logical choice.

Question 15: (D)
The psychologist is concerned with the cows. (Oh, those tree-hugging, hippie psychologists!) Clue phrases include, "mellow color...induce greater milk flow," and "diversity...reduce boredom." Match these to "produce more milk" and "bored" in (D) and you've got it.

Question 16: (C)
Beware the most frustrating question of the passage! Most people's instinctive answer to this question is "to be unfunny?" But remember, to ace the critical reading you have to become a "clue words robot," not a thinking, feeling human with opinions on the hilarity or lack thereof of "the old joke." Most people get this one down to (B) and (C). The reason why (B) is wrong is because to argue a point, you have to have something to argue against. Which, in this case, the author does not.

Question 17: (A)
Beware the second most frustrating question of the passage! Most people's instinctive answer to this question is "what the F*&#?!" Understandable. The key part of the passage here lies in lines 26-28: "The class of things that we do know.....one, maybe two hands." This tells us that physicists do not know very much. The author then compares this relative ignorance to Hollywood producers, so we can assume that they, too, do not know very much.

Question 18: (B)
Remember that clue word "details"? In line 36, in italics, the author states, "abstract out all irrelevant details!" Details are bad! We hate them!

Question 19: (D)
Again with the details?! Remember, once you grab hold of a "big idea," it's likely to be repeated over and over again in the answer choices. The only other answer choice concerning details, (A), also includes the phrase "ethical development," which the passage does not talk about.

Question 20: (C)
The wording of the passage starts to get real "physics-y" once Galileo is introduced, so try to focus on what you already know is important in the passage. Details are bad! This eliminates (A) and (D) as irrelevant. (B) is out because it comes to the opposite conclusion about "details." Which leaves us with (C) and (E). If you read (C) carefully, it basically echoes the "details are bad" mantra. In this case, the details are the "empirical facts," i.e.: that a feather, bowling ball, etc. behave differently.

Question 21: (B)
Of these choices, objects can only "find themselves" in their respective environments.

Question 22: (D)
This question builds on the ideas in question 21. (A) and (B) have nothing to do with anything. (E) is out because the word "beneficial" is too positive. (C) is out because you can't prove that the habitat an object finds itself in is necessarily it's "natural" habitat.

Question 23: (B)
These answer choices fall into two camps: Galileo is saying something positive v. Galileo is saying something negative. Clue phrases include, "he anticipated the onslaught of criticism," "I trust you will NOT follow the example of many others," and, "this is exactly what he argued Aristotle had done." What a negative Nancy! This leaves us with (B), (C), and (D). (C) is out because

it's not about rivals taking credit, and (D) is wrong because of the word "religious."

Question 24: (A)
Back to the main idea: Abstraction good, details bad.

Section 5: Math

Question 1: (B)
The quick way to solve this is to observe that the left side of the equation is some number x divided by two less than x, and the right side is 39 divided by a number that is 2 less than 39. Therefore, x equals 39, without the need for any algebra! Otherwise, it can be solved algebraically by cross-multiplying.

Question 2: (E)
The letter z represents the grand total, meaning that it is the sum of the right hand column (m + t = z) and it is also the sum of the bottom row (w + x = z). Unfortunately, neither of those expressions is one of our answer choices. However, based on the fact that m + t equals z, we can rewrite m as the sum of its row (m = k + n), and also rewrite t as the sum of its row (r + s = t). So we can replace m and t with k + n + r + s, and THAT matches answer (E).

Question 3: (C)
The angle next to the 60 degree angle must equal 120, because they form a straight line. So now we know that the angles in the triangle are 25, 120, and x. And good old triangles are nice and reliable: we always know that their angles add up to 180. So 25 + 120 + x = 180. x = 35.

Question 4: (D)
The difference between buying a new refrigerator for 900 and repairing the old one for 300 is 600. If the Martins save 15 dollars a month, it will take 600/15 = 40 months for the new refrigerator to be worth the investment (assuming it doesn't break before then!).

Question 5: (B)
The perimeter of DEF is 10. The perimeter of ABC is three times that, so its perimeter is 30. ONE SIDE of ABC is one-third of the perimeter, so we multiply 30 by 1/3 and end up with a side of length 10.

Question 6: (A)
We have to convert from smaller to bigger units of time, starting with seconds. The machine mints one coin per second. There are 60 seconds in a minute, so the machine mints 60 coins in a minute. There are 60 minutes in an hour, so we multiply by 60 again: the machine mints 3600 coins in an hour. The machine works

10 hours a day (apparently it needs to go home to see its machine wife and little machine kids at night), so we multiply 3600 times 10 to get 36,000 coins minted in one day. We want to know how many days it will take to get to 360,000 coins (which is just one more zero, so that means we would just have to multiply by 10 to get to 360,000). It takes 10 days.

Question 7: (C)
The average of x and 3x can be written by adding them up and dividing by 2.
(x + 3x) / 2 = 12. Then, solve by multiplying both sides by 2.
(x + 3x) = 24
4x = 24
x = 6

Question 8: (C)
This problem is a total jerk. Regarding the chess club, we only know that SOME members of the chess club are on the swim team, which is not very informative. Answers (B) and (C) seem pretty similar, but only one of them is 100 percent absolutely, positively certain from logical reasoning. Some members of the chess club are on the swim team, so THOSE kids can't be tenth graders. But we don't know about the rest of the chess club. They might be tenth graders or might not. So answer (B) isn't certain. But we can be certain about (C), because some chess club kids definitely aren't tenth graders (the ones who are on the swim team).

Question 9: (D)
We need to take the equation they give us and solve it algebraically for n.
3x + n = x + 1. Subtract 3x from both sides.
n = x + 1 − 3x. Combine like terms.
n = 1 − 2x. Voila!

Question 10: (E)
Remember that multiples are not factors! MULTIPLES of 5, for example, are 5, 10, 15, 20, etc. This problem is written in a confusing way, but what it really wants us to do is figure out which answer choice is a multiple of 2, 3, and 5. The number 60 is a multiple of 2, 3, and 5. That means that any multiple of 60 (like 120, 180, 240, etc) will also be a multiple of 2, a multiple of 3, AND a multiple of 5.

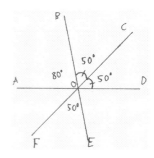

Question 11: (B)
See diagram. They drew this figure WAAAY off scale to trick people. Angle BOD forms a straight line with the 80 degree angle AOB, so BOD must equal 100. That 100 degree angle is bisected, so each half is 50 degrees. Angle BOC is one of those 50 degree angles. The angle we want, angle EOF, is a vertical angle to angle BOC, so it also is 50 degrees. Cool.

Question 12: (C)
The best way to do this problem is to try the answer choices and see which one could work for k. We need to multiply the number k by 5, divide it by 3, and then square root it, and have the result be an integer and not a messy decimal. Well, it would help if k has a factor of 3 inside of it, so that it divides evenly by 3. Also, since there is already a 5 under the square root sign, if k also contains a 5, the whole thing can be square rooted without creating a mess. Out of the answers given, we can check pretty quickly with our calculators and see that 15 works for k. (15 x 5 = 75, and 75 / 3 = 25, which has an integer square root).

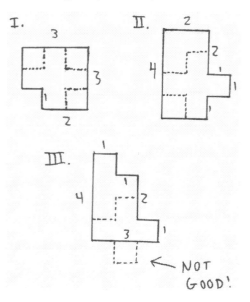

Question 13: (C)
See diagram. The most important part of this problem

is that the figures aren't allowed to overlap. The middle figure we're given on the top of the problem (the one that looks like a big plus sign) is the most helpful one because it is the biggest. Can it fit entirely inside each of the three possible figures in the answer choices? It can fit inside Figure I and Figure II, but not inside Figure III (unless you try to cheat with scissors and glue and make a mess). Going back to Figure I, the other small shapes won't fit properly around that unwieldy plus sign, but they do fit around it in Figure II, so II is the only answer that works.

Question 14: (D)
We need the products of two different prime numbers. It's helpful to write out the first bunch of prime numbers to see what we're working with:
2, 3, 5, 7, 11, 13, 17...
Starting with 2, what primes can it be paired with to multiply to a number between 20 and 30? 2 x 11 = 22, and 2 x 13 = 26. That's two possibilities.
Now we take 3. Can it multiply with any primes to reach a number between 20 and 30? 3 x 7 = 21. That's the only option we have with 3.
If we try multiplying 5 times any prime (like 7 or 11) we get numbers that are too big. So we have already found all of the possibilities. The total answer is THREE integers: 22, 26, and 21.

Question 15: (A)
It's helpful to wonder why this problem is looking for the value of $49 + x^2$. That's a weird thing to ask for! But it's a clue. The legs of the triangle we are given have values of $7 + x$ and $7 - x$, so getting to a value like $49 + x^2$ probably involves squaring them or multiplying them or something. The key is Pythagorean Theorem... we have to plug our values into $a^2 + b^2 = c^2$.
$(7 + x)^2 + (7 - x)^2 = 10^2$. We need to FOIL out each binomial on the left.
$(49 + 14x + x^2) + (49 - 14x + x^2) = 100$. Group like terms and cancel.
$49 + 49 + x^2 + x^2 = 100$. Notice the repetition of 49 and x^2. There's two of each.
$2(49 + x^2) = 100$. Divide both sides by 2 and we'll have what we're looking for!
$49 + x^2 = 50$

Question 16: (A)
The function h has a maximum when its x-value is 2. The problem wants to know what could be an x-value where the graph crosses the axis (that's where the height is zero). On the left hand side, the graph cross the x-axis somewhere to the left of the origin. So, starting from the maximum at x = 2, if we count the distance to where the graph crosses the axis, we have to go left past x = 0, so we have to go FURTHER than at least 2 units. The parabola could cross at x = -1.

But could any other answer work? Since parabolas are symmetrical, if we started at x = 2 and went to the RIGHT, the graph also would not cross the x-axis until we had gone some amount further than 2 units, which means that it has to cross the x-axis somewhere AFTER x = 4. Looking at the answer choices, the only possibility that is more than 2 units away from the number 2 is Answer (A), -1. Once again, multiple choice makes our lives easier!

Question 17: (D)
Basically they are just saying that the quadratic x² + kx + 7 has been factored into the binomials (x + 1) (x + h). By the rules of factoring, the last terms of the binomial must multiply together to give us the 7 from the original quadratic. So 1 times h equals 7. So h = 7. Now we can write (x + 1)(x + 7). We can FOIL that expression back into a quadratic and see what it gives us. It turns into x² + 8x + 7, so k in the original expression must equal 8.

Question 18: (A)
The straight line containing the point (4, 10) also goes through the origin, so we know that its slope (rise/run) is 10/4. Since A and B are both on that line, the slope between A and B is also 10/4 or 5/2. The slope between A and B equals (change in y)/(change in x), which really means that in this right triangle, the change in y can be thought of as the length of leg BC and the change in x can be thought of as the length leg AC. So the RATIO of leg BC to leg AB must be 5 to 2. Looking at the answer choices, 5 and 2 could be the length of the legs, in which case we would use Pythagorean Theorem to find the length of the hypotenuse: 5² + 2² = c². 25 + 4 = c². 29 = c². √29 = c. So Answer (A) contains values that work.

Question 19: (E)
When they mention f(√t), we have to plug √t in for x in f(x). So now we have f(√t) = 2√t − 1. But we're also told that one half of that whole function equals 4. So...
(1/2)(2√t − 1) = 4. Multiply both sides by 2.
2√t − 1 = 8. Add one to both sides.
2√t = 9. Divide both sides by 2.
√t = 9/2. Square both sides.
t = 81/4

Question 20: (E)
Trickier than it looks! The secret is that if we start with ANY integer k, we can get an EVEN integer by multiplying that integer by 2. So 2k is definitely an even integer, but that doesn't guarantee that we started with an odd integer. One way to definitely get an odd integer is take 2k and add 1. So 2k + 1 is the simplest way to get an odd integer. Now we want an even integer,

so we multiply the whole thing by 2. 2(2k + 1) = 4k + 2. Finally, we're back at an even integer, and now we know that it is double an odd integer. It's a good idea to plug in any positive integer for k into this answer to verify that it works. It does. How cool!

Section 6: Critical Reading

Question 1: (C)
Clue words "expressive movements" point to "gestures."

Question 2: (C)
Clue words "extensive experience," "practical knowledge," and "chief advice-giver" are all positive. (C) is the only choice with positive words for both blanks.

Question 3: (C)
Again, all clue words are positive. Even if you don't know the word "plaudits," you can most likely eliminate 3 or 4 of the other answer choices.

Question 4: (E)
The clue word "pungency," which means "strong smelling," points to "scent" or "aroma." However, in the battle of "identify" v. "cultivate," "identify" wins.

Question 5: (A)
It's difficult to figure out what the clue words are in this one. And what the hell does "raze" mean? "Distressing" is bad, but none of the answer choices seem to be negative. The real clue here is "announcement," which points to "disclosure."

Question 6: (D)
P2 is more negative than P1, and this shift should be reflected in the answer. This eliminates (C) and (E). The word "mocks" in answer choice (B) is too extreme, and although both (A) and (D) seem alright, P2 is more about questioning the assumption that the first three years are the most important than it is about calling for any "particular" changes.

Question 7: (D)
While the author of the second passage does not believe the first three years to be as crucial as the author of P1 does, he or she does say that it is widely acknowledged by others (i.e.: "much early childhood literature suggests") to be important.

Question 8: (B)
We know that the tone of P2 is more negative, which leaves us with (A) and (B). However, remember that extreme answer choices are usually wrong. "Skepticism" is less extreme than "indignation," so the answer is (B).

Question 9: (C)
Treat two-part answer choices as you would a double blank on the vocab: if it's half wrong, it's all wrong. Most people get this one down to (B) and (C), but are just so darned in love with "basic human needs" that they don't consider that "intellectual endeavors" is a weaker match than "scientific findings" for the clue phrase, "Now science has added stunning revelations."

Passage: How Harriet Jacobs Got her Groove Back
Main Idea: Harriet Jacobs wrote about abolition in language other women could relate to. Since this was pre-feminism, that language reflected traditional ideas about womanhood even as it attempted to transform ideas about race.

Question 10: (D)
As in many of these questions, it's not so much that the right answer is great, but that the wrong answers are worse. (A) is out because the passage doesn't really get into Jacobs' "emotions." (B) is out because of "comprehensive history." (C) is too broad and not enough about Jacobs, and (E) is wrong because, although the passage does make an argument about why Harriet Jacobs did what she did, it is not arguing for a "particular style of writing" in general.

Question 11: (D)
This one you can do in two parts. The clue phrase "firmly identified himself with the triumph of manliness and individualism" matches the "revered concept," and "the sufferings.....contravened their deepest principles of individualism" matches " its undermining." "It", in this case, is the idea of "individualism," which is mentioned in both parts.

Question 12: (D)
Okay, word substitution questions seem like they should be easy, right? I mean, they're short! However, sometimes these are the most infuriating questions because the answer choices all seem similar. Usually there's a "too literal" answer (in this case (A)), which you can immediately eliminate. The best strategy for these is to do what you would do in a vocab question. Figure out what word YOU would use without looking at the answers; then match your word. Let's say a good substitute in this case would be "figure out". The closest match is "formulate." If the sentence still looks like nonsense, think more specifically about the word that comes after "work out." Can you "struggle for" an analogy? No. Can you "solve" an analogy? Not really.

Question 13: (B)
Everybody hates this question. But the clue words here are "natural differences" and "domesticity." The phrase "true womanhood" has meant different things at different times in history, and it's hard not to put our own modern judgment on the phrase, so stick with "domesticity" for clarification. Domesticity has to do with the home and family, right? Therefore (B) is the only justifiable answer choice.

Question 14: (A)
The answer to question 14 can be found in lines 37-43. However, this question partially depends on whether you know the vocab. words in the answer choices. One of the most important vocab words to know for the critical reading section is "pragmatic." They love it! It's on every test! Pragmatic means "practical." Should be easy to remember. It's almost the same word.

Question 15: (B)
Remember "extreme answer choices" also include extreme emotions. Most of these passages are fairly dry. That's why they're so boring. Occasionally you'll hear an impassioned outcry, but not often. So when thinking about tone, stick with the more moderate words.

Passage: Trabb's Boy (Or: Oh my God, I am going to fail the SAT.)
Main Idea: The author fancies himself a celebrity slumming it back in a town where he once spent time, but he becomes humiliated when Trabb's Boy mocks him in public.

Question 16: (A)
The answer choices in this question suck! Most people shy away from the correct answer for two reasons: 1) Not sure if there were three encounters, and 2) What the *&^% does "ignominious" mean? So again, the best course of action is to eliminate. B) is out because the events are more tightly than "loosely" related. (C) is out because of "circular logic," which is a fancy phrase that the SAT people are trying to trick you into believing is right because it sounds smart. (D) loses because there is only one point of view, and (E) sucks because it is Opposite Day.

Question 17: (B)
Tone is very important here. Clue phrases such as "not disagreeable...to be stared after" and "I don't know whether they or I made the worse pretense; they of not doing it, or I of not seeing it," convey a superior attitude. That eliminates all but (B) and (E). However, the understated "not disagreeable" suggests that the narrator is more "distanced" than "nostalgic."

Question 18: (C)
Ironically, it is often the most stylized language that has the least to say. Think of those 19th century novels that take 3 pages to describe a man's overcoat. Wordiness

does not equal "a lot going on." All that's going on so far in this story is that the narrator is in a town he's been in before, he's full of himself, and he's walking down the street. You can't know any more than that, so every other answer choice but (C) falls victim to the "can I prove it" standard.

Question 19: (C)
This is a vocab. question in disguise. "Countenance," "feigned," "premonition"...these are all words that that, if you don't know them, make the question much harder to answer. If you know that "countenence" relates to ones' facial expression, you can get it down to (B) and (C). But by now we know that the narrator is not that friendly, so even if you do not know what "feigned" means, (C) wins by default.

Question 20: (E)
This one is usually between (D) and (E). The difference is in how specific you should be in defining these two words. "Haunted" insinuates that something supernatural is at work, while "afflicted" can be purely physical.

Question 21: (B)
The "joy" of the onlookers is CONTRASTED with the sense of being "confounded" felt by the narrator. This says that the townspeople are on the side of Trabb's boy and against the narrator.

Question 22: (B)
By now the "big idea" is all about the narrator's sense of himself as awesome v. the reality that he is being made fun of. Therefore we can understand the tone of Trabb's boy as mocking.

Question 23: (E)
The only even remotely provable choices are (C) and (E). However, (C) is the "sounds too smart for it's own good" answer, and (E) wins becaue of the phrase, "unpleasant personal experience."

Question 24: (B)
Wait, this thing is supposed to be funny?! I know, I know. But here's how to break it down: A) is wrong because the townspeople make no commentary, C) is wrong because the narrator DOES seem to comprehend what happened, D) is out because it's the "sounds too smart for it's own good" answer, and E) loses because it's Opposite Day.

Section 8: Math

Question 1: (A)
Each of the 8 dinners could be paired with 3 different desserts, so the total options are 8 x 3 = 24.

Question 2: (E)
The SUM of 3x and 5 means "3x + 5," and that EQUALS the PRODUCT of (multiplying) x times 1/3, meaning "(1/3)x."

Question 3: (C)
Out of 90 possible trash cans, we want the probability that the clerk lost a file in one of the 15 blue trash cans. So 15 out of 90 trash cans are blue. Our probability is 15/90 = 1/6. And what is the probability that the clerk will lose his job if the whole office gets stuck digging through the trash for that file? 99 percent.

Question 4: (E)
The equation x/y = 1/2 is referring to any pair of numbers where one number is twice as big as the other. How many pairs of integers satisfy that equation? Well, let's name some: (1, 2), (2, 4), (3, 6), (4, 8), (5, 10), (-1352, -2704)... umm, this could go on forever! There are literally infinite answers.

Question 5: (C)
You'll thank yourself later if you take a second and write in numbers as estimates for the height of each bar in the graph. It makes it much easier to read and compare values. Here are my rough estimates: June 7... July 40 ... August 10 ... Sept 32 ... Oct 25 ... Nov 30. Now we can accurately compare the answers.
(A) June plus July = 47
(B) July plus Aug = 50
(C) Aug plus Sept = 42 (Here's our LOWEST value!!!)
(D) Sept plus Oct = 57
(E) Oct plus Nov = 55

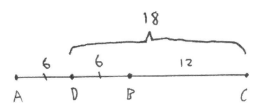

Question 6: (D)
See diagram. Since AB = BC, each segment must be 12. Then point D is in the middle of AB, so it must divide AB into two segments of 6. The distance from D to C includes one of those segments that is 6 units long, plus BC which is 12, for a total of 18.

Question 7: (B)
Since 6 and 1 are both being multiplied times 10 to the same power, we are allowed to add the terms. (Just like how $6y^2 + 1y^2 = 7y^2$). So we get a sum of 7 x 10^-n. A negative exponent can be rewritten as a positive exponent if you move it to the denominator. So 10^-n

moves down below and becomes 10^n. The 7 stays on top. Our final answer is 7 / 10^n.

Question 8: (B)
First of all, it's super important to remember that anytime circles are mentioned, you need to be thinking 360 degrees. So 1/4 of a circle is (1/4)(360) = 90 degrees. 1/5 of 360 = 72 degrees. To find how many MORE degrees are in the quarter circle, we subtract 90 – 72 and get 18 degrees.

Question 9: (B)
Let's translate this problem into normal-speak: "Based on the graph of the function f above (LOOK AT THE PICTURE!), what are the values of x (USING THE HORIZONTAL MARKINGS) for which f(x) is negative (WHERE DOES THE GRAPH DIP BELOW THE AXIS)?" The graph dips down below the axis at the origin and crosses back upwards into positive territory when the x-coordinate is 6. So the range of x coordinates we want is from 0 to 6.

Question 10: (C)
It's best to find the volume of each layer separately, then add them up. The top layer is 1 foot in each direction, so it has a volume of 1. The layer below it is 1 foot WIDER, so it has a base that is 2 feet wide. Since all the bases are square, that base is also 2 feet deep. It's still 1 foot high. So the volume of the second layer is 2 x 2 x 1 = 4. The third layer is 3 feet wide and 3 feet deep and 1 foot high, for a volume of 9. And the fourth (bottom) layer is 4 feet x 4 feet x 1 foot = 16. The total volume is 1 + 4 + 9 + 16 = 30 cubic feet.

Question 11: (A)
We can plug in numbers to make life easy here. Since we're looking for x in terms of y, let's plug in a number for y. How about 5. Then 2 ^ 5 = 32. So our equation now is 4(2 ^ x) = 32. We divide both sides by 4 to get 2 ^ x = 8. What power must 2 be raised to, to give us an answer of 8? 2 ^ 3 = 8, so x = 3. So we found that if we plug in 5 for y, then x = 3. Looking at the answers, x = y – 2. We still would have found the same relationship if we had plugged in a different number to start with.

Question 12: (C)
The important thing to remember with ratios is that you need to find the total of the ratio. So in the ratio of 2:3:4, we add the parts. 2 + 3 + 4 = 9. We can now set up a proportion: 2 out of every 9 degrees equals an angle of X degrees out of a total of 180. In math terms: 2/9 = X/180. If we cross-multiply and solve, X = 40. X is the smallest angle. We can do another proportion for the largest angle, which is 4/9 of the degrees in the triangle. 4/9 = Y/180. Y = 80. The largest angle is 80 and

the smallest is 40. The difference between them is 40.

Question 13: (D)
If you make a call for 10 minutes, the first minute is 50 cents and the other NINE minutes are 30 cents each. The first minute is always 50 cents, but you only pay it once. So in the equation, it will be 0.50. Then you pay 30 cents for each additional minute. That means 0.30 needs to be multiplied times one less than the total number of minutes. So, answer (D) fits the situation best. 0.50 + 0.30(n – 1).

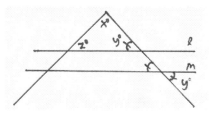

Question 14: (E)
See diagram. If we look at the small triangle with z and x in it, we can deduce that the missing angle is equal to angle y using the principles of parallel lines (Opposite Exterior Angles, anyone?). So the angles in the triangle are x, y, and z, and they add up to 180. x + y + z = 180. We need to solve for z. z = 180 – x – y.

Question 15: (C)
This question looks impossible at first. But the good news is that it's not impossible; it's just really hard! (Um… yay?) We can simplify the left hand side of the equation a bit by canceling one of the n's on top with the n that is by itself on the bottom. Now, on the bottom we have (n – 1)(n + 1), which simplifies to n² – 1. So now our equation is: n / (n² – 1) = 5 / k. But we still have two variables and only one equation. That's a bad thing, right? If we look at the answers, which are options for k, we might see a clue. The answers of 24, 25, and 26 are close to the value of 5². So the number 5 is key. Since 5 is on top of one fraction, why don't we make n = 5 on top of the other fraction. Then the bottom of the fraction, n² – 1, equals 24. And that means k = 24. The numbers check out, and that is the right answer.
(Note: It turns out that the values of 5 and 24 for n and k are the only INTEGER values when the equation is true. There are other solutions, but they are messy decimals that the SAT doesn't want us to worry about).

Question 16: (E)
The easy way to do this is plug in numbers. Let's say that there are m = 12 coworkers, and the total cost is y = 120 dollars. So the cost for each person should be 120/12 = 10 dollars. But what if p = 4 people don't contribute? Then the cost of 120 is split among only 8

people. 120/8 = 15. The cost is now 15 per person instead of 10. The ADDITIONAL cost per person is 5 dollars. If you plug those numbers into the answer choices, answer (E) gives the correct value of 5.

If you want to do it algebraically, the cost per person if everyone pays is y/m. But if p people don't pay, then the costs for the rest are $y/(m - p)$. The EXTRA cost per person is the second fraction minus the first (the amount they expected to pay). So, it's $y/(m - p) - y/m$. But that's not an answer choice. So we have to combine the fractions by getting a common denominator. Multiply the first fraction by m/m and the second fraction by $(m - p)/(m - p)$. Now we have $[ym / m(m - p)] - [y(m - p) / m(m - p)]$. If we combine the fractions and distribute on top, we get: $(ym - ym + yp) / m(m - p)$. Then we simplify and get $yp / m(m - p)$, and there's our answer. Plugging in numbers sure would have been easier!

Section 9: Critical Reading

Question 1: (C)
Clue words "co-wrote" and "mingling" point to "collaborative."

Question 2: (E)
The clue word "eager" makes the first blank positive, but the "but unfortunately" indicates an opposite, and therefore negative word for the second blank. Even if you are not familiar with the word "soporific," the incorrect choices don't satisfy the need for contrast.

Question 3: (E)
The clue word here is "touched," but this one usually comes down to knowledge of the words. After you eliminate the words you know don't mean "touched" ("archaic" and "rustic"), use any knowledge you have of prefixes to get rid of (A) and hopefully (C).

Question 4: (D)
If you know what "deft" means, you're halfway there. If not, use the clue word "astonished" to give the blank a positive connotation. This usually eliminates (E), (C), and sometimes (B). "Adroit" means "highly skilled," and it's one of the Top 10 SAT vocab words to know! You are hereby commanded to memorize this word!

Question 5: (D)
The first word "although" immediately tells us that there is an opposite happenin' here! The word "hero" means that the first blank is positive, and the clue words "lamentable" and "painful" confirm that the second blank is negative. The words in the second blank are easier to judge, so eliminate any positive second words before dealing with the first column.

Question 6: (C)
The clue phrase here is, "public declaration of motives." If you know the words, the top 2 contenders are "mandate" and "manifesto." The difference between them is that a "manifesto" is philosophical, whereas a "mandate" is concrete. In other words, the Communist Manifesto was a public declaration of how communism should work; however, a communist mandate would read more like, "Comrade Tutor Ted will report all suspicious activity to Our Dear Robot Overlords."

Passage: Colonial Williamsburg
Main Idea Passage 1: Williamsburg makes history accessible and is therefore awesome.
Main Idea Passage 2: Williamsburg is fake and is therefore stupid.

Question 7: (A)
Both passages agree that Williamsburg is "popular;" however, the authors disagree about whether this is a good or bad thing.

Question 8: (B)
The phrase, "unless one already knows a great deal," informs this answer choice. There are words in each of the other answer choices that cannot be substantiated by the evidence in the passage.

Question 9: (D)
Clue words like "forbidding" and "do not touch" signify a negative tone toward the "ribbon" and "sign." That gets rid of (A) and (B). The clue phrase "symbol of culture" matches the wording of (D).

Question 10: (C)
Support for (C) can be found in the clue phrases "Williamsburg guides have no set speeches," and "their own interpretation."

Question 11: (A)
These analogy questions can be tricky because they are not asking you about what is actually going on in the passage, but rather asking you to choose the answer that is most like what's going on in the passage. The examples "American spelling bee" and "Educational television shows," and the clue phrase "business and pleasure ought to be combined," express the idea that education can be fun. (B), (D), and (E) are not fun, and (C) is not educational.

Question 12: (D)
The word "studious," while seemingly positive, is followed by the phrase "fudging of facts," which reveals that the author actually has a negative attitude toward Colonial Williamsburg and its creators. (A) and (D)

are the only choices that are in any way negative, but "deliberateness" and "fabricated" are word matches for "studious" and "fudging." So congratulations (D)! You did it!

Question 13: (C)
Again, you can replace the words in the answer choices directly into the sentence. If you do so, (C) is the only one that both means what we want it to mean and sounds good in the sentence.

Question 14: (E)
We already know that the author's attitude is negative, which matches "ominous," and the clue phrase "established element of popular culture" matches "few people seem to be bothered."

Question 15: (D)
Build on the main idea of P2. Why does the author hate Williamsburg? Because it's fake. What's bad about being fake? The answer can be found in lines 60-63. ("Within those limitations….very nice time.")

Question 16: (E)
The academic historians in P1 treat Williamsburg as a "harmless but amusing example of American vulgarity." They don't like it, but they aren't too stressed about it. This one usually comes down to (C) and (E); however, do the academic historians actually say that people need their history simplified? No.

Question 17: (E)
The author of P2 is negative, so the answers are going to be negative. This eliminates (A) and (C). Both passages accept that Williamsburg is popular, so (B) is out. Finally (D) is out because, while negative, it's not so much the actual buildings as it is the fake sense of history with which the author of P2 has a problem.

Question 18: (C)
As in a two-blank vocab question, you can eliminate column by column. The first one needs to be positive, so (D) is out. The second one needs to be negative, so (A) and (E) are out. In the battle of "unprofitable" vs. "lamentable," lamentable wins.

Question 19: (C)
(C) pretty much echoes the main idea of each passage. P1 is about accessibility; P2 is about authenticity.

Section 10: Writing

Question 1: (B)
Two camps: "that" vs. "as." As wins. (B) is the most concise.

Question 2: (A)
Last words can be just as helpful as first words. "Is" vs. "are"? No matter how you begin this sentence, the subject is singular, so (B) and (D) are out. (A) is the most concise.

Question 3: (B)
Parallel structure! "Biographer" in the first clause must be matched by "biographer" in the second. This eliminates (C) and (D). (E) is out because of "being." And in the battle of "this" vs. "and" in (A) and (B)… drum roll please… "and" beats "this" because (A) would need a semicolon to be grammatically correct! What an upset!

Question 4: (A)
(D) and (E) are crimes against humanity. Of the three remaining choices, (A) is -- you guessed it -- the most concise.

Question 5: (E)
The rule of "first words" eliminates choices (A) and (B). Next, if "one of these things is not like the other" it's probably wrong, so too bad for you (C). Not only is (E) shorter, but also (D)'s use of "its" instead of "his" doesn't work for the subject "Shakespeare." Shakespeare is a person. You may have heard of him.

Question 6: (E)
Who is laughing because they had missed their stop? The tourists. This gets us down to (C), (D), and (E). (E) is short, sweet, and contains the past tense verb we are looking for.

Question 7: (D)
"Were" vs. "was"? ONE of the ballerinas "was." (D) is the most parallel and the inclusion of "that" creates the cause and effect relationship we want.

Question 8: (A)
Beware of wordiness! (A) and (D) are the least wordy, but only (A) uses the correct verb tense.

Question 9: (C)
Looking at first words tells us that (D) and (E) are probably wrong. (Two of these things are not like the others). A closer inspection confirms that they are indeed wordy. (B) is out because the phrase "damage is caused often" is awkward. Now think about which is a stronger subject: "The damage" or "strip-mining." Since strip-mining causes the damage, and not the other way around, strip-mining is the better subject.

Question 10: (A)
This is a hard one. Focus on punctuation and verb tense. (D) and (E) both have punctuation errors. (D)

needs a comma before "and," and (E) needs a comma instead of a semi-colon. (A) is the shortest, contains correct punctuation, and the past tense verb "slept" is stronger than either "sleeping" in (B) or "would sleep" in (C).

Question 11: (E)
Memorize this: "because they love because"! Just as "having" and "being" indicate that the answer is probably wrong, "because" often indicates a good answer. Nobody knows why, but they love because. "But wait a minute," you say! "I thought you can't start a sentence with because!" English teachers initially teach this as a black and white rule to prevent students from writing in fragments. You're right, "Because he was a werewolf" is not a sentence. However, "Because he was a werewolf, Teen Wolf became the star of his basketball team," is. As long as "because" begins an introductory clause, it's okay.

Question 12: (D)
Parallel structure. (D) is the only answer choice that is a full match. The phrase "as fascinating as" is the key here.

Question 13: (E)
Tricky! First off we've got two camps: "Nor" vs. "Or." Since the sentence does not contain the word "neither," we cannot use "nor." Once you get it down to (D) and (E), the issue is again one of parallel structure. Dr. Carl Sagan refused to do two things: "to accept" or "to profit."

Question 14: (A)
Looking at first words, (D) and (E) are probably out. Then it's about singular vs. plural. The compound subject, "convenience and availability" is plural, so (C) is out. However, "its" vs. "their" is referring to the paint itself, which is singular.

The Essay
How to Get a 12

Nothing freaks out a test-prepper quite like the essay. Relax! It's no big thing. Let's review the facts:

The essay is only about 30% of your writing test score and 10% of your overall score. That means you could SKIP the essay, do well on the rest of the test and still score over 2000. But **don't skip the essay.**

Everyone gets exactly 25 minutes to write this thing. William frickin' Shakespeare could not write a masterpiece in 25 minutes. The graders aren't expecting you to write one either.

The questions you are going to get are extremely generic. Sometimes questions like these are referred to as "softballs," because they're as **big as a grapefruit**, and as long as you keep your eye on it **you can knock it out of the park**. Here are a few examples:

> Do people need to keep secrets or is secrecy harmful?

> Can something unsuccessful still have some value?

> Is accepting responsibility the first step towards solving a problem?

Many of these questions will be followed by the instruction:

> Plan and write an essay in which you develop your point of view on this issue. Support your position with reasoning and examples taken from your reading, studies, experience, or observations.

What does that mean? It means that you can use **any** example you can possibly think of to support your argument, from the story about **the time when you went to school with your pants on backwards** to the **importance of water imagery in "The Great Gatsby."**

Oh, and don't listen to anyone who tells you that you'll get a higher score if you talk about a fancy book or historical figure. Write about whatever you know well. I've seen a great essay about Paris Hilton and a terrible one about Franklin Delano Roosevelt.

Two people will independently grade your essay on a six-point scale. If the scores they give are within a point of each other's, then the combined score (out of 12) is your final tally. If they disagree by more than one point, a third reader will evaluate it. The essay score is then **cross-referenced with your multiple-choice score to produce your Writing section score.**

Although there has to be some subjectivity when it comes to grading someone's writing, the graders are looking for **some specific things** when they assess your essay. Those things are, in order of importance:

Relevance—did the essay answer the question?

Argument—was the argument sophisticated and complete?

Evidence—was the argument supported by specific evidence?

Structure—did the essay have appropriate structure, with topic sentences

Length—did the student write enough to make his or her point?

Clarity—did the language of the essay get in the way of the argument?

Transitions—did they essay have 'flow'?

Sentence variety—did the writer make an effort to vary his or her rhythms?

Vocabulary—did the author use appropriate vocabulary?

Style—was it interesting to read?

Those are the priorities of the graders. To get a high score, you just have to make them your priorities as well.

The essays that we've seen that have scored a 10, 11 or 12 have a few things in common. **One is that they are long.** I have not come across an essay that scored a 12 that was shorter than 300 words. It makes sense: the essays that score the highest are the ones that are the best-developed, which means they generally are longer. The most obvious common factor among essays that score a 12 is this: they have **an argument** (that's the thesis plus the way that you support the thesis) **that goes beyond a simple 'yes' or 'no' answer to the question.**

Take the question "Do people need to keep secrets or is secrecy harmful?" for example. One approach would be to write an essay that proves the point, "Yes, secrecy is harmful." That essay, if written decently well, would probably score an 8. **Take the argument a little bit further and you're much more likely to earn a better score**. Here are some examples of theses on the same topic that would probably earn a score higher than an 8.

Secrecy is harmful because if we do not interact truthfully with those around us, we will not be able to trust any of our communication with others. This one goes beyond the question by including the idea of 'trust' and that secrecy can undermine it.

Whether secrecy is harmful or not depends on the scale of the secret. Secrecy is harmful when it comes to governments misleading their people, but between friends and loved ones we may keep secrets to prevent hurt feelings. You may have heard that you need to take ONE side and stick to it. Not true! What you need to do is take a position. This thesis does take a position—it says that secrecy is harmful on a large scale but not on a small one.

Secrecy is harmful only if the individual keeping the secret has malicious intentions. This thesis goes beyond the question in a really simple, elegant way: by adding a condition about the intentions of the person telling the secret.

After you've got an interesting thesis, your next task is to **prove your point with evidence**. One of the best things you can do to prepare for the essay is to have an **Idea Bank**—a list of evidence you can cite to make your argument. Complete the following lists and you'll have enough evidence to argue just about any question they could throw at you.

Three stories from your personal experience that taught you something:

_____

_____

_____

Three good books (no, "Harry Potter" does not count) **that I know really well:**

_____

_____

_____

Three historical events/figures (try to avoid the obvious: Martin Luther King Jr., Gandhi, Hitler) **that I can discuss:**

_____

_____

_____

Three highly regarded films (no, not "The Hangover") **that I know really well:**

_____

_____

_____

Three current developments in politics, technology or the arts about which I feel passionately but which avoid any potentially controversial subject matters like abortion.

_____

_____

_____

Here are examples of what essays from each score category 1–6 look like. When grading your own essays, compare them to these to get an approximate score. These are answers to the essay question on page 389 of the Big Blue Book.

The following essay received a score of 6.

Thoughtful challenges to the ideas of people in positions of authority have led, over the course of history, to some of the most profoundly positive developments that mankind can claim. Take Martin Luther's 95 theses as one example. One man's critique of authority led to the democratization of established religion. Look at the civil rights pioneers who marched on Selma despite Alabama Governor George Wallace's objections. With these and many other examples we can easily establish the repeated value of questioning those in authority. The question might then be about limitations to such challenges. Is there ever a time when we should not challenge the establishment? In order to create and maintain social justice, it is vital that we question the ideas of those in positions of authority, but we must be careful not to abuse this right to free expression simply because we can.

The Crimean War was the first war in which professional journalists ventured in the conflict area to document what they saw. And what they saw was frequently horrific. 19th century war power meant having a large number of soldiers, soldiers to stand in the way of rifles and cannons. After one particularly disastrous battle for the British army, journalists reported about the miscommunication that led to the complete annihilation of the "light brigade", soldiers on horseback, carrying only small weaponry. Poet Alfred Lord Tennyson wrote his poem "The Charge of the Light Brigade" in response to those reports. His poem affected not just the reading population of the time (who then demanded reforms in military communication and strategy) but also reverberated throughout the years as an effective criticism of mismanagement by those in authority.

Despite the many heroic examples we can cite when one person stood up to authority to fight for what's right, we can also look at examples of when someone stood up and the result was hostility and failure. Take the congressman who, during President Barack Obama's State of the Union speech, yelled, "you lie!" at the President. Many Americans viewed this act of defiance as an embarrassment. While the congressman viewed his statement as a heroic challenge to authority, it ultimately interrupted a moment of agreed-upon civil discourse. We should not challenge those in authority just because we can.

Comments: The most important thing that the author does to get the 6 is to go beyond a basic "yes" answer to the question. Within the first paragraph the author answers the question at face value and then proceeds to ask a follow-up question. Structurally, this essay does not follow a traditional 5-paragraph structure—that's OK, and works well in this essay. Mechanically, this essay is solid. It also contains varied sentence structure and vocabulary. So it's got structure, argument, a strong position, good vocab, sentence structure, good details, it's long, blah blah blah…but…it's not perfect. The last paragraph doesn't have the same level of analysis of the first two paragraphs. And the final idea, that we should not challenge authority, "just because we can" is a little thin. I'd definitely like to read more explanation of that idea. But the things that make this essay good place it squarely in the 6 category.

The following essay received a score of 5.

It is important to question ideas of people in authority, because if we didn't, we would likely still be governed by dictators and others who abuse their power. In looking at examples ranging from the civil rights movement in the United States to the Richard Nixon and the Watergate scandal, it is clearly important to question the ideas and positions of those in authority.

The civil rights movement in the 1960s was based on a simple idea: that organized, peaceful resistance can correct injustices in the world. Led by the Reverend Dr. Martin Luther King Jr., thousands of Americans participated in demonstrations, protests, sit-ins and marches. They were protesting the unequal treatment of blacks primarily in southern states, where segregation was legal and common. Through constant pressure, the people of this movement were able to overturn the unjust treatment of African Americans, a positive result.

When Richard Nixon ran for a second term as President, he had significant support among the

American people. Early polls suggested that he would be easily reelected. For Nixon, this was not good enough. He and his cronies hatched a plan to invade the headquarters of the National Democratic Party and install microphones so that they could overhear what their opponents were planning. As anyone who knows their history can tell you, they got caught. This eventually led to Nixon's resignation, even though he never did accept responsibility for his crimes. It was important for the public to know about Nixon's illegal activity because they then were in position to pressure him to leave office.

Without questioning people in positions of authority, America might still have Jim Crow laws. Taking it to the extreme, we might still have slavery! It is important to question the ideas and decisions of people in positions of authority because those questions can lead to impactful change.

Comments: This is a well-structured essay that answers the question thoroughly. There are two major differences between this and an essay that would get a 6. First, this essay does not push the analysis of the answer very far beyond the question. The author does include the idea that it's important to question those in authority BECAUSE it can lead to positive change. That's good. Now the author just needs to take the argument a little further, perhaps by exploring why questioning authority leads to positive change, or even asking if questioning authority always leads to positive change. Second, the sentence structure and facility with vocabulary is good, but a little bit less than what you might see in a 6 essay. The author should actively try to shake up sentence structures and increase the level of the vocabulary.

The following essay received a score of 4.

People should question the ideas of people in authority. Leaders are not always right and frequently need to be reminded what is right and wrong. Some examples include Stalin and my high school principle.

Josef Stalin was a leader of the Communist party in Russia. His ideas were that people should do equal work and receive equal payment. That's what he said his ideas were, anyways. In reality, Stalin was a mean dictator. He ruled his country through fear and violense. He killed thousands of Russian citizens to stay in power. He is an example of a person in a position of authority who's ideas and decisions needed to be questioned.

When my high school principle cancelled the pep rally before the state volleyball tournament, I was irate! Our team had worked so hard to get to where no other team from our school had ever got to before. Whenever a team gets to the state tournament, our school throws a pep rally. But our principle, Mr. Vang, cancelled it because "it was too close to Winter Carnival." My teammates and I wrote a petition and passed it around the school. We had 1000 signatures by the time we were done! We brought it to Mr. Vang and explained. Before we left, he agreed to schedule the pep rally for Friday.

Although we lost in the second round, the pep rally really psyched us up for our games. If we had not stood up for what was right, we would not have had this special event. Thus, it is important to question the ideas and decisions of people in positions of authority.

Comments: Now, nothing says that you can't write about Stalin and your high school principal in the same essay, or even in back-to-back paragraphs. But look: I don't know your high school principal, but I'm pretty sure he's got a less-evil track record than Josef Stalin. To include them in the same essay without pointing out that the two examples come from polar extremes on the scale of evil is, well, a little awkward. The author seems to have more to say about the volleyball tournament. I would tell him or her to write the whole essay about that. There must be many other details from the story to explore. What did other students have to say? When did the author realize that the team had the power to question the principal's decision? Why did they choose a petition? Exploring those ideas and expanding the pep rally story (leaving Stalin out altogether) would make this essay much stronger. The author also needs to improve sentence structure, vocabulary and spelling.

The following essay received a score of 3.

It is important to question authority because some of the gratest changes in the history of our times have come about because of this. Hitler is somebody who was in authority and did some of the worst things ever nown about. The Hollocost killed millions of innocent Jewish people and millions of other people too. Only when the United States and other nations questioned his authority and fought against him did the killing end.

Adolf Hitler was a man who started the worst war humans have ever seen. Worst of all, he killed millions of Jewish people in concentration camps. But he was in authority and maybe they should have just accepted it? Of course not! When Japan invaded Pearl Harbor, America stood up against Hitler because they knew he was wrong. We won the war and Hitler killed himself. Even though so many people died and suffered because of him, we might be speaking German today if someone hadn't questioned authority.

Hitler is someone who in authority and have to be questioned sometimes. Hitler should be questioned all of the time, of course. Some of the best things in the history of humans have happened only because people questioned authority. Sometimes people in charge are right, but they can also be wrong and when they are we need to question them.

Comments: This essay answers the questions, but the argument is not very strong. Hitler is certainly an example of a leader whose ideas needed to be challenged and defied, but that's a pretty simple point to prove. The author would have done better to pick a more interesting example to investigate. The key to receiving a better score is to make a more interesting point. Just because Hitler works doesn't mean you have to write about him. This essay also has some logical and mechanical issues, which don't help.

The following essay received a score of 2.

Questioning authority is important because people who are in authority are not always right. In "To Kill A Mockingbird," Atticus is a tough lawyer who stands up for what he believes in even though people in charge think he's wrong.

In "To Kill A Mockingbird," Boo is accused to committing a crime he didn't do. Everyone thinks he did it because he is black. All the people in the town to the judge to everyone else thinks he did it. But one great man has the strength and courage to do something about it. Atticus knows the facts don't add up and like a great crime fighter detective he figures it out! He makes everyone see that they are wrong when he proves it in the courtroom and Boo is a free man! By standing up for what he believes Atticus proves that people in authority are not always right.

Comments: Let's first focus on what's good here: the essay has a thesis sentence. That's clutch—the grader reads that first sentence and thinks, "hey, this kid's got a point." Unfortunately, it's downhill from there. Although you generally won't be penalized for factual errors, any English teacher reading this essay would immediately recognize that Boo Radley was not the character accused of the crime in the book. That can't help your grade. This essay is also very short. The author doesn't say enough to make an interesting point. He/she does try to answer the question, though, which is why this brief essay gets a 2 and not a 1.

The following essay received a score of 1.

Talking about authority it is always good to question it. Asking questions about everything and authority is very important in times like war. In the slavery and Civil Rights times the people in authority wanted separate schools and drinking fountains and later they said we couldn't go to the moon. People in authority are just people after all and all people makes mistakes and can be wrong.

Think about Santa Claus and the Tooth Fairy. Are we supposed to believe there real when we get old enough to figure out theys fake. Time after time it happens like that and the people has to stand up and fight for it. From war times to peace times its the same old story and your never going to fix it unless you do something about it.

If people didn't question authority Rosa Parks might still be on that bus today.

Comments: OK, we'll be honest. We included this essay just because we thought it was pretty funny. Santa Claus and the Tooth Fairy? Where did that come from?! The author doesn't make much of a point here. In the second body paragraph the author seems to be making a point ("it's the same old story") but doesn't share that point with his/her readers. The last sentence, though dramatic, doesn't make any sense. In addition to the logical errors, this essay is riddled with mechanical errors—verb conjugation problems, words that don't exist—so this essay receives a score of 1.

Glossary — By Section

Word	Definition

Section 1–2

foresight	forethought
nostalgia	wistful, longing
folly	foolishness
despair	misery
artistry	creativity
intricate	complicated
candid	sincere
ostentatious	showy, pretentious
fictional	imaginary
convoluted	elaborate
capricious	unpredictable, impulsive
bombastic	pompous
loquacious	talkative, wordy
dispassionate	calm
decorous	well-behaved
emotional	touching
intellectual	academic
chance	unintended
random	arbitrary
intuitive	instinctive
impulsive	spontaneous
deliberate	on purpose
instinctive	natural
intentional	planned, intended
logical	rational
streamlined	sleek, smooth, efficient
infighting	internal strife
mitigated	moderate, to make less severe
jingoism	patriotism
ossified	hardened
bureaucratization	to complicate through overregulation
politicized	to make political
innovation	originality
venerable	respected, esteemed
legislation	the process of writing and passing laws

Section 1–5

cowardice	fearfulness
prudence	carefulness
hospitality	generosity, kindness
aloofness	unfriendliness
loyalty	faithfulness
applauded	highly praised
derailed	wrecked, spoiled
acknowledged	recognized
permitted	allowed
anticipated	expected
condition	circumstance
highlight	focus
stimulus	incentive, motivation
dictum	saying, motto
respite	break
negotiate	discuss, bargain
concessions	the act of conceding or yielding
antagonize	irritate
friends	acquaintances
surrender	give up, admit defeat
enemies	foes
dominate	control, rule

inquiries	investigation
equivocate	be evasive, beat around the bush
denunciations	public condemnation
rousing	stirring
memorable	unforgettable
pedestrian	ordinary
evolving	developing
chaotic	disorganized
unprecedented	extraordinary
derivative	not original
inept	incompetent
spontaneous	impulsive
graceless	clumsy
cheapened	to decrease the quality of
affordable	reasonably priced
transformed	changed
viable	possible
revolutionized	radically altered
prohibitive	prevent or forbid, too expensive
provoked	aggravated
improbable	unlikely
stimulated	inspired
inaccessible	unreachable
cryptic	mysterious
judicious	sensible
jubilant	excited
supercilious	arrogant
pugnacious	confrontational
belligerence	hostility
indigence	poverty
perfidy	disloyalty
aspersion	criticism, slander
tenacity	stubbornness

Section 1–9

imprecise	inexact
straightforward	uncomplicated
deficient	lacking
obtrusive	sticking out
elliptical	indirect, oval-shaped
vast	huge
hollow	empty
sparse	thin, meager
thunderous	loud
enormous	huge
deafening	noisy
unimpressive	mediocre
muted	quiet
negligible	insignificant
rousing	inspiring
advanced	better
setback	delay
altered	distorted
revolution	uprising
contradicted	denied
truce	peace
reinforced	toughened
crisis	disaster
halted	stopped
breakthrough	step forward
credence	credibility
irrefutable	unquestionable
disrepute	disrespect
dubious	doubtful
acceptance	agreement

convincing	believable
momentum	drive
systematic	orderly
currency	popularity, money
inconclusive	uncertain
palpable	tangible, obvious
diaphanous	see through
variegated	multicolored
luxurious	comfortable
anomalous	abnormal, strange
egalitarian	equal
dowager	a respected, rich woman
dilettante	amateur
iconoclast	one who challenges tradition
purveyor	seller

Section 2–4

convincing	believable
misinterpret	misunderstand
misleading	deceptive
anticipate	expect
predictable	unsurprising
foresee	predict
ironic	sarcastic
endorse	approve
spellbinding	fascinating
ignore	pay no attention to
liquefying	to make or become liquid
founder	creator
contaminating	ruining
backfire	go wrong
purifying	to make pure
boomerang	rebound
saturating	fill up
reciprocate	give in return
polluting	to make unclean
prevail	succeed
dispassionate	unemotional
insubstantial	weak
esoteric	obscure
capricious	unpredictable
indignant	angry
conclusive	definite
reality	truth
tenable	reasonable
misconception	false impression
mythical	imaginary
possibility	likelihood
erroneous	mistaken
delusion	illusion
hypothetical	theoretical
digression	sidetrack
substantiated	proved
impugned	challenged as false
protected	sheltered
united	joined, combined
mollified	soften
flotsam	debris
reconnaissance	investigation
decimation	to destroy
raiment	clothing
sustenance	nourishment

disposition	temperament
cantankerous	irritable
anatomy	makeup
churlish	rude
outlook	viewpoint
benevolent	kind
personality	character
laconic	terse, using few words
stature	physique, standing
robust	healthy
mercurial	changing, unexpected
corrosive	destroy gradually
disingenuous	insincere
implacable	merciless
phlegmatic	apathetic, impassive

Section 2–7

ensured	to make sure or certain
approved	accepted
belittled	mock
eliminated	removed
defended	protected
amateurish	unprofessional
professional	skilled, qualified
lax	laidback, careless
harsh	cruel
selective	careful
inclusive	all-encompassing
judgmental	critical
discriminating	discerning
sensitive	responsive
insightful	perceptive
verbose	wordy
mundane	ordinary
concise	brief
elaborate	complex
comprehensive	complete
edifying	enlightening
succinct	short, to the point
enlightening	informative
provocative	stimulating
technical	related to mechanics or science
aggregation	collection of different things
inclination	tendency
prognosis	prediction
retrenchment	cutback
preeminence	supremacy
unequivocal	clear
effusive	overenthusiastic
incorrigible	persistent
tenuous	questionable
ineffable	indescribable

Section 2–9

lush	abundant
sprawling	expansive
desolate	deserted
gaudy	extravagant
monumental	immense
misnomer	wrong name
hybrid	mixture
vector	quantity with magnitude and direction

curative	healing
precursor	predecessor
stringent	severe
dispersive	spread, scatter
conditional	restricted
recessive	to go backward
obtrusive	unmistakable
revolutionary	innovative
promoted	further, advance
positive	encouraging
prohibited	forbidden
successful	triumphant
protested	disapproved of, fought against
divisive	disruptive
restricted	limited
militant	confrontational
fostered	promoted the growth of
bucolic	rural
prolific	productive
lugubrious	sad
sundry	various
metaphorical	symbolic
misguided	mistaken
remonstrance	complaint
absurd	ridiculous
erudition	sophistication
plausible	possible
lassitude	weariness
painstaking	thorough
fabrication	untruth
wrongheaded	foolish
chicanery	trickery
cosmopolitan	sophisticated

Section 3–4

defense	resistance
worldly	experienced
inspiration	motivation
moral	ethical
obligation	duty
stunted	underdeveloped
condition	state
limited	incomplete
center	middle
hinder	hold back
reconcile	settle, bring into agreement
control	organize
soothe	calm
extend	expand
coddled	to treat tenderly
taunted	teased
prodded	nudged
ousted	get rid of
chided	scolded
exhilarating	exciting
banal	dull
shocking	outrageous
prophetic	visionary
startling	surprising
revolutionary	ground-breaking
appalling	terrible
groundbreaking	innovative

unanticipated	unexpected
irrelevant	unrelated
digression	aside
proximity	nearness
expansion	growth
stabilization	to make permanent, stable
correlation	association
benign	kind
cantankerous	irritable
reticent	quiet
bellicose	argumentative
complacent	content
docile	submissive
aggressive	hostile
placid	peaceful
playful	lighthearted
frisky	lively
mentor	teacher
profiteer	one who makes excessive profits
counterfeiter	forger
clairvoyant	psychic
propagandist	one who spreads ideas, information
obscure	unclear
deferential	respectful
discriminating	selective
sanctimonious	self-righteous
unrelenting	insistent
replicated	simulated

Section 3–7

ignore	pay no attention to
perused	read thoroughly
discard	throw away
obliterated	destroyed
translate	interpret
recollected	remembered
conceal	hide
scrutinized	inspected
decipher	decode
deterrent	prevention
launched	began
panacea	cure-all
overcame	defeated
barrier	obstruction
awakened	wake up
catalyst	something that makes change happen
stirred	stimulated
provocation	irritation
mitigated	to make less severe
conducive	favorable
invaluable	important
imperative	essential
indistinguishable	identical
bereft	deprived of
miscreants	troublemakers
revisionists	people who revise, change
anomalies	irregularities
pacifists	peace lovers
extremists	radicals
tacit	unstated
fervent	passionate
unqualified	untrained

Glossary — By Section

impetuous	impulsive
conditional	restricted

Section 3–9

regal	majestic
imperial	royal
simplistic	basic
neutral	unbiased
liberating	invigorating
repressive	oppressive
totalitarian	dictatorial
absolutist	one who favors autocratic government
scandalous	shocking
compromised	negotiated
imagine	envision
worthlessness	insignificance
reconcile	settle, bring into agreement
superiority	dominance
embrace	hug
insecurity	uncertainty
dispel	dismiss
inferiority	weakness
fathom	understand
levity	lightheartedness
haughty	arrogant
impudent	rude
irresolute	uncertain
insolent	rude
presumptuous	arrogant
loquacious	wordy
arrogant	conceited
articulate	eloquent
reverential	respectful
contemptuous	disdainful, disapproving
satellites	followers, minions
antipodes	opposites
reversals	changes, to go back
bifurcations	divided into two parts
dichotomies	branching into two parts
filial	related to a child and his/her parents
symbiotic	close association
avuncular	friendly, helpful, like an uncle
convivial	welcoming
funerary	associated with a funeral
cacophonous	harsh sounding
syncopated	cut short
harmonic	good sounding
collaborative	shared
mellifluous	smooth

Section 4–2

erratic	unpredictable
informal	casual
elaborate	complicated
predictable	unsurprising
idiosyncratic	unusual
preventive	precautionary
regressive	reverting to a previous way
catastrophic	disastrous
unforeseen	unanticipated
moderate	normal
arrangement	agreement

devoid	lacking
entertainment	amusement
disparaging	disapproving
attitude	outlook
consisting	made up of
bargain	deal
worthy	admirable
misfortune	bad luck
trusting	unquestioning
meddle	interfere
scoff	make fun of
temporize	to draw out, take time
prolong	delay
misbehave	be bad
disrupt	disturb
sneer	mock
terminate	end
withdraw	remove
intrude	break in
conduct	transmit
release	let go
deflect	repel
transmit	convey
admit	let in
contain	hold
absorb	soak up
dispense	distribute
resist	oppose
trap	catch
reason	rationale
dalliance	idleness
infelicity	inappropriateness, an inappropriate act
conviction	certainty
rhetoric	oratory
substance	material
pragmatism	common sense
futility	pointlessness
boorishness	rudeness
integrity	honesty
fastidious	fussy
sedulous	persistent
vindictive	bitter
petulant	irritable
mercenary	motivated by money
treacly	sentimental
cursory	quick
prosaic	ordinary
meticulous	careful
consecrated	sacred

Section 4–5

remiss	careless
adept	skilled
humorous	funny
hesitant	uncertain
contemptuous	disdainful
rebellion	uprising
challenged	confronted
interrogation	examination
fortified	prepared
conflagration	fire
fostered	cultivated

denial	rejection
restrained	reserved
uprising	rebellion
quelled	put down
ineffable	indescribable
articulated	expressed
consummate	accomplished
presumptive	assumed
deleterious	harmful
vacillated	wavered
inconsistency	variation
sermonized	preached
fidelity	faithfulness
wavered	fluctuated, swayed
steadfastness	resoluteness
experimented	tested
inflexibility	rigidity
relied	depended
negligence	inattention
polarized	divided
vindication	justification
imaginative	original
discernment	judgment
holistic	complete, all of something
censure	criticism
complimentary	praising
animosity	hostility
equitable	fair
eulogy	tribute

Section 4–8

secretiveness	sneakiness
cooperation	collaboration
understanding	accepting
counsel	advice
concord	agreement
passion	enthusiasm
contagious	infectious
knowledge	information
inaudible	impossible to hear
contempt	dislike
praiseworthy	commendable
propensity	tendency
futile	pointless
commitment	dedication
impersonal	unfriendly
momentous	significant
formidable	tough
decisive	crucial
unavoidable	inescapable
unexpected	surprising
ambiguous	unclear
advantageous	helpful
beneficial	useful
catastrophic	disastrous
constructive	helpful
release	free
elevate	lift up
entangle	ensnare
shroud	cover
attain	achieve
opportune	well-timed

instantaneous	immediate
intermittent	irregular
dubious	doubtful
extravagant	excessive
experimentation	testing
eliminate	get rid of
arrogance	egotism
pursue	chase
humility	humbleness
advocate	supporter
smugness	overconfidence
legitimate (v)	prove something to be lawful
rigidity	inflexibility
console	comfort

Section 5–3

healthy	well
expensive	costly
wasteful	inefficient
toxic	poisonous
inane	absurd
idealizes	romanticizes
avoids	keeps away from
beautifies	makes pretty
scrutinizes	looks closely at
excludes	keeps out
argue	fight
contrast	difference
testify	give evidence
jeopardize	put at risk
sustain	continue
plentiful	abundant
subtracted	took away from
ornate	elaborate
retrieved	got back
multifarious	diverse
catalogued	documented, recorded
scarce	limited
extracted	took out
anachronistic	out of proper date, time
extrapolated	inferred, drew conclusions
byzantine	intricate, complicated
adroit	skilled
nefarious	evil
conscientious	careful
devious	tricky
lackadaisical	lazy
onerous	burdensome
slipshod	careless
predictable	unsurprising
compulsive	obsessive

Section 5–7

credit	as in a credit card, money to be paid later
loan	borrowed money
faith	trust
patronage	investment, financial backing
barter	trade, exchange
concern	worry
cooperation	collaboration
urgency	hurry
relevance	significance

dispute	argument	creating	making
autonomy	independence	erratic	unpredictable
incoherence	not understandable	egotistical	self-centered
intuition	instinct	flexible	bendable
sophistry	flawed method of argumentation	tactful	considerate
receptivity	openness	inconspicuous	not noticeable
supplement	add on to	resourceful	imaginative
integrates	mixes	courteous	polite
substantiates	validates	tenacious	stubborn
undermines	weakens	manipulative	scheming
remedy	cure	determined	resolute
compromises	negotiates	demonstrative	expressive
disparage	ridicule	resolute	unwavering
reinforces	strengthens	diplomatic	tactful
foster	encourage	outspoken	blunt
curtails	limits	indiscriminate	arbitrary
critics	opponents	consecration	blessing
epitome	essence	rationalism	based on reason
proponents	supporters	autonomy	independence
realization	understanding	effacement	modest behavior
advocates	supporters	simplicity	ease
embodiment	incarnation	rebellious	disobedient
debunkers	one who discredits, exposes falseness	conformists	traditionalist
rejection	refusal	apolitical	not political
belittlers	one who makes fun of	loyalists	people who are faithful
reversal	turnaround	seditious	disloyal
partisanship	bias	insurrectionists	rebels
intemperance	excess	subversive	rebellious
acumen	sharpness	nonpartisans	people who are politically neutral
irreverence	disrespect	supportive	helpful
interest	attention	opponents	enemies
deceiving	misleading	corrective	fix
ingenuous	honest	tribute	honor
arcane	mysterious	corollary	result
abstruse	obscure	stimulus	motivation
spare	light	precursor	predecessor
didactic	instructive		
lucid	clear		

Section 6–3

definitive	ultimate	indictment	condemnation
concise	to the point	illusion	false impression
esoteric	obscure	copy	duplicate
selfishness	self-centeredness	symbol	sign
inattention	lack of concentration	mockery	ridicule
insolence	disrespect	adept	skilled
virtue	good quality	temperamental	easily upset
magnanimity	generous	congenial	friendly
pettiness	small-mindedness, insignificant details	vulnerable	exposed
opportunism	taking advantage of circumstances	reclusive	isolated
ambition	determination	knack	ability
solicitousness	anxiousness	assess	evaluate
generosity	kindness	penchant	fondness
		pilfer	steal

Section 5–9

swimming	moving in water	purpose	reason
lessening	decreasing	dispense	hand out
descending	downward	predilection	liking
increasing	rising	disturb	upset
removing	taking away	remedy	cure
avoiding	keeping away from	raid	invade
returning	frequenting	inseparable	indivisible
seeing	witnessing	legitimacy	validity
climbing	going up	unconcerned	unworried
		prestige	status

derived	consequential
profundity	insightfulness
related	connected
accuracy	correctness
diminished	lessened
detachment	disinterest
elitist	exclusive
perquisites	benefits
monarchical	like a monarchy, fancy
tribulations	troubles
irreproachable	faultless
luxuries	comforts
reprehensible	in the wrong
afflictions	problems
commendable	admirable
privileges	benefits

Section 6–7

agnostic	disbeliever
eclectic	diverse
empiric	relies on observation and experimentation
phobic	fearful
quixotic	romantic
foster	cultivate
provide	supply
predict	guess
allege	claim
sustain	maintain
question	doubt
effect	result
ascertain	determine
anticipate	expect
ensure	make certain
presumption	assumption
gaiety	fun
conspicuousness	obviousness
unexpectedness	suddenness
brevity	shortness
oppose	fight
subdue	suppress
create	produce
postpone	delay
confirm	verify
indigenous	native
transitory	temporary
recessive	to go backward
pliant	flexible
arboreal	living in trees
unwitting	unsuspecting
unswerving	constant
inhibiting	restraining
elusive	hard to pin down
antagonistic	hostile
eliminated	abolished
extolled	celebrated
condensed	reduced
censured	criticized
expanded	extended
disparaged	mocked
intensified	made stronger
glorified	valued highly
rearranged	reorganized

endorsed	approved
naïveté	innocence
furtiveness	secretiveness
venality	corruption
indecisiveness	uncertainty
sarcasm	mockery

Section 6–9

neglected	ignored
coerced	forced
rediscovered	found again
inspired	motivated
limited	restricted
required	forced, obliged
collected	gathered
allowed	permitted
circulated	distributed
disinclined	made someone reluctant
evaluating	assessing
supplement	increase
envisioning	imagining
circumvent	avoid
ignoring	paying no attention to
depersonalize	take personal qualities away from
ameliorating	making better
revisit	return to
condoning	excusing
belabor	dwell on
mischievous	naughty
gluttonous	greedy
supple	flexible
adroit	skillful
docile	quiet
intensity	strength
precision	accuracy
scope	range
polish	shine
duration	length
suppresses	holds back
disseminates	distributes
undermines	weakens
confounds	confuses
foreshadows	predicts
repertory	collection
expendable	disposable
paucity	small number
meaningful	significant
barrage	bombardment
libelous	slanderous
rehash	go over
repetitive	recurring
cacophony	disharmony
orderly	neat

Section 7–2

guarantee	promise
lobby	petition
preclude	stop
enact	pass
ascertain	determine
consolidate	combine
compound	combine

contend	compete	revitalizing	stimulating
suppress	restrain	eradicating	eliminating
ratify	approve	augmenting	adding to
motley	diverse	candid	honest
callous	unfeeling	disarming	charming
languid	unhurried	empathetic	sympathetic
mysterious	strange	insightful	perceptive
humane	caring	hysterical	frenzied
meager	small	entourage	group of supporters
accumulated	collected	interfered	obstructed
illegible	unreadable	debacle	disaster
clarified	explained	concurred	agreed
copious	plentiful	faction	group
amassed	collected	pertained	related to
voluminous	huge	dearth	lack
excised	removed	intercepted	cut off
monotonous	repetitive	coalition	alliance
embellished	inflated	encompassed	included
dubious	doubtful	affluence	wealth
self-serving	putting personal concerns before others	affability	friendliness
enthusiastic	excited	equanimity	calmness
contemptible	shameful	resilience	toughness
disparaging	disapproving	truculence	aggression
sporadic	irregular	accessible	reachable
excited	thrilled	abstruse	puzzling
gratuitous	unnecessary	arcane	mysterious
disillusioned	disappointed	unequivocal	clear
benevolent	caring	esoteric	obscure
conflagration	fire	impenetrable	dense, hard to understand
distillation	refinement	hackneyed	clichéd
concordance	agreement	exotic	unusual
aberration	abnormality	lucid	clear
amalgamation	combination	grating	harsh

Section 7–5

		Section 7–8	
howling	crying	dismayed	distressed
noisy	loud	authenticated	genuine
maternal	motherly	overjoyed	delighted
shy	quiet	exacerbated	made worse
lone	single	intrigued	interested
social	communal	enveloped	covered
vicious	brutal	prepared	ready
dangerous	unsafe	enhanced	improved
hungry	starving	embarrassed	humiliated
famished	hungry	marred	flawed
obscure	unclear	standardize	regulate
severe	harsh	ignored	neglected
conventional	normal	offset	balance
erroneous	flawed	surrendered	gave up
noteworthy	remarkable	explain	describe
compromised	negotiated	dismantled	took apart
prediction	guess	compensate	make up for
rejected	discarded	established	created
insolence	disrespect	account	explain
substantiated	proven	administered	managed
endorsement	support	timeworn	unoriginal
confirmed	established	invariable	unchanging
intuition	instinct	edible	safe to eat
belied	contradicted	curative	healing
retraction	withdrawal	descriptive	expressive
alleviating	easing	celebrated	congratulated
distracting	disturbing	failing	not succeeding

promoted	endorsed
refusing	declining
denounced	criticized
neglecting	forgetting
spurned	rejected
hastening	hurrying
honored	praised
opting	choosing
artificial	fake
dependent	reliant
unique	distinctive
unnecessary	pointless
decorative	pretty
instrumental	influential
beautiful	good-looking
results	consequences
unrelated	unconnected
precursors	ancestors
supplant	replace
dramatize	perform
finagle	trick
winnow	examine to remove the bad parts
overhaul	renovate

Section 8–2

widespread	extensive
reinforce	strengthen
waning	declining
harm	hurt
diminishing	decreasing
reform	change
encroaching	intruding
disturb	upset
further	additional
aid	help
protected	sheltered
threatens	intimidates
located	situated
bypasses	goes around
limited	restricted
touches	contacts
surrounded	encircled
borders	touches
associated	connected
covers	includes
modicum	small amount
discrepancy	inconsistency
surfeit	excess
deficit	shortage
juxtaposition	combination
phlegmatic	unconcerned
apathetic	uninterested
conciliatory	peace-making
confrontational	challenging
empathetic	feeling
compassionate	caring
vigilant	watchful
reputable	of good reputation
penurious	poor
frugal	careful
flabbergasted	stunned
miffed	annoyed

jaded	cynical
wary	cautious
embittered	disillusioned

Section 8–5

preserve	protect
distort	warp
enlighten	inform
negate	undo
destroy	obliterate
tension	worry
conservatism	slow or unwilling to accept change
integrity	honesty
convergence	meeting
eradication	annihilation
tangential	peripheral
premature	early
exorbitant	excessive
indiscernible	unclear
cumulative	increasing
expressing	stating
hostility	unfriendliness
suppressing	holding back
conflict	disagreement
stifling	containing
temperance	restraint
disguising	masking
deceit	dishonesty
rousing	inspiring
wrath	anger
gradually	steadily
abruptness	suddenness
erratically	unevenly
solace	comfort
temporarily	momentarily
length	duration
inevitably	unavoidably
approach	come near
instantaneously	immediately
onset	start
foil	person serving as a contrast to another
expose	reveal
pioneer	founder
implement	put into practice
resource	source of information
squelch	smother
mitigator	moderator
promote	advance
critic	opponent
exploit	take advantage of
alacrity	enthusiasm
conformity	obedience
deliberation	consideration
recrimination	accusation
exasperation	frustration
censures	criticizes
exacerbates	worsens
explores	investigates
duplicates	copies
delineates	outlines

Section 8–8

neglected	deserted
adopted	accepted
avoided	stayed away from
criticized	disapproved of
encountered	met
corrected	fixed
displayed	showed
generated	produced
scrutinized	examined
accentuated	emphasized
demolition	destruction
inconsequential	unimportant
renovation	restoration
derelict	ruined
razing	destroying
salvageable	savable
protection	defense
venerable	respected
scouring	searching
grimy	dirty
amiable	friendly
ethical	moral
glacial	unfriendly
taunting	hurtful
nondescript	ordinary
unyielding	firm
tremulous	unsteady
emphatic	forceful
lithe	flexible
fickle	indecisive
reprieve	pardon
infusion	introduction
deferment	postponement
inducement	encouragement
rebate	refund
advance	payment in expectation of reimbursement
hearing	trial
security	safety
procurement	obtaining, purchasing something
account	explanation

Section 9–4

diverted	sidetracked
confined	limited
scuttled	abandoned
cleansed	washed
drenched	soaked
insure	protect against risk
inclined	tending
maintain	preserve
vulnerable	open to
squander	waste
liable	likely
stimulate	inspire
resistant	opposed to
retain	keep
immune	resistant, protected
orderliness	neatness
credulity	innocence
curiosity	interest

shyness	nervousness
morbidity	gloominess
cure	treat
flag	droop, decrease
foster	advance
thrive	flourish
combat	fight
abate	decrease
scrutinize	examine
prosper	do well
eradicate	eliminate
flourish	grow
impressionable	vulnerable
innocuous	inoffensive
unsuitable	inappropriate
insensitive	unfeeling
unapproachable	unfriendly
empathetic	feeling
indomitable	strong
expeditious	quick
idiosyncratic	distinctive
astute	smart
insolvent	broke
fraudulent	fake
prudent	careful
speculative	tentative
autonomous	independent
subordinate	lesser
bankrupt	penniless
charitable	generous
stable	steady
manipulative	scheming
obstinacy	determination
hubris	pride
impetuosity	impulsiveness
valor	courage
callousness	heartlessness

Section 9–6

limited	restricted
developed	advanced
diverse	varied
foundered	failed
variable	uneven
declined	weakened
lengthy	long
lasted	remained
sedate	calm
soared	improved, increased
refuted	disproved
theories	speculations
challenged	confronted
predictions	guesses
confirmed	verified
speculations	assumptions
validated	authenticated
disclaimers	denials
substantiated	proven
doubts	uncertainties
rambunctious	rowdy
indecent	offensive
extravagant	excessive

excessive	extreme
secluded	private
scrupulous	thorough
circumscribed	restricted
impulsive	reckless
irreverent	disrespectful
animated	lively
corroborated	supported
prospering	thriving
confirmed	established
extant	still in existence
belied	contradicted
dwindling	declining
diminished	reduced
debilitated	harmed
tempered	balanced, calmed
thriving	flourishing
irresolute	unsure
officious	bossy
rancorous	bitter
punctilious	thorough
myopic	narrow-minded

Section 9–9

engage	take on
alleviate	lessen
transport	move
regenerate	restore
trivialize	underestimate
apprehensive	anxious
agitated	troubled
furious	angry
serene	calm
considerate	thoughtful
peacefulness	calmness
placid	calm
forthrightness	outspokenness
reserved	quiet
fairness	evenhandedness
dilatory	tardy
meticulousness	care
accessible	available
peevishness	irritability
irritable	bad-tempered
conscientious	careful
despoiled	dishonored
incompetent	unskilled
sustained	continued
shrewd	smart
debilitated	harmed
innovative	new
fertilized	made productive
imprudent	reckless
denuded	stripped
dispatch	quickness
presumption	guess
durability	sturdiness
deliberation	consideration
reverence	admiration
induction	introduction, a method of reasoning
amalgam	mixture
immersion	complete involvement

occlusion	obstruction
estrangement	separation

Section 10–4

realized	understood
exonerated	forgiven
denied	rejected
reprimanded	scolded
perceived	saw
enlightened	informed
understood	knew
apprehended	caught
confirmed	established
obligated	required
implied	suggested
publicized	revealed
denied	refused
repealed	cancelled, revoke
stipulated	specified
disregarded	ignored
revealed	exposed
executed	carried out
insisted	firmly stated
honored	respected
disposal	discarding
repair	mend
sacrifice	give up
opulence	luxury
wastefulness	carelessness
comfort	coziness
spirituality	religion
worldliness	relating to this world, wise
humiliation	shame
charity	generosity
disclose	reveal
rearrange	reorganize
simplify	make simpler
conclude	end
ascertain	determine
compression	solidity
disintegration	breakdown
distension	swelling
deflation	reduction
dehydration	dryness
aptitude	ability
eccentrics	odd people
morality	principles
emancipators	people who free others
erudition	sophistication
enigmas	mysteries
devotion	loyalty
egotists	selfish people
altruism	unselfishness
exemplars	models
obsequious	flattering
mysterious	strange
lackadaisical	lazy
argumentative	confrontational
aggressive	hostile
dismissal	release
preparation	training
consumption	use

dispersion	spreading
harvesting	collecting
gathering	drawing together
exploitation	misuse
husbandry	careful conservation
stockpiling	hoarding
extirpation	destruction

Section 10–6

exposé	public revelation
verbalizations	articulations
gestures	body movements
cognitions	knowledge
intuitions	instincts
store	stockpile
condemned	damned
supply	amount, quantity
dismissed	forgotten
wealth	abundance
regarded	seen
modicum	small amount
abandoned	deserted
deficit	shortage
praised	admired
condemnation	criticism
sarcasm	mockery
plaudits	praise
irony	mockery
pathos	suffering
scent	smell
cultivate	develop
flavor	taste
conceal	hide
appearance	look
recognize	identify
texture	feel
locate	find
aroma	smell
identify	recognize
disclosure	revelation
evaluation	assessment
liberation	release
instance	occurrence
inquiry	investigation

Section 10–9

stratified	ordered by status level
fitful	disturbed
collaborative	joint
vicarious	experienced through another person
corresponding	related
interesting	exciting
rousing	inspiring
advantageous	helpful
beneficial	useful
rudimentary	simple
reassuring	comforting
insipid	dull
bland	ordinary
stimulating	exciting
soporific	sleep–inducing
odoriferous	strong smelling

archaic	old
aural	auditory, hearing-related
rustic	rural, country
tactile	tangible, related to touch
discernment	judgment
tenacity	stubbornness
hilarity	amusement
adroitness	skill
insecurity	uncertainty
recognition	acknowledgment
versatility	adaptability
ignominy	disgrace
inadequacy	insufficiency
prestige	status
finesse	flair
prominence	fame
ineptitude	incompetence
notoriety	dishonor
rectitude	goodness
invocation	chant
prospectus	official advance information
manifesto	written declaration of principles
arbitration	settlement
mandate	order, command